MW00583979

A NEW AMERICAN
LABOR MOVEMENT

A NEW AMERICAN LABOR MOVEMENT

The Decline of Collective Bargaining
and the Rise of Direct Action

WILLIAM E. SCHEUERMAN

Cover images: Photographer unknown. (11437) "End of Strike, Cadillac Motor Company, Detroit, Michigan, 1937." January 17, 1937. Walter P. Reuther Library, Wayne State University, Detroit MI. http://reuther.wayne.edu/node/5639

Bob Simpson (BobboSphere), "Fight for $15 in Chicago: May 15, 2014," Licensed with CC BY-SA 2.0. To view a copy of this license, visit https://creativecommons.org/licenses/by-sa/2.0/

Published by State University of New York Press, Albany

For information, contact State University of New York Press, Albany, NY
www.sunypress.edu

Library of Congress Cataloging-in-Publication Data

Name: Scheuerman, William E., 1943– author.
Title: A new American labor movement : the decline of collective bargaining and the rise of direct action / William E. Scheuerman.
Description: Albany, NY : State University of New York Press, 2021. | Includes bibliographical references and index.
Identifiers: LCCN 2021024223 | ISBN 9781438485492 (hardcover : alk. paper) | ISBN 9781438485508 (ebook)
Subjects: LCSH: Labor movement—United States—History—21 century. | Direct action—United States—History—21st century.
Classification: LCC HD6510 .S34 2021 | DDC 331.88/0973—dc23
LC record available at https://lccn.loc.gov/2021024223

10 9 8 7 6 5 4 3 2 1

To my grandchildren—
Lizzy, Zoe, Lily, Erik, Charlotte, and Genevieve—
the youth of today who will help
create a better tomorrow for all of us

Arise ye workers from your slumber,
Arise ye prisoners of want.

(The Internationale)

Contents

Acknowledgments

The determination and commitment of those battling for social and economic justice inspired me to write this modest book. I thank them for the many sacrifices they make and the hope they give us for a better future. My great appreciation also goes to those participants in the struggle who found the time to talk to me and tolerate my often naïve questions. Edward Escobar of the Alliance for Independent Workers was a fantastic source of information. His patience and willingness to assist went well beyond anything I could have expected. As one who has felt the sting of abusive corporate power, Edward helped me understand why some California gig drivers want to become "real" independent contractors rather than corporate employees. Freelance worker Halley Bondy put the concerns of freelance workers in perspective, as did the recently appointed head of the Freelancers Union, Rafael Espinal. And many thanks to Bob Simpson for allowing me to use his photo of a Fight for $15 rally on the book cover. Two good friends and former colleagues in the New York State United Teachers union, Alan Lubin and Brian O'Shaughnessy, invited me to meetings of the Rural & Migrant Ministry and spent hours with me analyzing issues facing farmworkers. Many of my academic friends and former colleagues contributed to this work as well. Mike Urban reviewed several chapters and made a number of insightful comments. Sid Plotkin, Ray Petersen, Ray Borycka, Vinnie Seravallo, and Artie Siegel, my childhood friend from the old neighborhood, also read the manuscript during its various stages of development. My son and namesake, Bill, read parts of the manuscript and was not shy in pointing out some shortcomings he found in an early draft of the conclusion. I thank him for his intellectual rigor and honesty. My wife Louise deserves thanks for reading the various drafts of the book and living through months of my self-imposed exile to libraries or meetings or to my study. Finally, I owe my greatest thanks to all my sisters and brothers in the labor movement who have dedicated their lives, often at great personal cost, in the seemingly endless struggle against the forces of economic and political oppression. Needless to say, the book's shortcomings are the sole responsibility of the author.

Introduction

On a crisp October day in downtown Albany, New York, a small coalition of fast-food, retail, and transportation workers and their supporters took to the streets. The sound of a voice through a bullhorn pierced the air. "What do we want?" the voice roared.

"Paid sick leave!" the crowd answered.

"When do we want it?"

"Now!"[1]

This Central Avenue rally wasn't their first. Previously, coalition members conducted silent protests before the Albany County Legislature to secure a law requiring all area employers to allow both part-time and full-time workers to earn paid sick leave. Strategically, the coalition linked its demands to the larger communal good of protecting public health. All the protesters wore surgical masks. "I Served Food With the Flu," read one protester's sign. Their actions worked. The county legislature drafted such a bill.[2] But on that October day in 2018 the group marched in protest of an amendment that weakened the bill in favor of small business owners. Caught in the struggle between local business interests and protesting workers, in November 2018 the county legislature temporarily tabled the bill. As of this writing, the coalition is still waiting for the county legislature to reconsider the bill. Meanwhile, the workers take hope from the successes of similar coalitions throughout the state. The Westchester County legislature passed a mandate that now provides a new opportunity for paid sick leave to over 100,000 workers, almost a third of whom are women.[3] In New York City, 1.2 million workers gained paid sick leave for the first time in 2014.[4]

There's a new spontaneous energy in the labor movement, and a new kind of direct action is its engine of change, born of the decades-long war against unions that has blocked vast numbers of American workers from the bargaining table. These direct action movements are taking place mainly outside the realm of organized labor and are in the process of reshaping the American labor movement. Conscious of their economic vulnerability and no longer willing to accept the economic and social status quo, tens of thousands of exploited workers in industries running the gamut from farm laborers and gig drivers to freelance artists and fast-food employees have taken to the streets in a collective attempt to attain a living wage and decent working conditions. This spontaneous new militancy, an upsurge of vibrant democracy from below, expressed through mass demonstrations, strikes, sit-ins, political action, and similar activities, has already achieved some successes and offers models for workers to exercise their power in the twenty-first century.

The history of the union movement in the United States has been the subject of an endless number of studies. And recent decades have produced countless analyses of why unions are in decline. Along the way, this book will briefly recap that history and summarize various factors cited as contributing to the union movement's current sorry state. This work argues that all these analyses are partially correct, but they fail to address the core of the problem: *the structure and culture of organized labor no longer serve the larger labor movement.*

This book frames the rise and development of the new labor movement in light of organized labor's decline by asking a number of important questions. The first series of questions arises from the historical contributions of labor unions, their current condition, and their future prospects: Why are unions important, and why does it matter that they're on the decline? Why are they losing members? What, if anything, can they do to reverse this decline? Finally, what are the social and political implications of a weak and ineffectual union movement? A second group of questions examines the new labor movement that has emerged outside the parameters of organized labor: What economic and social changes have given birth to this new militant labor movement? What are the goals of these new organizing groups, and what are they doing to realize them? What is their relationship to unions and to electoral politics? How might this relationship evolve? A third, and not inconsequential, set of questions looks at the impact of the Covid-19 pandemic on these workers and their direct action movements.

Before proceeding with a brief synopsis of the chapters, a few words on the idea of direct action are necessary. The genealogy of the concept "direct action" goes back to the nineteenth-century anarchists, syndical-ists, and others for whom direct action meant not just grassroots activ-ities such as taking to the streets, demonstrating, and so on, but those activities that directly and immediately brought about the new world they envisioned. For example, when anarchist squatters occupy buildings, as they still do today, they are not merely protesting housing policies. They're also attempting to start living the new utopia they seek without private property and beyond the tentacles of the political state.[5] Martin Luther King Jr.—no anarchist—also described civil disobedience as direct action, holding onto the old idea that protest itself already anticipates and prefigures the new social order sought by activists. That's why he supported nonviolence and respect for one's opponents.[6] This book does not use the principle of direct action in its classical sense. Instead, the idea as used here refers specifically to those grassroots activities aimed at improving the terms and conditions of employment outside the insti-tutional structure of organized labor. It embraces a host of working-class efforts to win representation, benefits, and voice outside the traditional union framework.

The opening chapter begins with an examination of the so-called "golden years" of organized labor and documents why unions are of vital importance to America's economy and its political institutions. The chap-ter argues that unions helped build the middle class and erased much of the economic inequality of the pre-union age through the creation of the most egalitarian level of income distribution in U.S. history. A viable union movement also enhanced America's version of democracy by providing working people with an institution powerful enough to countervail the power of giant corporations. John Kenneth Galbraith, for instance, hailed organized labor's ability to advocate for ordinary workers against powerful corporations as fundamental to American democracy. But as unions declined, all these gains began to disappear. Today, with only about one in ten workers belonging to a union, America's middle class is shrinking, economic inequality is reaching new heights, and in the absence of a strong union movement, our institutions of procedural democracy increasingly favor the rich and powerful. More bluntly put, in the words of a recent presidential primary candidate, "the rules of our country have been rigged" in favor of the rich.[7]

The second chapter examines the causes of organized labor's decline. There are almost as many reasons for the decline of unions as there are observers. Explanations include its tendency to reject organizing in favor of business unionism, ineffective organizing techniques, a lack of militancy and refusal to strike, an emphasis on electoral politics, a failure to articulate union values, a hostile legal system, the globalization of capital, and, finally, its failure to develop into a larger social movement.[8] This work recognizes that these diagnoses are correct as far as they go, but they fail to address the core of the problem: *The structure of corporate power, the forms of labor and its new workplaces, and the very character of employment itself have changed since unionism's golden era, but the structure of organized labor has simply not kept pace. Unions are fighting twenty-first-century battles with early twentieth-century tools.*

There are two aspects to organized labor's structural deficiency, one external and one internal. Externally, the U.S. economy has undergone a rapid change from manufacturing to one that is primarily service and knowledge-based and contingent. So much of today's labor is contingent that the world of work has a new Orwellian concept: "perma-temps." According to Louis Hyman, 94 percent of new jobs created between 2005 and 2015 consisted of some form of temporary work. As the French political economist Andre Gorz predicted decades ago, conventional full-time jobs are disappearing for vast swaths of the working class.[9] This fact has broad implications. Polls indicate that young workers or millennials— those born between 1981 and 1996—know they'll frequently change jobs and, consequently, have little or no interest in joining a union. In the tech sector, the fluidity of jobs and preponderance of contract employees, many of whom work offsite, seriously impede labor's practice of organizing permanent workers at brick-and-mortar work sites. In low-pay sectors such as child care, home health care, and the fast-food industry, workers are often unwilling to pay a portion of their paltry earnings to union dues. Many of these workers support the growing sector of informal non-union organizations that build public support for legislative action to address their needs.

This chapter also examines the external threat to unions posed by hostile political forces bought and paid for by the corporate sector and a handful of extreme right-wing multibillionaires, some of whom see democracy and its key institutions, such as unions, as the primary threat to their liberty. Backed by the wealthy Koch brothers and other billionaires, the neoliberal attack on popular sovereignty and unions provides an ideological justification for corporate power. Operating on the premise that liberty exists only when individuals pursue their private interests by making choices in the so-called free market, neoliberals view any interference in the market place as an assault on individual liberty. Therefore, social movements that countervail or otherwise interfere with the power of capital, as Friedrich Hayek argues, are sure to lead to some form of totalitarianism, and the social movement most likely to do that is none other than the one the Koch brothers dub "the labor monopoly movement." In other words, capital can become as huge and powerful as it wants, while workers are advised to cherish their individualism: the preservation of individual liberty necessitates the crushing of unions.[10] Put simply, this is a formula for weakening worker organizations and strengthening business. And the Kochs, among others, have spent lavishly to convince us that it is the right formula for America.

Factory shutdowns, outsourcing, and illegal firings of union supporters are squashing private sector unions. A hostile legal system, highlighted recently by the Supreme Court's *Janus* decision, which exempts non-union members from paying their fair share for union servies they receive, is likely to cost public sector unions—the most powerful arm of the union movement—tens of thousands of dues-paying members.[11] The Kochs and other billionaires who also underwrote the Janus campaign are more than willing to spend unlimited millions to smash organized labor thanks to another Supreme Court ruling. In *Citizens United v. Federal Election Commission*, the Court ruled that political spending was a protected form of free speech, which meant that corporations and unions could now legally spend as much as they wanted in the political arena. Unfortunately for unions, they lack the fiscal resources to compete with the corporate sector and the likes of the Koch brothers. The fiscal disadvantage is nothing new to organized labor. In the past, the corporate sector outspent Big Labor by about 15 to 1. Today the gap in spending is far greater. Campaign dollars helped Tea Party members win control of a number of state governments, including former union-dominated states in the Rust Belt. Once they assumed positions of power, these anti-government advocates were not reluctant to use the powers of the state to crush unions. To make matters worse for organized labor, the Trump presidency sought to aggressively tear unions apart, not only by promoting a hostile Department of Labor and National Labor Relations Board but also through appointing right-wing federal judges hostile to labor. After all, it was Trump's appointee to the Supreme Court, Neil Gorsuch, who cast the deciding vote for Janus.

The chapter concludes with an examination of how external pressures on unions expose the internal conflicts inherent in organized labor's structures. As membership numbers shrink, pressures increase on union leaders to organize new members. After all, membership numbers and, most importantly, union dues are vital organizational imperatives to elected labor leaders who depend on rank-and-file support to keep their own jobs. Without sufficient dues revenue, unions cut staff, reduce membership services, and produce a lot of dissatisfied members internally. The union fractures. But too frequently union leaders have mistaken the survival of individual unions with the survival of the labor movement itself. As membership and influence declined, organizational survival became the name of the game. Consider, for instance, the formation of Change to Win (CtW).

In an effort to promote organizing and save the labor movement, seven large unions split from the AFL-CIO in 2005 to form Change to Win. But CtW didn't save the movement; in fact, its formation created many new problems. First, it fragmented and weakened the organized labor movement. It also created new levels of divisiveness and conflict within CtW as well as the broader labor movement. For instance, the flagship of CtW, the Service Employees International Union (SEIU), almost immediately became embroiled in internal battles when a 155,000-member local of health care workers in California broke away to form a national union of their own.[12] SEIU subsequently spent millions fighting this defection. This tale has been repeated many times over, creating tension and conflict within the larger union movement. Take, for instance, the case of the United Auto Workers, an industrial union, gaining the right to represent college faculty. What do professionals trained in industrial relations in the automobile industry know about higher education? Maybe we'll gain a more profound understanding of the inappropriateness of this practice by envisioning a higher education union, the United University Professions (UUP), for example, representing auto workers. Would that create hard feelings within organized labor? You bet. Would it give auto workers effective union representation? Unlikely.

What follows in each of four subsequent chapters is a study of five relatively successful non-union organizations, or, as they are more commonly known, alt-labor organizations. The rise of the alt-labor movement generates daily coverage in the mainstream media and has led to some highly popular books that analyze the movement's actions and future prospects. David Rolf's *Fight for Fifteen: The Right Wage for a Working America*, Annelise Orleck's *We Are All Fast-Food Workers Now: The Global Uprising against Poverty Wages*, and Eric Blanc's *The Red State Revolt: The Teachers' Strike Wave and Working Class Politics* are among the best. These works scrutinize the proliferation of such movements across the globe. Orleck examines the travails of a plethora of international low-wage workers, ranging from McDonald's workers in Brazil to Filipino rice farmers.[13] Rolf traces the rise of the Fight for $15 movement, closely examines the struggle in Seattle, Washington, and looks at the Our Walmart movement, home care workers, and others while making the argument in favor of a $15 minimum wage.[14] Blanc's *The Red State Revolt* studies the collective action of workers in a single occupation—teachers who in 2018 waged illegal strikes in Arizona, Oklahoma, and West Virginia that brought gains they failed to win by other means.[15] The scope of this book is not as broad as Orleck's work or as wide-ranging as Rolf's study, and unlike Blanc's tome, it focuses on more than a single industry. It takes an in-depth look at five alt-labor movements that represent a good cross-section of the many direct action strategies now being utilized by exploited workers throughout the United States.

The five non-union organizations studied are the Immokalee Workers of Florida and New York's farmworkers; Gig workers in California, mainly Uber and Lyft drivers, who are not much better off than the highly exploited farmworkers; the Freelancers Union, an organization that attempts to mitigate rather than reverse changes in the economy; and, finally, fast-food and tipped restaurant workers involved in what some observers view as the birth of a new labor movement, the Fight for $15. All five groups rely on direct action to improve terms and conditions of employment, and all point to ways the labor movement can achieve successes while operating *outside* the union structure.

All these different groups of workers achieved significant gains without paying union dues or facing the many legal hurdles unions confront when trying to organize or secure contracts. Each chapter studies the structure and strategies of these action groups, including the important role now played by social media in fostering internal cohesion. This book searches for areas of commonality and differences among the groups. How do they define success? What have they achieved? Why are these groups successful? What is the relationship between direct action movements and the union movement? Why are these groups thriving outside the organized union movement? Most crucially, what can unions learn from these direct action groups? It's important to note that direct action is not a recent phenomenon. In fact, such actions helped form the modern labor movement. For example, think of the 1937 sit-in strikes at auto plants that led to the creation of the United Auto Workers of America.

Will this scenario be repeated? If not, what is the future role of these direct action groups?

The first of the four analyses focuses on the farmworkers in New York State and the Immokalee Workers of Florida. The National Labor Relations Act did not provide farmworkers with the right to organize a union. Nevertheless, farmworkers in both states formed non-union organizations to promote their economic interests. In Florida the Immokalee workers, unhindered by restrictive labor laws, won a major victory by waging a boycott prohibited by labor laws. In New York, farmworkers have used their political clout to gain significantly better working conditions and have secured legislation allowing them to form a union.

The fourth chapter explores the plight of Uber and Lyft drivers in California and their struggle to fight back against their classification as contract workers—Hayek's heroic free individuals—who are not entitled to the benefits and protections available to traditional employees. This chapter documents how California's gig workers successfully took to the streets en massé to correct what many characterized as a corporate-driven misclassification of their employment status. After years of struggle the California legislature passed a law—California AB5—that classified most gig workers as employees, but a ballot initiative exempting rideshare drivers from the law passed in the November 2020 election. Not only did Uber and Lyft oppose AB5, but many drivers and gig workers did too.

Chapter 5 investigates the growth and political and social impact of the Freelancers Union. According to a recent report issued by the Freelancers Union and Upwork, a freelancer website, more than one of three workers in the entire labor force identify as freelancers. Many of these workers are younger than thirty-five and a large majority find their work online. Full-time freelance workers, however, do not have many of the same legal protections afforded other full-time employees.[16] Most are contract workers not protected by the NLRA; they frequently do not get paid for their work, are not protected against discrimination, and have little or no recourse to contest arbitrary and capricious behavior by their contractor. To address these issues, many have joined the Freelancers Union, which, contrary to what the name might suggest, is not a labor union. The Freelancers Union doesn't do collective bargaining. But it offers much-needed services to its members and advocates effectively in the political arena. The organization now has nearly 500,000 members and is growing at a rate of one thousand each week. Unlike traditional unions, the Freelancers Union does not charge dues. Instead, it is financed through grants and fees from the insurance plans and other services it offers, and supports its members through political action. For example, in New York City, the Freelancers Union secured legislation requiring the use of contracts and mandating payment within thirty days. Freelance work is the fastest-growing segment of work in the United States, and, since polls indicate that freelancers are among the most politically active groups, the organization's future in the political arena bodes well.

Chapter 6 studies the Fight for $15 and its sibling struggle of tipped workers, the fight for One Fair Wage. Unlike the previous groups of workers studied here, these workers are classified as employees and are protected by existing labor laws. Nevertheless, restaurant workers—both fast-food and tipped employees—are among the most exploited in the U.S. workforce. The chapter opens with a brief analysis of the plight of these mostly minimum-wage restaurant workers. Despite the common belief that most of these workers are teenagers working at their first job, the average age of these workers approaches thirty, and many have families to support. The chapter critically examines the strategy and tactics of restaurant workers and their connection with organized labor, and evaluates future prospects and what their efforts mean to the growing new American labor movement.

All the workers examined in this book have taken to the streets either because labor laws have excluded them from the bargaining table or because the nature of their work and full-frontal corporate attacks on unions have made them almost impossible to organize. But these workers can't go it alone. The book's conclusion proposes ways a new direct action movement can work in conjunction with a smaller, reimagined organized labor movement to reduce economic inequality and rebuild the middle class. And one key way the labor movement can be reimagined is to adopt the model of European unions that operate within a larger framework of industry-wide sectoral bargaining.

Chapter 1

Why Unions Matter

There she stood on a freezing day in February, in the shadow of the long-idle textile mills of Lawrence, Massachusetts, Elizabeth Warren declaring her candidacy for the 2020 presidential election. Warren began by delivering a moving account of the abysmal working conditions that led to the historic Bread and Roses strike in Lawrence over a century ago: Not only were workers paid starvation wages, literally, "Children were forced to operate dangerous equipment. Workers lost hands, arms, and legs in the gears of machines. . . . One out of every three adult mill workers died by the time they were twenty-five."[1] Warren ended her tribute to these long ago workers by reminding onlookers that it was because of the Lawrence strike that we now have forty-hour work weeks, a national minimum wage, weekends, a ban on child labor, and national safety laws. "Unions built America's middle class," Warren said, and "unions will rebuild the middle class."[2]

Chapter 2 examines the reasons underlying the American union movement's decline. This first chapter sets the stage by describing the state of organized labor in the first two and a half decades following World War II, its relationship to a strong middle class, the subsequent decline and loss of union power, and the implications of the decline. The answers that emerge illuminate the importance of organized labor to American society and our democratic political institutions.

Unions and the Middle Class

Former Secretary of Labor Robert Reich has dubbed the years in post–World War II America between 1947 and 1975 as The Great Prosperity.[3]

The Great Depression was past, the war was over, and the economy was buzzing. Union membership grew, as did the political and economic clout of organized labor. In 1950 the United Auto Workers and the General Motors Corporation reached a groundbreaking agreement dubbed the Treaty of Detroit. The agreement increased the prospects for labor peace by giving management greater control over the productive process. In return, it tied wages and benefits to increases in worker productivity, thereby channeling a share of the productivity increases into the pockets of workers in the form of higher wages and benefits, including pensions and vacation time. The Treaty of Detroit set the standard for the labor movement. Union membership continued to grow and the wages of working people climbed steadily.[4] Economic inequality, which had peaked in the roaring twenties, dropped precipitously. In the twenties, the top 1 percent earned close to a quarter of all income, but by the late 1940s they could claim only about 10 percent of the nation's total income, a loss of more than half. This leveling off in income level would not change for the next two-plus decades. Americans were buying consumer goods, including televisions and automobiles, and moving in droves from cramped inner-city housing to new homes built alongside newly constructed roads and highways in suburbia. In short, postwar America developed a large and prosperous middle class. And organized labor—unions—were the backbone of this middle class. Indeed, by the mid-1950s one in three American workers belonged to a union.

Unions contributed to the growth of America's middle class in many ways. Most obviously, study after study has found that union workers earn more than their non-union counterparts. An Economic Policy Institute (EPI) report, for instance, concluded that unions raise wages of unionized workers by about 20 percent. Other studies find that the wage premium— the difference in wages between union and non-union workers—is even greater for the least skilled workers and workers of color.[5] Employees in a union shop are also more likely to have significantly better fringe benefits than non-union workers. In terms of earnings, the fringe benefits enjoyed by union workers give them an additional 8 percent advantage. Included among their benefits are health plans with lower deductibles and co-pays. When unionized workers retire they are 24 percent more likely to receive health care coverage from their employer. They also receive 26 percent more vacation time and 14 percent more paid leave. Unionized workers are up to 54 percent more likely to have employer-provided pension plans, and their employers contribute approximately 28 percent more toward their pensions.[6] In addition to all this, let's not forget, unions brought us the weekend, the eight-hour work day, and paid vacations.[7]

Unions also increase the earnings of those employed in non-union settings. The threat of collective bargaining leads some firms to raise wages and benefits to a competitive level to keep unions out. Walters and Mishel, EPI economists, use the example of a high school graduate who works in a unionized plant within an industry that is 25 percent unionized. That worker generally receives 5 percent more than similarly situated workers in less unionized industries. Another EPI study by Rosenfeld, Denice, and Laird found that men working in the non-union private sector in 2013 would have earned an additional 5 percent weekly if union density had remained at its 1979 level. The study estimates that the 40.2 million workers affected by Big Labor's decline lost over $109 billion in wages.[8] The fact that highly unionized states have higher minimum wages is another indicator of organized labor's cultural push on wages.

A study by Christain Weller, David Madland, and Alex Rowell from the Center for American Progress (CAP) summarizes the positive effect unions have on American families. If owning a home is the fulfillment of the American Dream, union families are more likely to realize that dream than their non-union counterparts. In 2013, 71 percent of middle income union households were homeowners, as opposed to 63 percent of comparable nonunion domiciles.[9] Based on the Federal Reserve's Survey of Consumer Financing, the study found that between 2010 and 2016 union families had a median wealth of $80,993, as opposed to $45,025 (2016 dollars) for non-union families—an 80 percent difference. While four in ten American families cannot easily come up with $400 to meet an unexpected emergency, union workers are positioned to put aside savings to meet future contingencies. In short, the higher salaries, better benefits, and job stability associated with union representation allow workers to own homes and plan for the future, an option becoming increasingly rare in today's America.

Historically, as unions grew in strength and numbers, so did their political clout. Unions provided workers with an institutional structure to effectively represent their interests in political arenas on the local, state, and national levels. There was a time in the 1950s when U.S. presidents would meet regularly with labor leaders to find a way to accommodate labor's needs with the interests of big corporations. As John Kenneth Galbraith observed,[10] the political power of unions served as a countervailing force to the growing political power of large corporations. The

AFL-CIO's George Meany concurred in a more blunt way. The primary role of unions, Meany observed, "was to see that the big guys didn't kick the little guys around."[11] In the mid-1950s, the American economy was thriving despite the concentration of economic power among huge private corporations. Nineteenth-century classical political economy would have called for the restoration of a competitive marketplace by breaking up the power of the relatively new corporate leviathans. But Galbraith rejected that solution. The way to keep the economy working smoothly in a democratic setting was to meet power with power. Large institutions such as unions, he argued, could countervail the power of corporations. Powerful unions, then, were key institutions of democracy in an era of concentrated economic power. A strong union movement ensured that the country's political institutions addressed the needs of ordinary working people, rather than just promoting the interests of the very wealthy and powerful.

Unions have effectively countervailed the power of big corporations in a number of ways. One way is by relying on their members to get to the polls and vote for union-backed candidates. In so doing, they promote political participation among the entire citizenry, not just union members. Helen Marot, a labor organizer, summarized the political role unions play when she observed that "unions are group efforts in the direction of democracy."[12] And that's just what unions do. They endorse candidates, educate their members on the issues, and work at getting out the vote. Union members knock on doors, donate to labor's political action funds, attend political rallies, and work as volunteers in the campaigns of endorsed candidates. Unions, in short, are good for democracy. In fact, a study by Notre Dame's Benjamin Radcliff and the State Department's Patricia Davis indicates that a 1 percentage point increase in union density is associated with a jump in the voter turnout rate by 0.2 to 0.25 percentage points.[13] Other studies back this finding. Roland Zullo of the University of Michigan, for example, concludes that those who identify as working class—unionized or not—vote with the same frequency in congressional elections when unions run campaigns in their district. But these same voters are 10.4 percent less likely to vote when unions don't conduct electoral campaigns.[14] Organized labor's foray into the political arena promotes the value of civic virtue among the citizenry and strengthens America's democratic institution of popular sovereignty.

Times have changed since the days when unions built the middle-class and were strong and active enough to countervail the power of the corporate sector. Working people and union members are not doing very well these days, and many are taking it out on their unions. Scores of union members felt sufficiently dissatisfied with an economy that's booming for everyone but them that they broke rank with their unions by rejecting their leader's endorsements of Hillary Clinton in the 2016 presidential election. Frustrated union members in what we now call Rust Belt states—former bastions of the alliance between unions and the Democratic Party—voted for that outspoken champion of the working class, Donald Trump, ensuring his election to the presidency.[15] As discussed in some detail later, the Trump presidency has shown open hostility to unions and the working class, including the many that supported his candidacy.

Rank-and-file rejection of Big Labor's political endorsements is just one example of organized labor's loss of power and political significance. More significant is the continued hemorrhaging of members. Measured in terms of union density—the percentage of workers belonging to unions—organized labor reached its zenith in 1954 when unions represented 34.8 percent of the labor force. In absolute numbers, 1979 represented the high point for organized labor when an estimated 21 million workers belonged to unions.[16] In 2017, according to the United States Bureau of Labor Statistics, 10.7 percent of all wage and salary workers belonged to unions, a low point not seen since 1928, the eve of the Great Depression. Union density in the private sector mirrors the numbers of the pre-union era of 1900 at 6.5 percent. In absolute numbers, 14.8 million workers were union members in 2017, up by 262,000 from the previous year but down 6.2 million from Big Labor's 1979 membership apex. A further breakdown of labor's numbers reveals that representation in the public sector at 34.4 percent is more than five times greater than the private sector density rate of 6.5 percent,[17] which helps explain recent attacks by Tea Party–backed governors and legislators on public unions in their states. Indeed, since the 2010 elections, Wisconsin, Michigan, and Indiana have laid off thousands of public sector employees and enacted Right to Work laws prior to the recent Janus decision. This reduced the unions' political power and lowered wages for many of the remaining workers.[18]

Significantly, union membership is concentrated in just seven of the fifty states. Although these states account for only about one-third of the nation's wage and salary workforce, they're home to slightly more than half the country's 14.8 million union members. Union membership is clustered in the Rust Belt states of Illinois at 0.8 million, Michigan at 0.7

million, Pennsylvania at 0.7 million, and Ohio at 0.6 million, along with California's 2.5 million, New York's 2.0 million, and New Jersey's 0.6 million.[19] This geographical concentration raises several important questions. On the one hand it might suggest that labor's predicament isn't really that dire. It's just a matter of trying to organize in different geographical areas. On the other, it also indicates that union efforts to organize outside their traditional locales have failed over many years. These numbers also reflect that unions are having trouble maintaining membership levels in traditionally pro-union areas. Subsequent chapters examine why union numbers are in decline. In the meantime, it's essential to explore how union decline has affected our economy and political institutions.

The slow but steady contraction of the middle class is directly related to the decline of unions. In 1928, when union density was about the same as today, the top 1 percent of the population received 23.9 percent of all income and the top 10 percent captured about 50 percent of all wages and salaries. Today the top 1 percent holds 22 percent of all income, just 1.9 percent less than the 1928 high.[20] In contrast, during the heyday years of union power between 1945 and 1973, income inequality leveled off as the top earners captured only 4.9 percent of income growth.[21] As more workers began to form unions in the mid-1930s, the gap between the rich and poor narrowed significantly. By the early 1970s the top 1 percent received less than 9 percent of all income and the share of income going to the top 10 percent slipped to slightly less than one-third.[22] Union membership continued to rise, but union density started to plummet and by 2013 income disparity had skyrocketed to pre-Depression levels. A RAND Corporation study concluded that the aggregate annual income of workers earning less than the top 10 percent would have been $2.5 trillion more in 2018 alone if income distribution ratios had not declined after 1974. The $2.5 trillion constitutes about 12 percent of the GDP. The RAND study also found that these last four decades of income inequality growth have taken about $47 trillion out of the pockets of workers.[23]

This change reflects a new dynamic: as union power declined because of shrinking union density, corporations shifted from sharing productivity gains with workers to taking the lion's share of these gains for themselves, their CEOs, and their stockholders. Remember, the Treaty of Detroit gave auto companies more control over the labor process and brought labor peace. In return, workers' compensation packages were tied to productivity. In essence, workers and owners would all share the fruits of any productivity gains. This arrangement contributed greatly to economic leveling. Between 1948 and 1973, for instance, as workers' productivity nearly doubled, so did their earnings.[24] After 1973, when productivity gains were no longer shared, income inequality took off. Productivity continued to increase, but wages flattened. An EPI study found that between 1979 and 2017 productivity grew by 70.3 percent while hourly compensation increased by 11.1 percent. In short, during this period, productivity increased six times faster than hourly wages.[25] As Reich and others observe, beginning in the 1980s, median household incomes stopped growing when adjusted for inflation. Wage stagnation became so severe that many American workers actually lost ground. In fact, by 2013 median household earnings slipped below their 1989 level. Reich shows the decline in wages in concrete terms. Fifty years ago, he observes, when General Motors was the country's largest employer, the typical GM worker earned thirty-five dollars an hour when controlling for inflation. Nowadays, Walmart is the nation's largest employer. The average hourly pay at Walmart is less than twelve dollars.[26]

If productivity grew six times faster than wages, the jugular question becomes, where did the surplus productivity go? Some of the excess, of course, took the form of corporate profits, which reached a record-breaking $2.12 trillion in 2014 and have remained comfortably over the $2 trillion mark ever since.[27] Corporate profits are just part of the story. Not surprisingly, according to an EPI study, a large share of the surplus found its way into the pockets of the top 1 percent on the income scale. Between 1979 and 2015, the real earnings of the top income group grew by 229 percent, compared to a 46 percent increase for the remaining 90 percent of wage earners. By 2015 those at the apex of the income scale earned 26.3 times more than the remaining 99 percent of the population.[28]

Within the top 1 percent, CEOs in command of the corporate sector managed to pocket large amounts of the productivity surplus that once went to workers. According to the AFL-CIO's *PayWatch*, for 2017, CEO pay of Standard and Poor's 500 Index companies grew by 6.4 percent to an average salary of $13.94 million annually. At least two S&P CEOs earned over $100 million that year. During the same period, production and nonsupervisory workers received wage increases amounting to a meager 2.6 percent.[29] The 361 to 1 earnings ratio between CEOs and workers illuminates the rise in income inequality. Thanks in large part to the weakening of organized labor, the United States today has the highest level of economic inequality among industrialized nations. But this situation took place in a larger context that deserves a brief examination here before moving on to an examination of the causes behind the decline of unions.

Several other factors besides the decline of unions helped fuel the rise in economic inequality. Nobel Prize–winning economist Joseph Stiglitz agrees that the decline in union membership is a primary cause of America's growing income inequality, but he and many others also point to government policies as a significant contributor to the contraction of America's middle class. When asked how best to understand rising income inequality in the United States, Stiglitz responded: "I think the change in labor law that has weakened the bargaining rights of workers obviously had a very adverse effect."[30] Stiglitz's response illuminates the role of government in directly attacking organized labor. Government hostility to unions, to be discussed in chapter 2, is a major contributor to the decline of organized labor. But public policy affects the middle class in many other ways.

After World War II, government policy contributed to middle-class growth through a host of legislative acts. Government-backed mortgages that allowed working people to move out of crowded tenements and the G.I. Bill that paid college costs for returning soldiers played an instrumental role in building America's middle class. The federal government was indispensable in providing opportunities to members of the postwar generation. The Truman Commission outlined a plan to expand affordable public higher education in the United States, thus leading to the expansion of institutions of higher learning throughout the country. For instance, in 1946 New York became the last of the forty-eight states to establish a public university system when Governor Dewey through his Dewey Commission created the State University of New York.[31] A progressive tax structure with a top rate of 91 percent for the wealthiest during the Eisenhower administration made sure the rich paid their fair share. In 1969 the income tax rate was still 77 percent and, as Robert Reich observed, high tax rates on the very wealthy "did not reduce economic growth . . . they enabled the nation to expand middle-class prosperity, which fueled growth."[32]

These days things are different. The country's tax laws are less than fair, with the top rate dropping to 37 percent of earned income and even less on investment income such as rent, dividends, interest earnings, and capital gains. These sources are taxed at a rate of about 20 percent. This category of income has expanded more and more to benefit the very rich, who derive a large share of their incomes from these non-labor sources.[33] Joseph Stiglitz reminds us that the bottom 90 percent of all income earners get less than 10 percent of all capital gains. Compare that to the wealthiest 400 taxpayers as measured by income. Wages and salaries accounted for just 8.8 percent of their income, with 73 percent of their income deriving from capital gains.[34] They also reap 5 percent of the country's dividends alone. Lowering the capital gains rate from 35 percent gave each of the wealthiest 400 an average gift of $45 million in 2007 while lowering government tax revenues that year by $18 billion.[35]

Tax cuts to the rich also run up the federal deficit, shifting more burdens to the states while simultaneously reducing the flow of federal dollars back to them. As the spigot of federal funds to the states gradually closes, states cut programs beneficial to the middle class. Spending on infrastructure drops and with it the quality of public transportation, public drinking water, and sewage treatment systems. Medicaid is usually at the top of the list of programs targeted for cuts, but reduced spending on public health, nutrition, housing, and schools is becoming standard practice. In addition to reducing spending, states attempt to raise revenues in a number of ways.[36] Regressive sales taxes are common, including the imposition of large tuition hikes on public colleges and universities, restricting a prime source of admission into the middle class. Higher education is becoming increasingly out of reach of too many Americans. The tax reform of 2017 exacerbated the already precarious state of the middle classes by running up a record-smashing national budget deficit that leaders of the Republican Party now cite as the reason to cut Medicare, Social Security, Medicaid, and other vital programs. While the average American stands to lose Medicare, Social Security, and the rest of the so-called safety net, 83 percent of the benefits of the Tax Cuts and Jobs Act of 2017 goes to the richest 1 percent of the population.

Corporations Grow, Unions Shrink

As union membership has plummeted to pre-Depression lows, the private corporate sector has thrived, growing bigger, more centralized, more profitable, and more politically powerful. The urge to merge has become the driving force of corporate behavior. Since 2008, for instance, more than $10 trillion in mergers have taken place in corporate America. The ongoing consolidation of corporations and the decline of market competition continue to increase. In 2015, American companies established a new record for most mergers in a single year, and the month of October 2016 set a new standard for most mergers in a single month.[37] The merger movement and its accompanying control of market share is an issue of international concern. In June of 2018, Jason Furman, former chair of the Council of Economic Advisors to President Obama, testified on the increase of economic concentration in U.S. industries at a hearing on economic concentration held by the Organization for Economic Co-operation and Development. In commenting on market power and economic concentration in the United States, Furman concluded that "most industries have seen a few large players account for an increasing share of their market."[38]

The implications of concentrated corporate power are far-reaching. Concentrated corporate power allows for price gouging. Price gouging produces super high profits. And super high profits can be used to buy political power and to obliterate the countervailing power of unions. Recent examples abound. In an op-ed piece written in 2015, presidential candidate Hillary Clinton condemned legal price-fixing in the airline and pharmaceutical industries. Some drug companies, she observed, raised prices by as much as 5,000 percent for drugs that have been on the market for years. Today the four major U.S. airlines—down from ten less than two decades ago—have not lowered ticket prices or removed special fuel cost fees despite the cost of oil dropping by one dollar a gallon.[39] The four largest domestic airlines—American, Delta, United-Continental, and Southwest—control 73 percent of the market.[40] Price-fixing? Stiglitz agrees with Clinton that "monopoly corporations are the primary reason that drug prices in the United States are higher than anywhere else in the world." As for consumer choices, Stiglitz asks, if we find our internet company not to our liking, what are the alternatives, and if there are any, are they any better?[41]

Corporate price-fixing, whether legal or illegal, exacerbates the effect of workers' stagnate wages by raising the cost that workers pay for consumer goods. While workers pay more, corporate profits surge and CEO salaries skyrocket. Profits earned by corporations during the second quarter of 2018 clearly illustrate this fact when they reached a record-breaking high of $2.0075 trillion. Is it any wonder that the average CEO salary increased by 8.5 percent in 2017? As noted above, the average CEO salary of $13.94 million in 2018 is 361 times greater than the average pay of nonsupervisory workers.[42] But average salaries don't tell the complete story. Just look at Broadcom's Hock Tan, who received a 318 percent raise to boost his annual salary to $103.2 million. [43]

Just as important, corporate centralization has a negative effect on workers' wages, particularly when unions are weak or absent. Numerous studies indicate that in concentrated industries where there are very few employers, workers have limited options for employment and even less leverage once they are employed. Such monopsonistic markets, of course, affect wages, for lack of competition among employers allows them to keep wages down.[44] The sheer size and market power of corporations also impacts workers' earnings. Decades prior to the 1980s saw a direct positive correlation between corporate size and worker earnings. Large unionized companies such as U.S. Steel, General Motors, and General Electric paid their workers middle-class wages. Beginning in the 1980s this correlation began to disappear. Today, the wage premium huge corporations paid is gone and the correlation between firm size and employee earnings is muted. The shift from manufacturing to a service economy also contributed to this change, as has the dependence on outsourcing as a means to cut labor costs.[45] But the sheer size and power of the corporate behemoths allows them to drive down workers' wages. A 2018 paper by the EPI finds that economic concentration has, indeed, increased over time and that market concentration does suppress wages. The EPI study applauds the growing literature on economic centralization but concludes that "rising concentration by itself cannot explain a significant portion of key trends in American wages over recent decades."[46] Fighting economic concentration is no silver bullet, the EPI concludes, for corporations of any size can lower wages if workers lack bargaining power.[47]

The decline of unions and the growth of corporate centralization mean lower wages for workers, higher salaries for CEOs, greater economic inequality, and higher prices for consumers. The implications for American democracy are far-reaching. In the mid–twentieth century, Galbraith and others rationalized the end of competitive markets and the rise of giant corporations by arguing for the force of countervailing powers such as organized labor and, at times, the federal government. Now, with 93 percent of all workers in the private sector employed in non-union jobs and under 11 percent of the total labor force unionized, organized labor's ability to countervail the power of the behemoth American corporate sector has all but disappeared. Unions remain politically active, but their influence has receded. Giant corporations have more political resources than the diminished organized labor movement. Big corporations can always blackmail politicians by threatening layoffs, plant closings, and the like. But corporations also have apparently unlimited cash to protect their political interests. In 2012, for instance, the corporate sector spent $56 on lobbying for every dollar spent by labor unions.[48] A crucial turning point in union's ability to influence election occurred in the Supreme Court's 2010 ruling in the *Citizens United v. the Federal Election Commission* case. The decision gave corporations and unions the ability to spend unlimited funds on political ads and other political means to convince voters to support or oppose a political candidate. Interestingly enough, the AFL-CIO apparently felt good about its political muscle and initially submitted an *amicus* brief in favor of removing the spending prohibitions. After evaluating their resources compared to potential corporate spending on elections, the AFL-CIO came to its senses and withdrew its brief in support of the change. *Citizens* ruled, first, that corporations are persons and, second, that as persons, their speech is protected under the First Amendment. Then a lower court ruling in *SpeechNow.org v. FEC* used *Citizens United* as precedent to kick open the floodgates to unlimited campaign spending by removing limits on contributions to PACs and dark money[49] groups that make independent political expenditures.[50] This ruling, combined with the Supreme Court's restrictions on disclosure, led to the formation of super PACs and made it possible for individual right-wing billionaires such as Las Vegas casino magnate Sheldon Adelson to pour about $40 million into conservative and anti-labor causes.[51] With no limitations on political spending, the weakened union movement is at a great disadvantage. During the 2012 election cycle, for instance, the conservative Koch brothers' political networks alone poured $407 million into various right-wing campaigns. Super PACs are playing an increasingly bigger role in campaign financing, but disclosure protections hide the identity of contributors.[52] That's why it's called dark money.

In light of a smaller organized labor movement, *Citizens United* delivered another blow to labor's power by reducing its influence within the Democratic Party. When Big Labor was actually big, unions were one of the top contributors to the Democratic Party. In fact, in the 1980s and into the early 1990s, contributions to the Democratic Party by unions and the top 0.01 percent of the population were about equal. As unions shrunk and restrictions on campaign spending were removed, the top 0.01 percent outspent unions by a 4-to-1 ratio during the 2012 election cycle.[53] This helps explain why studies show that, increasingly, Democrats do not support policies that would reduce economic inequality as much as in the past.[54] In short, as unions become smaller and weaker, they lose political power, which, in turn, weakens them even more.

When it comes to political spending, unions are at a clear disadvantage. But money is only one of many other political resources. Union membership is associated with higher political participation rates, first, because organized labor's sheer number of voters has in the past compensated for its lack of dollars. Second, union members have been a traditional source of volunteer labor to get others out to vote. Unfortunately for organized labor and American democracy, both roles are now vastly diminished. It's still true that union members are more likely to vote in midterm elections than non-union workers. In 2014, for instance, only 39 percent of non-unionists voted, compared to 52 percent of union workers. This voting gap is even greater at the lower end of the income spectrum, where 40 percent of union workers earning less than $25,000 voted, as opposed to 15 percent of non-union employees. The problem today isn't just the drop in percentage of participation by union members, it's their declining numbers. As the number of union members decreases, so does voter turnout. In 1940, 34 percent of eligible voters cast their ballots. As labor union membership grew, voter turnout increased. In 1950, some 43 percent of eligible voters cast their ballots, and by 1967 turnout rate peaked at 48 percent. Voter participation has declined steadily since 1967, dropping to 36 percent in 2014.[55]

The fading size and strength of unions within the context of economic centralization and the growth of the corporate sector does not augur well for American democracy. The power of a strong union movement, along with other powerful institutions, including the government itself, would, so the theory of countervailing power goes, serve as a counterweight to offset the potential economic and political domination of giant corporations. In so doing, these institutions of countervailing power would ensure that America's workers and middle class would gain a fair share of the country's wealth. This theory may have held true when unions were strong and could countervail the power of corporations. In fact, in the early 1960s, President Kennedy acknowledged Big Labor's political clout in promoting the interests of unionists and the entire middle class by dubbing the AFL-CIO "the people's lobby."[56] But that's not the case today. On the economic front, the data on Big Labor's decline and the rise of income inequality tell the story. Working- and middle-class people are not sharing the wealth. In fact, the middle class is rapidly disappearing.

At the political level, the democratic value of civic participation, a value crucial to the culture and practice of democracy, is vanishing. As the size of unions diminishes, fewer people participate in political campaigns, and voter turnout declines. Big-moneyed interests fill the political vacuum by defining the political dialogue and shaping public policy. A recent study put contemporary American democracy to a test by analyzing different theories of who rules, who really governs? In answering these questions in a near post-unionized society, the authors arrived at a troubling conclusion. Their findings indicate that the American public has little influence over governmental policies. The authors applaud our institutions that are democratic in form: free speech, regular elections, a wide-spread voting franchise, the right to assemble, and so on, but conclude "if policymaking is dominated by powerful business organizations and a small number of affluent Americans, then America's claims to being a democratic society are seriously threatened."[57]

Chapter 2

The Long Slide

As president of the National Labor College, I was sitting at a table with a dozen or so other top level members of the AFL-CIO's management team. To the best of my recollection it was the spring of 2009. At the previous manager's meeting, President Sweeney's chief of staff, Bob Welsh, had told us that the AFL-CIO was on the verge of a major organizing victory. It was just a matter of working out the remaining details. Now, a month later, we were all patiently sitting around that same table anticipating the big announcement. The chief of staff, a very bright guy whom we all respected, walked into the room, took his seat, and finally announced the great victory: some 800-plus California car washers had agreed to join the United Steelworkers of America (USWA). I was shocked. Our big victory wasn't 80,000 new members, or even 8,000. It was just 800. A few decades earlier, 800 new members would have been treated as business as usual. But that was then. Today, given the current state of unions and the difficulties of organizing in the United States, signing 800 new members in an industry that was not unionized was indeed a major victory.

This scenario depicts the current state of organized labor in the United States today. For decades, the steady loss of members and union power has plagued the U.S. labor movement, leading most observers to agree that unions are in crisis. While there's overwhelming agreement that unions are on the brink of disaster, there is no consensus on the reasons for organized labor's decline. As noted earlier, some attribute it to organized labor's focus on business unionism; others point their finger at unions' ineffective organizing techniques. Still others fault labors' lack of militancy, its emphasis on electoral politics rather than organizing, the globalization of capital, or labor's failure to develop into a larger social movement.[1] All these analyses are at least partially accurate, but they fail to address the core problem. Simply put, the organizational structure no longer serves the mission of the labor movement for two reasons, one external and one internal. Externally, big business and its cronies are waging an all-out war against organized labor as the last bastion of resistance against corporate hegemony. Internally, labor leaders too often mistake the survival of individual union organizations with the survival of the union movement itself. The first section of this chapter explores the questions of why, after years of labor peace and cooperation, the corporate sector launched its intense war on unions and how they are waging this war. To answer these questions this chapter first examines labor struggles immediately following the war, the emerging social contract between capital and labor, and how this contract helped shape the economy. It then analyzes the consequences of the changing economy on this social contract, the transformation of work in the United States, and how corporations are using their power to marginalize and crush unions. The second section of the chapter investigates attempts by unions to meet the challenges presented by this corporate warfare, the loss of members, the changing economy, and the resultant decline of organized labors' economic and political clout.

Labor and the Postwar Economy

Post–World War II America sets the scene for organized labor's rise and decline. The Great Depression in the United States finally ended with the onset of World War II. Massive government military spending brought full employment by creating seventeen million new civilian jobs and expanding industrial production by 96 percent. Although the war effort directly consumed more than one-third of the nation's industrial output, for the first time in years consumers had money to spend on consumer goods.[2] The idle factories, long unemployment lines, and chronic deflation that characterized the Great Depression were in the past. The American economy was, indeed, humming along, but it was not without problems. Despite government restrictions on prices and wages, inflation had become a serious issue. In fact, between January 1941 and June 1945, the cost of living had jumped by 30 percent.[3] Inflation was just one issue. There was also much uncertainty as to whether the war economy could successfully make the transition to peace time without slipping back into a depression. Given the huge cuts in military expenditures, it was reasonable to ask if the twelve million returning soldiers would have jobs. The end of military spending meant an annual loss in wages alone of about $2 billion. Uncertainty was the order of the immediate postwar world.

Postwar economic uncertainty put organized labor in a tough position. Despite continued government controls, wages and prices continued to rise. A growing anti-labor sector of government, consisting mainly of representatives from the border and southern states where unions were weak, blamed unions for the wage-price spiral. Not surprisingly, the corporate sector, which had reaped great profits during the war, was more concerned with controlling wage costs than keeping prices down. Consequently, they appealed to the magic of the marketplace, calling for an end to government's wartime restrictions on prices. Corporations and anti-labor politicians from the South were joined by an emerging segment of the general population that blamed union wage increases for rising prices. This combined anti-union force encouraged many elected officials to look for ways to weaken the Wagner Act, Labor's Bill of Rights.[4]

Unions also found the wage-price spiral unacceptable. The different positions of capital and labor were crystal clear. Whereas corporations viewed high wages as the issue, labor defined rising prices as the problem. The conflict between these two competing perspectives was at the heart of the immediate postwar struggle between labor and industry, triggering a hard-fought power struggle between unions and the corporate sector. The playing out of this conflict would have a significant long-term impact on unions, corporations, and, in fact, the American political economy.

CIO president Phillip Murray recognized the implications of industry's commitment to control prices by keeping wages down. Fearing corporate induced labor strife, he warned both management and labor that "only chaos and destruction" would result if anti-labor employers forced unions to take militant actions, including strikes. To avoid a destructive conflict, Murray sought a continuation of the tripartite bargaining cooperation among labor, industry, and the government that began to collapse after the war. In his view, labor would benefit through business policies that favored high wages, high employment, and a commitment by business not to amend the Wagner Act. In return, unions would continue the war-time no-strike pledge and recognize industry's right to direct its own operation; in other words, labor would not seek price controls.[5] Government would oversee the agreement between labor and capital. Murray's proposal, as labor historian Nelson Lichtenstein observes, was essentially a form of corporatism similar to what developed in the advanced European countries after the war.[6]

Murray's plan was not well received by corporate interests that had felt overly constrained by government wage and price controls during the war. But industry was not alone in rejecting Murray's corporatist idea. Led by the United Auto Workers (UAW) First-Vice-President, Walter Reuther, a large segment of the union movement also rejected Murray's program. With government spending on the wane, Reuther argued that workers needed a large raise to sustain the economy and to compensate for lost pay when the postwar work week was cut by eight hours.[7] Given industry's resistance to price controls and large wage increases, he saw direct militant action as the only realistic way to realize the dual goals of raising wages while holding prices down. Reuther's brother Victor clearly articulated the rejection of Murray's proposed cooperative agreement when he publicly stated, "It is time to debunk the notion that labor can meet in parlays with government and management and by some miracle, fashion a compromise that will keep all parties happy and contented."[8] Consequently, Walter Reuther presented General Motors with a strike demand for a 30 percent wage increase. After the automaker rejected the wage demand by claiming it couldn't afford it, Reuther petitioned the company to prove it by (1) opening its books to the public, and (2) not raising car prices as a result of any negotiated wage increase. Holding auto prices steady, Reuther believed, would generate community support for the union's position, hold the line on inflation, and boost the economy. General Motors' profit margin, he argued, was sufficient to meet the union's wage demands without raising car prices. Not surprisingly, GM found these "socialist" demands unacceptable, triggering the start of a hard-fought strike by 320,000 autoworkers that lasted 113 days.[9]

While the autoworkers were striking, other industrial workers walked off the job, too. In the largest strike wave since 1919, between November 1945 and June 1946 more than three million workers went on strike.[10] All the strikes were about wages and working conditions, but what made the UAW strike unique was its attempt to limit the automaker's ability to set prices. After more than two million striking workers in other industrial sectors returned to work, the UAW was the last holdout.[11] Increasingly feeling the pressure to settle, the UAW finally agreed to a raise of about 19 percent, but without realizing its goal of restricting management from raising car prices to cover the cost of wage increases.

Inflation took off as the cost of living jumped by about 14 percent in an eight-month period between March and November 1946.[12] This inflationary spiral led the major unions to return to the bargaining table the following year, prompting labor's enemies to intensify their attacks on unions as the cause of rising prices. Unions came under further attacks after the CIO attempted to organize southern states in its highly publicized and well-funded "Operation Dixie" campaign. Although the massive organizing drive failed, it galvanized Southern Democrats to join with their Republican colleagues in Congress to pass the Taft-Hartley Act in 1947, a law that undercut many of the rights guaranteed labor in the Wagner Act.[13] Anti-union sentiment in Congress was so strong it overrode President Truman's veto of the bill. At the same time, big industrial corporations also needed labor stability. America's manufacturing sector was making huge investments to convert to peacetime production. General Motors, for instance, had undertaken a multibillion dollar expansion plan and another major strike would undermine these plans. To achieve the stability and predictability needed for long-range planning, in 1950 GM and other major automakers made significant concessions to the UAW, an agreement that *Fortune* magazine dubbed the Treaty of Detroit. The treaty, which eventually spread to other industrial sectors, provided pensions, health care, and pay raises tied to the cost of living in return for a five-year contract that guaranteed labor stability. *Fortune* magazine observed that the treaty was the first to accept "the existing distribution of income between wages and profit as 'normal' if not 'fair.' "[14] The agreement allowed large corporations to make long-range plans and investments with knowledge of labor costs and assurances of labor stability. With a contented labor movement no longer seeking to limit their internal activities such as setting prices, big corporation's used their sufficient power to maintain their system of administered pricing that passed production costs onto the consumer.[15] Both unionized workers and corporations benefited from this arrangement. This system of mutually beneficial cooperation worked as long as competition remained minimal.

Since the war had devastated foreign industries, American companies dominated the world economy. The Marshall plan rebuilt war-devastated Europe and provided U.S. manufacturers with additional markets to prosper. During the 1950s, for instance, American steelmakers employed approximately 700,000 workers and produced over 40 percent of the world's steel.[16] The four largest U.S. steelmakers alone accounted for nearly 30 percent of the world's steel production.[17] Concentration in other industries was even more extreme. The Big Three domestic automakers, as late as the early 1970s, produced 93 percent of all cars made in the United States, and the four largest cereal companies turned out 90 percent of all breakfast cereals.[18] The absence of any significant domestic or international competition, combined with the ability to pass on labor costs in product pricing, contributed to high profitability for the companies and decent wages for the unionized labor force. This controlled market arrangement generally led to higher product prices. In fact, prices tended to rise faster than labor costs. Again, looking at steel, an industry characterized by follow-the-leader pricing, in the ten years from 1947 to 1957, labor costs increased by 5.2 percent annually while steel prices rose by 7 percent a year.[19] Controlled or oligopolistic markets also inhibited technological innovation. During the 1950s and into the '60s, automakers changed the tailfins of their cars every year but neglected quality issues.[20] American steel producers avoided the financial risks associated with new technologies and instead invested in forty million tons of open hearth capacity while the rest of the industrial world invested in modern basic oxygen furnaces. *Business Week* claimed this decision put American steel companies at a disadvantage they couldn't overcome.[21]

Although the controlled markets functioned as designed for American corporations and their unionized workers for a generation after the war, the problems inherent in noncompetitive oligopolistic markets eventually undercut the foundation of this arrangement.[22] The first signs of trouble appeared as early as the late 1950s when lower-priced foreign steel, primarily Japanese, flooded the U.S. market, making the United States a net importer of steel.[23] Rather than modernize their facilities, U.S. steel companies, in conjunction with the steelworkers' union, used their massive political clout with the federal government to gain protection against foreign imports. Concurrently, the steel industry underwent a massive restructuring: some steel companies merged, while others were swallowed up by conglomerates or invested in non-steel industries. In 1968, for example, the LTV corporate conglomerate added Jones and Laughlin Steel to its vast portfolio. Lykes similarly bought Youngstown Sheet and Tube, which it milked for revenue it invested in areas other than steel. Then U.S. Steel Corporation purchased Marathon Oil, a not-so-subtle signal about where U.S. Steel thought the market was heading.[24] Steel was threatened by imports earlier than other industries, but by the late 1970s it had become clear that lower-priced foreign imports threatened virtually every domestic industry.[25] The 1973 oil crisis propelled the purchase of small, fuel-efficient Japanese cars, imports that captured 29 percent of the U.S. market by 1981. Japanese companies also dominated the electronics industry and made inroads in farm equipment and the growing computer industry. Germans and Swedes captured the high-tech machine tool industry, and Italians made inroads in the fashion scene.[26]

The Coming of Post-Industrial Society: Won't It Be Grand

The consequences of foreign competition were far-reaching. First, U.S. company profits dropped. In the early 1960s the annual average return on investment for nonfinancial corporations was about 15.5 percent. After 1975, the rate of profit fell below 10 percent. Second, in response to declining profits, corporations rejected the social contract between labor and capital that had been in effect since the Treaty of Detroit. General Electric's Jack Welch famously summarized the new corporate attitude toward labor and local communities by suggesting that corporations owed their allegiance to stockholders, not employees.[27] Now, the driving corporate philosophy became making as much money as possible as quickly as possible. In short, as Gordon Gecko declared, greed is good.

The stockholders Welch spoke about were largely financiers, because during the early 1970s financial institutions—banks and insurance companies—became major shareholders in American industrial companies. By 1980, for instance, Chase Manhattan Bank had become the largest shareholder of the General Electric Corporation. The central question for finance capital is always, "Where do I make the most money?" So long-term investing in manufacturing began to take a backseat to financial ventures that could turn a quicker and bigger buck short term.

No longer able to raise prices at will and crippled by outdated, inefficient industrial infrastructure, U.S. companies were in a bind: how do they make a buck under these conditions against foreign competitors? Capital seeks its most profitable outlets. Operating on the time-tested principle that labor is stationary and capital is mobile, corporations initially sought cheap labor in the non-union South. Additionally, companies intensified overseas investments in countries where labor costs were even lower and unions virtually nonexistent. Thanks to their political power, American companies also benefited from the financial incentives the nation's tax laws provided for foreign investments.[28] This led to massive plant closings and shutdowns that destroyed more than fifteen million U.S. jobs between 1969 and 1976.[29] This massive corporate flight, dubbed by Bluestone and Harrison as deindustrialization, reshaped the labor force. Since the bulk of the lost jobs were in unionized industries, union membership declined in both percentage and in absolute numbers. By the early 1980s only 19 percent of the labor force was organized.[30] Corporate flight continues to this day, thanks in part to the North American Free Trade Agreement (NAFTA) of 1994.[31] During the first decade of the twenty-first century the United States lost another 5.5 million manufacturing jobs, about one-third of the total. In the 2016 presidential campaign candidate Trump loudly proclaimed that "A Trump administration will stop the jobs from leaving America."[32] Unfortunately for American workers, during Trump's first two years in office jobs fled overseas at a record rate.[33]

The new era of foreign competition prevented corporations from passing on labor costs through higher prices. Deindustrialization was one response. Another response was to increase production efficiency by modernizing and introducing new computerized and robotic technologies in the domestic facilities they choose to keep operating. This too reduced the unionized workforce. Consequently, U.S. automakers today are about even with Germany and slightly behind China in the use of robotics. In fact, 55 percent of the U.S. demand for robotics comes from the U.S. auto industry, where robotics are currently 1,141 units per every 10,000 workers.[34] Labor-saving technology is even more extreme in the American steel industry. Productivity has increased drastically while the labor force has declined.[35] In the 1980s, in large integrated mills, it took 10.1 work hours to produce a ton of steel. Today modern, efficient mini-mills use electric arc furnaces to make steel out of scrap metal. It now takes just 1.5 work hours to produce a ton of steel. Some super-efficient mills can make a ton in 0.5 work hours. Domestic steel production today is just slightly below a fifty-year average, but the industry employs just over 140,000 workers, about a fourth of its postwar high employment level.[36] The developing robotics technology, according to a Brookings Institute report, could take 25 percent of American jobs.[37]

The millions of high-paying jobs that disappeared were generally replaced by low-paying service sector jobs. Clerical work had been the fastest-growing occupation in the economy since the end of World War I and into the mid-1980s, when one in six people worked as clerks or in sales.[38] This marked a sea change in the nature of work that began to take place in the 1970s as U.S.-based corporations moved from manufacturing to service to the gig economy. During the 1970s, about 90 percent of all new jobs created were in the low-paying, non-union service sector.[39] In a study for the Joint Economic Committee, Bluestone and Harrison found that most of the twenty million new jobs created between 1979 and 1984 were at the low end of the wage and salary scale.[40] During that same period more workers took jobs as independent contractors in short-term operations, a trend that prefigured the rise of the gig economy. Today, over 80 percent of the American workforce is employed in the low-paying service sector.[41]

While blue-collar workers lost their jobs to corporate flight overseas, the white-collar workforce also took some hard hits. Initially, the virtual absence of unions gave managers the ability to rely on poorly paid temporary workers. As early as the 1960s, firms outsourced through temporary agencies. Since these workers were not employees, they lacked stable long-term employment and the possibility of wage increases, health care, and pensions, all benefits that unions had previously won at the bargaining table. Later, white-collar jobs were outsourced domestically and overseas. Louis Hyman describes what happened to white-collar workers in clear terms: "Call centers, accounting, and many other formerly internal functions were subcontracted to the lowest bidder . . ."[42] The rise of the digital age accelerated the outsourcing process, enabling business firms to set up work centers anywhere in the world and freeing them from their dependence on temp agencies for workers. Early on, Craigslist gave companies easy access to a willing labor force, but by the 2000s new digital labor platforms appeared, TaskRabbit, Uber, and Elance, to name just a few. Following the Great Recession of 2008–2009, employers and jobseekers could now use a proliferation of websites as the middleman. This short-term, temporary work attained through the new technology is the gig economy.[43] Nowadays, when someone says they have a gig, they don't necessarily mean a club date for a musical performance. The gig economy runs on non-union, usually low-paying and insecure jobs that contribute significantly to the steady disappearance of America's middle class.[44] As journalist Philip Dine has observed, "Plunging union levels don't reflect workers' opting out of unions but . . . a shifting balance between the manufacturing and tertiary sector jobs."[45]

War on Unions: The Disappearing Middle Class

While the corporate sector engaged in deindustrialization and restructuring, they simultaneously initiated an all-out political war on labor unions.

The threat of shutdowns, backed by the reality of corporate flight and declining membership numbers, reduced labor's leverage at the bargaining table. A turning point for collective bargaining in heavy industry came with the highly publicized Chrysler bailout of 1979. Threatened with bankruptcy, Chrysler had arranged for a massive line of credit that the U.S. government promised to guarantee. Despite the government's guarantee, the banks wanted concessions from the union. On the premise that concessions would save jobs, the UAW agreed to a giveback package worth hundreds of millions. Union workers surrendered paid holidays, took pay cuts, and deferred their pension increases. Labor's concessions did not solve Chrysler's financial issues; nor did they keep Chrysler from closing some facilities. But they did two things crucial for all major industrial producers. First, the givebacks at Chrysler broke the tradition of industry-wide pattern bargaining. By ending the decades-old tradition of pattern bargaining,[46] corporate managers could negotiate lower wages and benefits by pitting plant against plant in a competitive race to the bottom. Failure to participate in this competition of givebacks could result in a plant closing. In fact, the breaking of pattern bargaining played an instrumental role in fostering concession bargaining and weakened unions. Second, the agreement opened the door to a pattern of concession bargaining that exists throughout industry even today. Shortly after the Chrysler givebacks, workers at Ford and General Motors made concessions. Union workers at the seven companies covered by the Basic Steel Agreement initially rejected proposed concessions, but after givebacks in airlines, trucking, rubber, and other industries, the steelworkers also joined the ever-growing giveback club. Initially concessions focused on cuts in wages, benefits, and pensions. They split the labor movement further by imposing two-tier wage and benefit programs. Today, new hires at Chrysler, Ford, and General Motors make between $14 and $19 an hour, about half of what their senior co-workers earn. Eventually the givebacks went even deeper, shifting other financial obligations from management to the union. Automakers, for example, dodged their health insurance obligations to some 800,000 retired members of the UAW by putting up $59 billion in cash and stocks to create a new health fund, the Voluntary Employees Beneficiary Association (VEBA), that the UAW would now administer and finance.[47] No doubt, $59 billion is a large sum of money. But look what it bought. The UAW alone is now responsible for the management and fiscal solvency of a fund that pays for retiree health care benefits, and the benefits provided are no longer guaranteed. They are a function of the fiscal health of the fund. Should the VEBA's earnings fail to keep up with rising health care costs, the UAW, not the company, would cut retirees' health benefits. Management is now off the hook.

Some labor organizers view the strike as the most effective tool in organized labors' tool box.[48] That is debatable. In the early days of unions, workers struck to secure a host of improvements to the terms and conditions of their employment. In contrast, for at least the last forty years, workers strike just to hold on to what they have. In 2019, for example, 50,000 UAW members joined the ongoing national wave of walkouts by initiating a strike against the General Motors Corporation (GMC). Like most of the other strikes, this one was defensive. GMC had earned over $35 billion in North America alone over the preceding three years while closing plants in the United States. Worse yet, compensation to GM executives had skyrocketed, but workers' inflation-adjusted pay continued its two-decade decline. Other issues leading to the walkout included a GM demand that workers pay a larger share of the costs of health benefits and the company's reliance on lower-paid temporary workers.[49] When the forty-day strike ended, workers received raises plus bonuses equivalent to their lost wages; health care costs remained the same, and temporary workers benefited from a process to become permanent employees; and the strike averted a previously announced plant closing. However, during the strike the company announced it was closing more plants and cutting up to 6,000 jobs, including its Lordstown, Ohio, factory. *Vox* characterized the settlement as not "terrible for workers, but it's hardly a victory."[50] So much for strikes bringing capital to its knees.

The relentless decline of wages has now made some parts of America attractive for foreign investors. In 2011, a study by a Boston consulting firm concluded that labor costs of factory workers in Shanghai would approach the costs of production in Mississippi by 2015. According to the study, America is flexible compared to all economies with the exception of China. By flexible, of course, the authors mean low wages. The report's conclusion that jobs will return to the United States is proving accurate, given its definition of the United States in geographical terms: the South.[51] General Electric re-shored its production of water heaters and refrigerators from China and Mexico into the U.S. South. Aerospace manufacturers and auto makers find the South a good place to invest. In the period between 1980 and 2013, auto industry jobs grew by 52 percent in the South while declining by 33 percent in the Midwest. Much of the investment is coming from overseas. Today, Nissan has two facilities in the

South, in Tennessee and Mississippi; Volkswagen has a plant in Tennessee; Mercedes has a factory in Alabama and will soon open a new one in South Carolina; BMW also has a plant in South Carolina, in Spartanburg; and Volvo built a plant in Ridgeville, South Carolina. All manufacturing jobs rose by 196 percent in Alabama, 121 percent in South Carolina, and 103 percent in Tennessee. Germans chose to invest in the United States rather than China, a German union leader at Airbus explained, because "it's cheaper to do the final assembly in the U.S." Despite the opening of auto plants across the South, wages for workers at auto parts plants fell. Between 2001 and 2013, Alabama workers took a 24 percent wage cut, and their colleagues in Mississippi suffered a 13.6 percent wage loss.[52] In the meantime, the Rust Belt is getting rustier as manufacturing continues to plummet: since 1980, Ohio has experienced a 36 percent decline in manufacturing, Wisconsin a 43 percent slide, and Michigan a 49 percent reduction.[53]

Manufacturing wages continue to decline in the South for several reasons, even while the number of jobs continues to increase. Five states have no minimum wage law, and another has a minimum below the national standard. Perhaps more importantly, unions are virtually nonexistent in the South. Union density in Georgia is 4.3 percent, 3.7 percent in Mississippi, a mere 2.2 percent in South Carolina, and 1.9 percent in North Carolina. Many workers are employed through temporary agencies. About half of Nissan's workforce in its southern plants are temps. State and local governments support companies that prevent unions from organizing. In Tennessee, Volkswagen announced its neutrality but allowed union organizers to enter its plant. The company viewed the unionization of its facility as a means to set up German-style work councils that they believe give them a competitive advantage. Tennessee's anti-union Republican establishment quickly responded to what they perceived to be VW's pro-union position by threatening to kill additional tax incentives for the company.[54] To make sure workers understood the "need" to defeat the union's organizing efforts, the state governor and U.S. Senator Bob Corker also publicly opposed unionization. Corker went so far as to proclaim during the certification election that VW would expand its facilities and create more jobs if workers rejected the union.[55] These anti-union attacks initially paid off. In a close certification election, the UAW lost by less than a hundred votes. But Volkswagen wanted the workers councils that came with union representation. In a decision that defied the hostile political environment, the company formally recognized the

UAW as the worker's official bargaining agent. By April 2015, a majority of the workers had joined the union.[56] A year later, following the company's emissions scandal, Volkswagen's management team reversed its decision and openly opposed the UAW's efforts to unionize the plant. In 2018 Volkswagen announced plans to expand their Tennessee facility.

The legal deck is stacked against organizing unions in the United States. In fact, the power of American organized labor is restricted by a hostile legal environment. The Wagner Act of 1935 gave employees the right to organize and form a union for collective bargaining without interference. This union-friendly law gave impetus to the massive growth in unions during the 1930s and into the 1940s. In the decade following the passage of Wagner, some eight million new workers joined unions.[57] But the wave of postwar strikes and the fear of communist infiltration of unions, a fear that raged through the 1950s, led to the passage of laws restricting unions' power. The favorable legal framework changed drastically in 1947 with passage of the pro-business anti-union Taft-Hartley Act. In amending the Wagner Act, Taft-Hartley made organizing more difficult, prohibited sympathy strikes, outlawed secondary boycotts, and allowed states to pass right-to-work laws.[58] The Act also required union leaders to sign anti-communist affidavits, which later led unions to purge members of the left. As CIO President Murray put it, "If communism is an issue in any of your unions, throw it the hell out."[59] Reports of communist infiltration weakened public confidence in unions.[60] Nevertheless, according to an AFL-CIO report, the new law's impact on unions' power was minimal throughout the 1950s and '60s, as "employers by and large complied with their legal duty to bargain . . . in an honest effort to reach a contract."[61]

The profit squeeze brought by foreign competition changed all that. U.S. corporations raised profits and weakened unions by closing plants and investing in facilities overseas and outsourcing work to low-wage areas. But that was not enough. They also decided, in the words of President Nixon's Assistant Secretary of Labor, to "zap" labor.[62] This meant that management would now resist union efforts to organize and do whatever else it took to smash unions. Taft-Hartley gave management a host of tools to beat back unions. Additionally, what protections workers still enjoyed under the Wagner Act were now often ignored by anti-labor appointments to the NLRB. An AFL-CIO report noted that by the mid-1980s, 95 percent of all employers actively resisted union organizing efforts and three-quarters collectively spent over $100 million on union-busting consultants.[63]

Taft-Hartley's impact on union organizing is huge. It sent a clear anti-union message to employers and gave management the legal tools and political incentive to maintain a union-free environment. In fact, labor scholars Freeman and Medoff estimate that 25 to 50 percent of the decline in union density is attributable to management opposition.[64] Among the anti-union tools Taft-Hartley provides are a more restrictive definition of employees who could form unions. By excluding supervisors and independent contractors, the law not only keeps potential union membership numbers down, it prohibits many in today's growing gig economy from forming unions and earning a livable wage. Taft-Hartley also places tight restrictions on the ability to organize. Union supporters, for instance, can organize only on break time, but the law's "free speech" provision allows employers to wage anti-union campaigns twenty-four hours a day, seven days a week. Employers are also free to legally intimidate workers in any number of ways, depending on their creativity. A study by Cornell's Kate Bronfenbrenner found that employers threatened to close plants in 57 percent of certification elections, discharged workers in 34 percent, and threatened to reduce benefits and wages in 47 percent of elections. It's not unusual for employers to force workers to attend anti-union meetings, punish union supporters who do not attend, distribute anti-union literature, and even force employees to watch anti-union videos. In 63 percent of the cases investigated by Bronfenbrenner, employers forced workers who seemed favorably disposed to unionization to attend one-on-one sessions with a supervisor who interrogated them about other workers who might back the union.[65] If it appears that workers may win a certification after a rigorous campaign, management can contest the makeup of the bargaining unit, removing or adding job classifications favorable to management. Managers also have the right to call for a pre-election hearing. On average, these hearings delay the certification election by 124 days and give management more time to wage an anti-labor campaign, which often proves to be a successful union avoidance strategy.[66] Managers can also call for the certification election even if the union is unprepared. If the organizing drive is defeated, as is often the case, Taft-Hartley mandates a lengthy waiting before the next election.[67] In a report prepared for President Clinton's Dunlop Commission, Cornell's Richard Hurd summarized the current legal obstacles to forming a union: "If an employer is determined to oppose unionization, it is virtually impossible for workers to achieve collective bargaining protections through the NLRB process."[68]

Given management's resistance to unions and a hostile legal structure, it's no surprise that organizing through the process established by
the NLRB and modified by Taft-Hartley has declined drastically over the
years. The number of NLRB elections has plummeted from more than
7,000 annually in the 1960s to less than 2,000 by the end of 2009. While
there are fewer certification elections, the union win rate has increased
from less than 50 percent in the 1980s and 1990s to almost 67 percent in
2009, a winning percentage that mirrors the mid-1970s. This leads to the
obvious conclusion that despite the severe limits of the NLRB, workers
still rely on the process when they believe they will win the election.[69]

Should workers beat the odds and vote for union representation,
they are likely to face stringent resistance from management in negotiating a first contract. The Wagner Act still requires employers to bargain in
good faith. Management often refuses to do so because they know long
delays in negotiating an agreement might result in workers turning on
their union, which is often the case. Other times, employers are more
tactful and discreet. But the data indicate that about one-third of new
unions fail to negotiate a first contract. The legal remedy often comes after
members of the newly formed union give up. Between 1975 and 1985,
union decertifications initiated by discouraged union members increased
by 73 percent.[70]

More than ever before employers now are quick to violate the law
by discharging union supporters. In addition to punishing union activists
with bad job assignments and disciplinary action, the practice of firing
union supporters has increased drastically. In 1957, the NLRB reinstated
922 workers who had been fired for union activism. By 1980, the number
soared to 10,000. Findings by President Clinton's Dunlop Commission
on the Future of Worker-Management Relation's support these data. The
commission reported that illegal firings of workers adversely affected one
in 700 union backers in the 1950s. By the late 1980s, one in fifty union
activists was fired. The report also found that most illegally dismissed
workers fail to take advantage of their right to a reinstatement process
and most of those who do are "gone within a year."[71] During this same
period the number of unfair labor practices against employers rose by 750
percent, in large part because employers knew they could get away with
it. After studying a hundred cases of workers' rights violations, Richard
Hurd concluded that "the right to an independent voice for workers has
become a mirage."[72] The penalties for violating workers' rights are minimal
even when the law is enforced, which is frequently not the case.[73]

The anti-labor bias of the law goes beyond organizing. In the 1938 case of *NLRB v. MacKay Radio and Telegraph Company*, the Supreme Court ruled that it was legal to hire permanent replacement workers during a strike. Respectful of growing union power and influence, employers ignored the court's ruling and did not fire striking workers. The election of Ronald Reagan changed all that. In the summer of 1981, over 13,000 Professional Air Traffic Controllers (PATCO), one of the few unions to endorse Ronald Reagan for President, went on strike. Reagan responded forcefully, warning the strikers to return to work within forty-eight hours or he would fire them. When they didn't return, Reagan fired them. This unprecedented anti-union action by the president gave a green light to employers to crush unions and punish strikers. Not surprisingly, then, companies hired permanent replacement workers in almost one in every five strikes during Reagan's second term. Given corporations' ability to neutralize labor's strike weapon, it's no wonder that the number of strikes has fallen precipitously since the 1980s. In 1974, the high-water mark for strikes involving a minimum of one thousand strikers, there were 425 strikes in which about 1,796,000 workers participated. Compare that to 2017, which saw a total of seven strikes involving 25,000 workers. Just when the strike as a weapon of union action appeared dead in the United States,[74] 425,000 workers, mostly educational workers, walked off their jobs in 2019.[75] This gave hope to some that labor had regained its traditional weapon of the strike. But such hope appears premature given that hundreds of thousands of federal employees continued to report to work despite not getting paid during President Trump's government shutdown of 2018–2019, the longest in American history. European observers questioned why these workers didn't call a general strike as they most certainly would have in Western European countries.[76]

Reagan's appointments to the NLRB and the subsequent anti-labor actions of the board also sent a loud and clear anti-union message. Donald L. Dotson, formerly a management lawyer who publicly and vociferously blamed unions for the decline of entire industries, was anointed by Reagan to take the reins of the NLRB. Under Dotson's guidance, the board reversed previous rulings in more than two dozen cases and allowed a backlog of complaints against employers to develop that was more than three times longer than before Reagan took office, leading some to observe that the board had become the Anti-Labor Relations Board.[77]

It is important to remember that the Wagner Act established the NLRB to promote collective bargaining. Beginning with PATCO and Dotson, Republican administration appointments have been openly hostile to collective bargaining and unions. The board under the Trump administration was perhaps the most extreme anti-union NLRB in history. Trump's board quickly began reversing eight years of labor protections won during the Obama years, leading one legal reporter to observe that "Trump's appointees . . . are contracting the law in a manner that's utterly incongruous with the policy of the board as prescribed by Congress. All indications are that they'll succeed in this partisan mission, and American workers will pay the price."[78] To rub salt into labors' wounds, President Trump honored union-busting Ronald Reagan by inducting him into the Department of Labor's Hall of Honor. As if that weren't enough, Trump further showed his disdain for unions by appointing Peter Robb as counsel to the NLRB. There was absolutely no expectation that Robb would protect organized labor, given his long history of anti-union actions, including his aggressive prosecution of the fired PATCO workers trying to get their jobs back. Ironically, as counsel, Robb was charged with protecting workers' rights by prosecuting violations of the law. In the words of AFL-CIO's Director of Government Affairs, "the decisions and actions of the NLRB general counsel make the difference as to whether or not the rights provided to working people under the NLRA are real rights or just paper rights."[79]

The increasing enmity of the NLRB and the overall hostility of federal and state labor law to unions is a function of organized labor's declining political power. Organized labor has made several serious efforts to amend hostile labor laws. With the backing of President Johnson, in 1965 union groups attempted to repeal the Taft-Hartley Act's provision allowing states to enact right-to-work laws. A Senate filibuster killed their efforts. Today, twenty-seven states have right-to-work laws. In 1978, with limited support from President Carter, unions sought reform aimed at expediting the NLRB's decision-making process and making it easier to organize. Again a lengthy Senate filibuster killed the bill. In 1994, labor groups mounted an effort to prevent employers from hiring permanent replacements for striking workers. This reform bill, too, died in the senate. Following the national elections of 2008, the Employee Free Choice Act (EFCA) was going to be labor's reward from the newly elected Democratic-controlled Congress and White House. During his campaign Obama supported EFCA, a law that would make organizing somewhat easier. But even with Obama's support and Democratic control of both houses, the 111th Congress finished without acting on EFCA. Passage of this law, unions said, would provide an impetus to organizing that would stop the long-term hemorrhaging of membership. Obama did reward labor for its support by appointing labor's candidate, Craig Becker, to the National Labor Relations Board. Since then, the federal and state elections of 2010 thru 2016 went badly for labor, to say the least.[80] Unions helped Democrats gain control of the House in 2018, but with Trump in the White House and the Senate under the control of a Republican Party openly hostile to organized labor, there was no chance that any pro-union legislation would be enacted into law.

As outlined in chapter 1, unions simply do not have the fiscal resources to compete with corporations and their anti-labor supporters. The passage of the Federal Election Campaign Act in 1974 allowed corporations to form PACs, a campaign tool unions already enjoyed. Corporate PACs quickly outgrew and, according to the Center for Responsive Politics (CRP), now outspend their labor counterparts by a margin of more than four to one. Bundling is a second way in which corporations gain access to politicians. The cap on individual contributions encourage bundling, a practice in which a would-be power broker collects contributions from many other individuals and presents them "in a bundle" to a candidate. Corporate lobbyists are expert in this practice. A third of campaign contributions is soft money in the form of issue ads by outside groups that are supposed to be independent of the campaign. The practice was eventually banned but replaced in 2002 by "527" tax-exempt organizations formed to influence elections. According to CRP, for every one dollar unions give to political campaigns, business interests spend fifteen. These numbers reflect campaign contributions prior to the January 2010 Supreme Court decision in *Citizens United v. Federal Election Commission* that removes caps on campaign contributions by organizations. Given business' superior financial resources, their campaign contributions continue to outstrip labor's, further reducing the ability of unions to compete.[81] When it comes to campaign contributions, as labor activist Kim Moody suggests, labor is in a race it can't win.[82] That's why it is difficult to understand why the AFL-CIO submitted an amicus brief urging the Court to remove the restrictions. Thankfully, the AFL-CIO eventually reconsidered and withdrew its support.

Organized labor functions in a hostile political and legal environment. To survive and prosper it needs favorable policy changes, and to do this it must get politicians elected who support labor. Some critics complain that labor's forays into electoral politics are wasteful. Aronowitz and others, for example, are critical of the Sweeney administration's shift of its priorities from organizing to electoral politics.[83] Labor, they argue, now lacks the power to conduct effective "get out the vote" campaigns and can't compete with corporations when it comes to campaign contributions. Besides, the money spent on such political efforts should go into organizing new members. That's how you build a movement, their argument goes. But corporate flight, outsourcing, and the rise of the gig economy place such severe limits on union organizing that it's anything but a panacea to unions' problems.

This is not to suggest that unions are powerless in electoral politics.[84] In 2003 the AFL-CIO created Working America, an organization that allows nonmembers to join with the larger union movement and participate in its political campaigns. Working America recruited tens of thousands of members and played an important role in the elections of 2006, 2008, and 2018, proving that unions remain relevant players despite their many disadvantages. But their power is limited. Many of labor's forays into electoral politics fail, and some apparently backfire. A good example of the latter is the union efforts to unseat Senator Blanche Lincoln in a 2010 Arkansas primary contest. A coalition of the AFL-CIO, SEIU, AFSCME and other unions spent $10 million in an effort to defeat Lincoln with the goal of sending a clear and threatening message to other anti-labor Blue Dog Democrats. Ten million union dollars later, Lincoln, with the help of former Presidents Clinton and Obama, both favorites of the AFL-CIO, secured a narrow primary victory. Weakened by labor's opposition in the primary, Senator Lincoln lost in the general election to a conservative, more virulently anti-union Republican, John Boozman. Given its failure to defeat Lincoln in the primary, the only message labor sent was its growing political irrelevancy.

If organized labor took a beating in the Arkansas senatorial primary election, the general elections in 2010 through 2016 on both the state and national levels proved much worse. In the House, Republicans in 2010 gained more seats (sixty-two) than either party had gained in a midterm election since World War II. The Democrats managed to retain their Senate majority, but Republicans took it back in 2014 and controlled both houses for the next four years. The results in gubernatorial races were, perhaps, even worse. Tea Party governors, led by Wisconsin's Scott Walker, the newly elected governor of the first state to give public employees the right to collective bargaining, launched their assault on public sector employees. According to Walker and his likeminded colleagues across the country, public workers have more than most of the tax payers who foot the bill: they are overpaid and have costly Cadillac health care plans and pensions that tax payers can no longer afford. More, the argument went, when public workers don't get what they want at the bargaining table, they get it from legislators they control through enormous campaign contributions. So how do you protect tax payers? The Tea Party answer: by breaking public sector unions. And that's just what they did.

Not surprisingly, the claim that public workers make more than their counterparts in the private sector is false. A study by the Economic Policy Institute, for example, found that Wisconsin's public sector workers earn about 5 percent less than similarly situated private workers, and the gap widens significantly for public workers with college degrees.[85] The salary differential in Wisconsin is not unique. According to the Center for State and Local Government Excellence, even after accounting for public workers' benefits and pension plans, the earning gap between public and private sector workers has widened in favor of private workers over the past fifteen years.[86]

The charge that unionized public workers "buy" legislators with campaign contributions is equally misleading. Of course public unions make campaign contributions. In fact, they are one of the last bastions of organized worker power against corporate political domination, a fact that helps provide insights into what the attacks on public sector unions are really all about. Fueled by campaign contributions from the Koch brothers and their ilk, Tea Party governors wanted to destroy one of the last major sources of campaign funding for the Democrats, namely public sector unions.[87] They added to the number of right-to-work states, which reached twenty-seven by 2018; cut the public workforce; and reduced employees' salaries and benefits. And they cheered loudly when the Supreme Court's *Janus* decision overturned a forty-year precedent by ruling that a union cannot force a nonmember to pay fees to cover the costs of collective bargaining, even if the nonmember benefits from the protections and enhancements the union provides. It is too early to tell whether the 2018 elections may have thwarted the tidal wave of anti-union actions in the states because Democrats replaced Tea Party governors in Michigan and Wisconsin, but not the gerrymandered state legislatures controlled by Republicans.

Organized labor still works effectively on the political front with groups that have similar electoral interests. In the midterm elections of 2018, for instance, unions joined a coalition of women and minorities to vote five incumbent anti-union governors out of office, including the sweetheart of Tea Party governors, Scott Walker. On the national level this energetic but loosely knit coalition lost two seats in the Senate but took control of the House by picking up forty Democratic seats. The success of the coalition suggests that unions may regain political clout by joining a larger social movement within the limitations proscribed by Taft-Hartley.

The Union Implosion

Union leaders are not without blame for organized labors' decline. Rank-and-file activists typically complain that some union leaders are overly bureaucratic, unresponsive, and perhaps even out of touch with their members. They look at commonly accepted union procedures as bureaucratic obstacles that stifle rank-and-file militancy. The expansion of the grievance procedure has allowed management to resolve issues peacefully, which, they claim, has diffused militancy and created a sense of frustration among rank-and-file workers. Automatic dues checkoff, they say, allows leaders to take their membership for granted. The literature on how the bureaucratic tendencies have hurt organized labor is voluminous.[88]

It's also evident that union leaders, much like leaders elsewhere, are sometimes less than perfect. They can be corrupt, ineffectual, or simply out of touch with membership. In the 1950s, for example, new public outcries of alleged union corruption, together with ongoing stories about communist infiltration, lowered public confidence in organized labor and tarnished labor's public image.[89] In 1957, the Senate Select Committee on Improper Activities in Labor and Management (the McClellan Committee) was created to investigate labor racketeering. These hearings resulted in a five-year prison sentence for Teamster President David Beck for tax fraud, the expulsion of the teamsters from the AFL-CIO, and the continuing loss of public support for unions. Congress responded in 1959 by passing the Landrum-Griffin Act, which instituted a host of new restrictions regulating the internal affairs of unions. Under the law, union members could now file unfair labor practices against their union; the federal government had the right to supervise union elections; unions had new financial reporting requirements; and the prohibitions on secondary boycotts were expanded. The public furor in response to charges of communist infiltration and internal corruption—remember the movie *On the Waterfront*—undercut labor's reputation and made it easier for corporations to justify their war on unions.[90]

Poor leadership has occasionally contributed to the decline of unions. More recently, however, structural issues galvanize unions to take actions deleterious to the union movement. For instance, as membership declined, unions responded by turning on one another. The inspirational "Solidarity Forever" is the unofficial anthem of organized labor. In these tough times, solidarity is a casualty as individual international unions and their locals engage in a dog-eat-dog fight for survival. This fight is driven by two dynamics. First, union officers are democratically elected, which means they must prove they can move their unions forward, or at least retain what the union has. Otherwise, they face defeat in the next union election. Second, and more important, unions need dues revenue in order to provide services and maintain staff. No services, no union. In this atmosphere, unions try to organize workers in any sector they can. In their desperation to survive, unions aren't rationally dividing the organizing pie, they're grabbing the first piece they can get their hands on. The decentralized structure of organized labor allows this free-for-all to happen.

Consider the structure of the AFL-CIO. The AFL-CIO is a federation of autonomous international unions with very few restrictions on union autonomy. This decentralized structure has many of the same problems the United States experienced under the Articles of Confederation when the power of individual states dominated a weak central government. In this sense, the president of the AFL-CIO is little more than a titular head whose main weapon is the use of the bully pulpit to get autonomous unions to follow his lead. In recent years, the pressure to organize more workers and rebuild the union movement has exposed the weaknesses inherent in this fragmented structure.

The drive to organize or die came to a head in 1995 when John Sweeney of the Service Employees International Union (SEIU) challenged Tom Donohue, the incumbent president of the AFL-CIO, for the office. The insurgent Sweeney's New Voice team prevailed primarily by promising to rebuild the house of labor through aggressive organizing. On taking office, the Sweeney administration put more resources into organizing new members and urged affiliate unions to do the same. Yet, within a short time it became clear that continuing deindustrialization, a hostile legal setting, and a pro-management NLRB appointed by President George W. Bush made organizing extraordinarily difficult. Moreover, since the AFL-CIO is a federation, Sweeney lacked the power to force recalcitrant union officers to follow his lead. Consequently, despite Sweeney's emphasis on organizing, many AFL-CIO unions had other needs and priorities. Unions in the building trades, for example, concentrated on finding work for their members rather than expend limited resources on organizing. Other unions chose to use their limited resources to provide services for existing members. By 2002, when it appeared that organizing wasn't the panacea to save organized labor, the Sweeney team switched its emphasis to electoral politics. At this juncture, several large units openly questioned the direction taken by the AFL-CIO. The leaders of the SEIU; the Hotel Employees and Restaurant Employees (HERE); the Union of Needle Trades, Industrial and Textile Employees (UNITE); the United Brotherhood of Carpenters (UBC); and the Laborers' International Union of North America (LIUNA) created an informal partnership called the New Unity Partnership (NUP). Claiming that they planned to work within the AFL-CIO, the newly formed group pressured Sweeney to promote organizing more aggressively.

Turmoil within the AFL-CIO worsened following the 2004 elections. After the AFL-CIO spent tens of millions in a losing effort to elect John Kerry in 2004, the dissidents made demands that split the labor movement. Andy Stern, the new head of SEIU, led the coalition of reformists who demanded that the AFL-CIO help affiliates by giving them more financial assistance and reducing affiliate fees due the AFL-CIO. They also called for a streamlined structure that would merge smaller unions with larger organizations and reduce overlapping areas of jurisdiction. After the AFL-CIO executive board rejected this proposal, the NUP dissolved and formed a new and larger coalition that disaffiliated from the AFL-CIO. Calling their organization Change to Win (CtW), the newly created alternative to the AFL-CIO consisted of the original NUP members plus the International Brotherhood of Teamsters, the United Food and Commercial Workers, the Carpenters, and the United Farm Workers. Collectively, the CtW unions represented about one-third of the AFL-CIO's membership and paid approximately one-third of the organization's dues revenue. As a consequence, the AFL-CIO had to lay off about a quarter of its staff.[91]

Change to Win set out to save the labor movement, but that didn't happen. A review of the NLRB's certification elections between 2006 and

2011 reveals that both CtW and the AFL-CIO had participated in about 4,000 certification elections; CtW unions won 58 percent of their elections compared to the 64 percent won by the AFL-CIO.[92] CtW had a net gain of 170,000 new members during this time. But that number doesn't provide an accurate picture. SEIU alone increased its membership rolls by 300,000, which counterbalanced declining membership in other CtW unions.[93]

The schism within the AFL-CIO that led to the formation of CtW was just the start of the implosion. Some observers argue that the split actually obfuscated other fissures among the CtW unions and within them.[94] The SEIU, the flagship union of Change to Win, soon became embroiled in internal battles of its own. Succeeding John Sweeney as president of SEIU, Andy Stern ruled with a heavy hand in an attempt to consolidate his power and increase union density within his industry. Stern frequently placed oppositional locals under trusteeship, replacing recalcitrant union leaders with loyalists. Initially, SEIU's membership grew substantially, but eventually the limitations of Stern's anti-democratic approach created conflicts and divisiveness within SEIU. Stern approached organizing based on the theory that the greater the union density, the better the contract. To get the union's foot in the door, so to speak, he relied on negotiating moderate contracts that reduced management's willingness to resist unionization. Increased union density would then place workers in a more advantageous position to negotiate better deals. Some SEIU locals committed to organizing disagreed with this approach, including a recently merged California health care local with more than 140,000 members, the Union of Healthcare Workers-West (UHW). After elected leaders of the local strenuously objected to SEIU's top-down attempt to remove some 60,000 nursing home health care workers from the UHW without a vote, Stern placed the local in trusteeship.[95] A battle ensued, one in which rank-and-file members of UHW decertified their SEIU affiliated union and created a new independent local, the National Union of Health-care Workers (NUHW).[96] Legal battles followed, costing SEIU about $110 million. The newly formed NUHW attempted to bring tens of thousands of other SEIU members into their new organization, precipitating further hostilities within the movement.[97]

Stern's leadership style precipitated a number of similar conflicts. Another worth mentioning is a jurisdictional battle between SEIU and the California Nurses Association (CNA). After the nurses rejected SEIU's organizing approach, the SEIU head accused them of sabotaging an unsuccessful Ohio organizing campaign. The animosity between the two unions resulted in fist fights when SEIU members and staff attacked CNA members attending a *Labor Notes* conference in Dearborn, Michigan.[98] While this was going on, the president of the hospitality division of the recently merged UNITE-HERE accused SEIU of meddling in the union's internal affairs and raiding its membership. Finally, after spending millions fighting internal battles, defections, and attempts to organize new members, Andy Stern in 2010 called it quits and retired. His anointed successor then immediately retired, perhaps after looking at the SEIU's political landscape.[99]

The struggle for union survival galvanized a seemingly endless number of conflicts within the movement, resulting in a wasteful expenditure of limited resources. Another example worth noting is the battle emanating from the merger between HERE and UNITE in 2004. UNITE brought significant financial resources to the merger, including the nation's only union-owned bank, but the cash strapped HERE had a larger membership and more votes on the executive board. Terms of the merger agreement allowed UNITE's Bruce Raynor to become president, while HERE's John Wilhelm headed the hospitality division. Within a few years the merger began to fall apart. Wilhelm criticized Raynor for his Stern-like heavy-handed approach to organizing. Raynor responded by claiming that Wilhelm had spent tens of millions to organize with disappointing results. Amidst all this infighting, in 2007 UNITE HERE workers at a Vancouver General Motor's plant disaffiliated to join with the Christian Labourers Association of Canada. In May 2009, Raynor resigned his presidency and took as many as 150,000 members to form a new union, Workers United. The newly formed organization affiliated with SEIU, which immediately began to raid UNITE HERE's membership, triggering an aggressive response by UNITE HERE. Raynor's efforts to recover UNITE's financial resources, including the $4 billion Amalgamated Bank, further exacerbated the situation and led to even more costly legal battles for UNITE HERE and SEIU.[100] These costly internecine struggles led one labor scholar to make the obvious observation that "[t]he sooner labor stops putting millions of dollars into fighting each other, the sooner they can put those resources where they should go—into organizing and political battles."[101]

Not only did Change to Win fail to bring much change, it also failed to win. The organization itself has shrunk in size and power. After experiencing internal battles that led to the formation of a splinter group affiliating with SEIU, UNITE HERE re-affiliated with the AFL-CIO. The

Laborers International and the United Food and Commercial Workers then followed suit. The CtW organization now consists of a downsized SEIU, the Teamsters, the small United Farmworkers of America, and the Communication Workers of America (CWA), which is also affiliated with the AFL-CIO. Union activist and commentator Steve Early estimates that the CtW split cost the AFL-CIO over $150 million in dues and special assessment revenues over a six-year period through 2011.[102]

The need for unions to generate revenue in order to service members, maintain staff, and provide elected union leaders with some political cover underlies a series of other conflicts within the union movement. Crucial among these are the efforts by all the unions to organize whoever they can, regardless of the industry or occupation. Since there is virtually no one left to organize in the industries where they started out, unions are now organizing in different occupations where they lack both expertise and experience. For example, part-time faculty and graduate assistants in higher education across the country are now represented not only by the American Federation of Teachers (AFT), the National Education Association (NEA), and the American Association of University Professors (AAUP), but also by the UAW, the USW, CWA, and SEIU, among others. Health care workers running the gamut from physicians and nurses to home health care aides and virtually every occupation in between are represented not only by SEIU and National Nurses United but also by United Food and Commercial Workers; the American Federation of State, County and Municipal Employees (AFSCME); the UAW, the USW, and AFT, not to mention the National Union of Healthcare Workers and others. Name an unrepresented sector of workers and you'll find an alphabet soup of international unions vying to organize them.

The strategy of seeking membership beyond their core industry produces not only these internecine squabbles but two other critical issues that go to the heart of union survival. First is the question of expertise. Can a union effectively represent employees outside its historical field of experience and specialization? The second is a question of resources. Many newly organized sectors consist of low-paid part-time and contingent employees who make union membership numbers look better but whose dues don't cover the cost of the union services they expect. The following story illustrates how these two issues feed off each other.

The author of this book is a former fourteen-year president of the United University Professions (UUP), an AFT local representing more than 30,000 faculty and professional staff at the state-operated campuses of the State University of New York (SUNY). In the 1990s, SUNY graduate students and teaching assistants wanted to organize, but the state labor board determined that UUP couldn't represent them because it would be a conflict of interest for SUNY faculty to represent their own students. The students subsequently formed the Graduate Student Employee Union (GSEU) as a local of CWA. During their first rounds of contract negotiations, the student leaders relied heavily on UUP staff to mentor them through the bargaining process. The students came to UUP because the CWA just didn't have a grasp on how to negotiate for higher education and couldn't provide them with staff sufficient to the task.

In order to survive, unions must grow, but the way they're growing now is likely to kill them in the long run. During organizing drives it's not uncommon to hear workers complain of past negative experiences with a union. They never see their union rep or they feel the union didn't protect them or they think their contract is a sweetheart deal with management. Ineffective representation is sure to weaken labor's already precarious prospects for growth. One way organized labor has tried to address the issue of growth is to remove the conditions that promote this cannibalism by reforming national labor laws. As previously discussed, EFCA was a modest reform that would make organizing easier, but it went nowhere, even though Democrats controlled both houses and the executive branch during the first two years of Obama's presidency. Since then Democrats have proposed similar bills that have gone nowhere. In February 2020, the new Democratic majority in the House passed the Protecting the Right to Organize Act (PRO Act), a bill that makes it easier for workers covered by the NLRA to unionize, but Senate Majority Leader Mitch McConnell (who self-identified as "the Grim Reaper") killed the bill in the Republican-held chamber. The House passed the PRO Act again one year later, but with Democrats controlling only 50 Senate seats, it won't become law without a filibuster-proof Senate.

Stephen Lerner's proposal of several years back, "An Immodest Proposal: Remodeling the House of Labor,"[103] could provide a way out of this dynamic. He suggests that organized labor needs to consolidate, rationalize, and reorganize. By this he means that unions should radically restructure to evolve from sixty-six amalgamated international unions into a small number of unions defined by large economic sectors. However reasonable Lerner's proposal, entrenched unions are not likely to give up their autonomy. The fragmentation and infighting are likely to continue.

Even while organized labor continues to shoot itself in the foot, a recent Gallup poll shows that 62 percent of Americans approve of unions, although a large percentage fear their political power. Other polls indicate that nearly half of non-unionized workers would like to have union representation.[104] More than anything, the polls suggest there is hope for labor, but such hope rests outside the confines of the organized labor movement. In recent years unions have focused their organizing resources on low-paid, low-skilled workers such as recent immigrants and the poor. Attempts to organize Walmart and fast-food workers have in general failed. Workers receiving poverty wages are often unwilling to pay union dues, and the U.S. legal structure is hostile to unions, to say the least. In addition to providing hurdles to organizing, the law prohibits unions from partaking in secondary boycotts and waging sympathy strikes. Fortunately, workers outside the union movement do not face these obstacles. Unfettered by restrictive laws, many of these poorly paid and poorly treated workers are taking to the streets to wage campaigns to pressure state and local governments to back them in their fight for decent wage and benefit packages. The ongoing national Fight for Fifteen movement is a stellar example of what workers can achieve through collective action.[105] Farmworkers, unorganized teachers, and others are taking militant actions outside the union movement. The following chapters of this book examine the activities of groups of workers who are the new face of the labor movement.

Chapter 3

Farmworkers Fight Back

It's 1960 in Immokalee, Florida. The sun has just come up but the open lot is already crowded with desperate men, women, and even some children looking for a day's work in the fields. Hawkers yell out the going piece rate for the day as the job seekers squeeze into trucks so cramped with humanity that only a rope tied across the back of the beds keeps workers from falling out. As the crowded trucks pull out to the fields, a farmer tells a reporter, "We used to own our slaves. Now we just rent them."[1]

The award-winning documentary *Harvest of Shame* opens with that scene. The film goes on to describe the life of the hundreds of thousands of poorly paid, poorly clothed, and poorly fed workers who for decades traveled from Florida to Maine to pick the crops that end up on our dinner plates. A lot has changed since 1960. But even today the average salary of a farmworker is under $10,000, with a median income of less than $7,500; working and living conditions are often abysmal; and, sadly, involuntary servitude is not that uncommon. Indeed, the lives of migrant farmworkers are still harsh as they follow the crops along both coasts of the United States, but across the country farmworkers are pursuing different strategic paths to significantly improve their working and living conditions while pushing back against Jim Crow era labor laws. By banding together they are gaining the power to challenge the growers and others who control the food industry.[2] Some have chosen traditional union organizing to achieve their goals. On the west coast, for instance, migrant farmworkers who lived for decades much like the Joads in Steinbeck's *Grapes of Wrath* succeeded against all odds to organize a union— the United Farm Workers (UFW). This chapter briefly touches upon their efforts, but in keeping with the theme of this book, its main focus is on models of labor organizing that have achieved similar success outside the union movement. In particular, this chapter traces how Florida's Immokalee workers developed successful strategies and actions, including the use of the secondary boycott, that provide organizing models for workers in other industries to emulate. A third path is a hybrid model like that of New York state farmworkers, who formed coalitions similar to those of Immokalee workers, but who also seek legislative mandates addressing various work issues while they pursued their ultimate goal of getting the New York state legislature to pass legislation allowing them to form a union. This chapter begins with an examination of the racist laws that historically blocked farmworkers from unionizing. It then examines the strategies and tactics of the Immokalee and New York farmworkers, studies their successes and failures, and compares their achievements to those of unionized farmworkers.

Racism Drives Progressive Reform: Compromises Cripple Farmworkers

Regardless of where in the country farmworkers have fought to achieve basic workers' rights, they are all bound together by the historical forces of racism that denied them these rights in the first place. The American legal system is replete with racist-driven compromises that excluded farmworkers and domestics, the majority of whom were people of color, from those labor laws that guaranteed the right to collective bargaining and provided a minimum wage and other fair labor standards. These exclusions contributed to the extraordinary poverty and exploitation of migrant farmworkers.

Without the legal protections available to industrial workers, farmworkers struggle just to survive. They work long hours for below-poverty wages in the fields with no sanitation facilities. They don't receive paid time off or retirement benefits, and most are ineligible for safety net programs such as food stamps. Agricultural is also one of the most dangerous occupations. Farmworkers suffer back problems from stooping over for ten or more hours a day. With little or no real occupational safety regulations, they experience a disproportionate share of physical injuries, and they and their children, often just infants, are routinely exposed to harmful pesticides. Why are their children exposed? Migrant farmworkers have no child care, and many children cannot attend school.[3] When the day ends and farmworkers go home, their homes are likely to be overcrowded, dilapidated old shacks that may lack a shower, warm water, a working stove, and other basic amenities. With conditions for good hygiene usually absent,[4] it's no wonder that the deadly Covid-19 virus spread like wildfire among Immokalee workers.[5] As for food, their diets depend mostly on potatoes and beans. Most do not have transportation, so they must shop at local or company stores where they pay high prices for low-quality goods. Farmworkers lack health coverage, so when they get sick or injured most of them try to avoid doctors altogether. On those rare occasions when they do seek medical care, they can only hope that a translator is available. Sadly, such extreme exploitation is not that uncommon.

The passage of the Thirteenth Amendment ended slavery, but as one scholar so lucidly put it, "Slavery was too integral a part of the social life of the South and too vital to the interests of certain classes to be suddenly eliminated by a mere constitutional amendment."[6] Agriculture was the predominant industry of the South, and southern landowners responded to the end of slavery by instituting new ways to exploit black farm laborers. They developed an almost infinite number of schemes to keep the freed blacks in a condition of dependency and subservience, but the institution of tenant farming was the most prevalent.[7] Tenant farmers lived on the property of white landowners to whom they paid rent, purchased food, tools, and supplies at exorbitant prices, and frequently took high-interest loans to pay for their expenses. Needless to say, at the end of the year many tenant farmers couldn't meet their debt obligations. Since failure to pay the landlord was a criminal offense that would lead to imprisonment, this debt bondage confined sharecroppers to work the farm until the debt was paid, a most infrequent event. White landowners often supplemented the promise of jail with threats of violence to keep tenant farmers working their land. The Thirteenth Amendment outlawed slavery, but black tenant farmers in the South still lived in a state of peonage.

The compromise of 1877 that settled the disputed election of 1876 consolidated the power of southern landlords and white supremacists over black farmworkers. In a secret deal, Democrats agreed to concede the disputed presidential election of 1876 to Republican Rutherford B. Hayes over Samuel Tilden, who had won the popular vote. In return for not blocking a Hayes victory, the new Republican president backed his commitment to honor the principle of "home rule" by withdrawing federal troops from the South. This political deal ended the period of reconstruction. Without federal troops to protect the civil rights of the newly freed slaves, the economic and political conditions of African Americans worsened. The absence of federal supervision gave the Ku Klux Klan free reign to intimidate and terrorize black citizens. The Klan's use of violence and terror against African Americans ensured that blacks in the South were not free to participate in the basic activities of America's civic and political culture. Indeed, throughout the South, white-dominated state legislatures took away the basic rights of citizenship from blacks by enacting a series of state laws, including literacy tests and poll taxes that prevented blacks from voting. On those occasions where these Jim Crow laws failed to keep southern blacks from attempting to cast their ballots, the unfettered use of violence by the Klan usually guaranteed an all-white electorate.[8]

The economic exploitation of blacks in the South was the foundation of the region's agricultural economy. But these social arrangements of exploitation could not endure unless landowners and white supremacists held and maintained unchallenged political power. The compromise of 1877 made that possible by giving the Democratic Party political control of the South and with it a free hand to exclude blacks from the political process. For most of the next one-hundred years the Democratic Party's southern alliance of white supremacists and landowners relied on the political process to promote white supremacy and maintain the economic and political subordination of the black population. Even today, the consequences of this coalition, as many scholars have observed, is responsible for the plight of contemporary farmworkers.[9]

The flagrant racism of the one-party South that excluded blacks from the electoral process allowed southern members of Congress to accumulate seniority and gain a stranglehold on the legislative process.[10] By the time of the New Deal, southern representatives controlled a disproportionate share of committee chairmanships and leadership positions in both the House and Senate. [11] Acting on the premise that his New Deal legislation would not pass Congress without the support of Southern Democrats, President Roosevelt compromised and signed a series of laws that precluded the nation's poorest and most politically vulnerable from coverage. Consequently, farmworkers and domestics, the vast majority of whom were black, were deliberately excluded from progressive legislation aimed at boosting wages and improving working conditions. The race-neutral language of exclusion by occupation permitted Northern Liberals to back the exclusionary language without losing black political support while allowing Southern Democrats to receive needed federal benefits without disrupting the racial status quo.[12] Four of these laws—the National Industrial Recovery Act (NIRA), the National Labor Relations Act (NLRA), the Fair Labor Standards Act (FLSA), and the Social Security Act—still today negatively impact agricultural workers, most of whom are now Latinos.

The NIRA, the predecessor to the National Labor Relations Act, recognized the right to collective bargaining and established codes of competition in each industry, including setting a minimum wage. Southern Democrats were joined by other farm interests in supporting the exclusion of agricultural workers from the legislation since previous attempts by the International Workers of the World (IWW) to unionize farmers had resulted in strikes at harvest time.[13] These NRA codes enlarged the definition of agricultural worker to include other primarily black occupations that were not directly involved in agriculture. Consequently, tens of thousands more black workers in food packaging and food-processing plants, cotton ginning, and tobacco warehouses were not protected by the law.[14] In 1935, after the NIRA was declared unconstitutional,[15] Congress strengthened the right to collective bargaining by passing the National Labor Relations Act, commonly known as the Wagner Act. But this law, too, excluded the millions of black workers employed in the agricultural and domestic service industries. As mostly northern industrial workers unionized, their earnings and standard of living improved, while the wages and job conditions of agricultural workers actually declined.[16] The racist policies in these federal laws have yet to be corrected, so labor's actions have been primarily at the state level. As of today, only twelve states have granted agricultural workers the right to form a union, but some placed restrictions on the right to strike.[17]

The FLSA (1938) set a federal minimum wage, provided for weekly maximum working hours, and prohibited child labor. Excluded from the law's provisions, farmworkers did not have a minimum wage until a sub-minimum was established in 1966. By the late 1970s most farmworkers were entitled to the full federal minimum wage, but the rules of eligibility still exempt many from coverage. Farmworkers also remain outside the law's overtime regulation. Only in 1966 did the federal government establish a separate set of rules for farmworkers that cover children, but the law still allows children as young as twelve to work the fields under certain conditions. Perhaps the crown jewel of the New Deal, the Social Security Act (1935), as originally passed provided unemployment compensation and old-age pensions. Subsequent amendments, including Medicare and Medicaid, gave benefits to dependents, the aged, and the indigent. Southern members of Congress were initially reluctant to support the bill because plantation owners thought the income security provided by the law to farm laborers, however slight, might weaken their control over their captive labor market. Congress again responded by excluding agricultural and domestic workers—who represented about two-thirds of black workers in the South—from coverage. By 1956, amendments to the law formally covered agricultural workers but contained so many restrictions that many still lack protections.[18]

What can farmworkers do to improve their standard of living? All but a handful of states prohibit agricultural workers from unionizing, and, politically, there's not much they can do since most migrant farmworkers don't meet the citizenship or residency requirements necessary to vote.[19] They also lack the financial resources to make their case in the political arena. This is why they're often called a "voiceless population." Migrant farmworkers are among the weakest and most vulnerable groups in the United States, but that doesn't mean they are powerless. Power takes many forms, and organizing is a proven method for the disenfranchised to achieve their collective goals. After years of struggle, farmworkers on the West coast and in the Midwest organized and formed unions. Westcoast farmworkers, led by Cesar Chavez and Dolores Huerta, drastically improved their working and living conditions by organizing and eventually forming a union. After negotiating the first collective bargaining agreement between growers and farmworkers, the United Farm Workers raised the standard of living of its members by negotiating benefits enjoyed by most other union workers.[20] Under the leadership of Baldemar Velasquez, a group of about 700 Midwestern farmworkers joined the Farm Laborers Organizing Committee (FLOC) and affiliated with the AFL-CIO. Their numbers grew to over 2,000 after FLOC waged a six-year boycott of Campbell's Soup.[21]

Westcoast and Midwestern migrant farmworkers are not alone in escaping the dismal existence lived by generations of agricultural workers. The Immokalee farmworkers of Florida and New York's agricultural workers have made gains, too. New York's farmworkers still face many of the abysmal working and living conditions typical of the farmworker experience. They work long hours, receive low pay, and have substandard housing and health care, but working with community groups, they have made some notable incremental gains. Their long-term goal now is to secure the right to collective bargaining. The Immokalee farmworkers of Florida do not aspire to form a union in Florida's right-to-work legal environment, but they may not need one because their unique strategy, unrestricted by labor laws, has already brought a great deal of success. Some observers have suggested that Florida's Immokalee farmworkers at one time may have had the worst working and living conditions of all migrant workers, but thanks to their collective efforts and incessant struggles, that has changed. In fact, the Immokalee workers may now have the best working conditions of all migrant farmworkers in the nation.[22] An examination of the strategies and tactics, successes and failures of the Immokalee and New York farmworkers should provide important insights for the growing part of the labor movement not yet unionized.

Immokalee Farmworkers: Community-Based Power Fights Back

Over the years, Florida's exploited farmworkers have attempted to use the power of organizing to get better wages and achieve a higher standard of living. In the early 1930s, for instance, the non-union United Citrus Workers of Florida waged a number of job actions that heightened growers' fears of organized farmworker power and contributed to its exclusion from New Deal reform legislation. [23] In the 1970s, the UFW's Manuel Chavez, Cesar's cousin, unsuccessfully attempted to organize citrus pickers in Florida, a strong anti-union, right-to-work state.[24] Where these past attempts at organizing failed, the non-union Immokalee farmworkers have succeeded for several reasons. Key among these is that they are not restricted by laws governing the activities of unions, their organizational structure is not hierarchical, and they do not define themselves solely as a workers' rights organization. An analysis of the formation, strategies, and activities of the Immokalee farmworkers suggests that non-union working-class people could benefit significantly by emulating this model.

In 1993, a pair of community organizers recently hired as community specialist paralegals by Florida Rural Legal Services (FRLS) arrived in Immokalee, Florida, a place characterized as "ground zero for modern slavery."[25] The legal advocacy organization had a total of three lawyers and six paralegals in all of Florida to play gotcha with growers who violated the human rights of pickers. Success was defined as gaining reparations for workers on a case-by-case basis. Trouble is, workers had to step up publicly and file a complaint, something that most, for obvious reasons, were reluctant to do. The newly arrived organizers, a married couple, Laura Germino and Greg Asbed, recognized the limits of this legalistic approach taken by sympathetic outsiders and, instead, directed their efforts at changing the workers' culture. Their goal was to bring the workers together in a self-organized collective community, a non-hierarchical worker center where farmworkers could collectively begin work to improve their wages and working conditions. To realize this objective they initially went door to door to introduce themselves to the workers and to discuss working conditions and future prospects. They founded the Southwest Florida Workers' Project, a human rights organization, by holding weekly meetings at a local Catholic church, where discussions focused on work in the fields and the larger issues affecting that work.[26] The majority of the pickers migrated from Haiti, Mexico, and Guatemala. Highly influenced by the peasant upheavals in these countries, including the Zapatista's struggle in southern Mexico, the new organization, now called the Coalition for Immokalee Workers (CIW), was guided by two fundamental principles. The first—"we are all leaders"—illustrates the non-hierarchical structure of the organization, which contrasts sharply with the organizational policies of many unions, including the United Farm Workers and its historical reliance on charismatic leaders. The notion that all are leaders is clearly expressed by CIW's practice of tying wages to field work and requiring all elected staff to work the fields from May until September. Compare these requirements to the practices and salaries paid to staff by the vast majority of U.S. labor unions.[27]

The second organizational principle elaborates on the first by developing a critical consciousness among the farmworkers, captured in their motto "consciousness + commitment = change." Consciousness, or "conscientization," is essential to understanding the situation workers face. This consciousness is based on mutual learning rather than lecturing and develops through a series of jugular questions discussed at weekly meetings: Why are farmworkers poor? What are the causes of their poverty? Why are workers abused? What can we do about this?[28] During the initial stages of organizing, early coalition members helped create a sense of community by establishing a food co-op as an alternative to the exploitative stores in the area. Pickers were also given a manual, the *Green Book of Workers Rights*, that enumerates their rights as workers. This Green Book (not to be confused with the Green Book guide for African Americans traveling the South) emphasizes that farmworkers are human beings with human rights, not the passive objects of the grower's seemingly unlimited and arbitrary power. For a $2 membership cost, CIW members receive membership cards resembling a driver's license that allows them to shop at the co-op. These official-looking membership certificates also serve as ID cards.[29]

Since most of the Immokalee farmworkers are uprooted from their home cultures and live a precarious economic existence, it's not surprising that substance abuse is rampant. But CIW provides an alternative to copping out on drugs by offering workers a vision of farmworkers organizing themselves in a self-governing community that could change their lives. In short, participating workers must forgo substance abuse and accept the responsibility of the collective if they are to change their lives. Once workers gain this critical consciousness, they make their commitment to the collective's vision by signing cards authorizing the CIW to represent them. Although not a union, CIW has become the voice of the Immokalee farmworkers by collecting thousands of these authorization cards.[30]

CIW's fundamental approach of having the farmworkers involved in all the organization's decisions, combined with the individual's responsibility to the collective, was expressed in one of its early actions. Traditionally, labor contractors mediated between the growers and the pickers by recruiting and hiring the workers. They could do this because they owned the conveyor belts, a piece of equipment essential to harvesting. After CIW members raised enough money to buy a conveyor belt, they no longer needed a labor contractor. Without a contractor to take a cut of the revenue, the workers earned more, divided the income as they decided, and shared the harvesting tasks as they saw fit. Just as importantly, they saw the value of collective action and gained a sense of empowerment.

Bypassing the contractor helped, but the CIW still had to pressure growers to improve wages and working conditions. This was especially important because wages for Florida's tomato pickers were declining and workers were often treated as subhumans; some pickers were even forced into slavery, unpaid and held against their will. As a human rights organization rather than a labor union, the coalition attracted many allies from the faith-based community. The Presbyterian Church, for instance, was among the first to assist. In working with allies, CIW made clear the nature of their relationship. The activities of allied organizations would be autonomous but dedicated to following CIW's lead.[31] Since the plight of migrant farmworkers was not known to the general public, CIW's overall strategy was to build public awareness of the issues, and its tactics all aimed at achieving this end. These tactics included several work stoppages and a thirty-day hunger strike by six coalition members. In declaring, " 'This is just a faster death' than that experienced by other farmworkers," the hunger strikers generated significant news coverage.[32] A well-publicized march from Fort Myers to Orlando also drew national media coverage. The farmworkers gained more favorable attention after public revelations of pickers being forced into involuntary servitude resulted in the conviction and sentencing of two crew leaders to fifteen years in prison. The protests forced growers to increase wages by up to 25 percent, from forty cents to fifty cents for a thirty-two-pound bucket. On the surface, that sounds good, but given the long-term decline of pickers' wages, the increase brought earnings only back to the pre-1980s mark. Just as importantly, the illegal practice of involuntary servitude continued. Virtually every year some crew leaders would end up in prison for modern-day slavery. Still, nothing really changed. Workers still had to pick more than two tons of tomatoes to earn the minimum wage, wage theft remained a problem, and workers remained subject to physical and sexual abuse.[33]

The concessions gained by farmworkers after years of actions and sacrifice amounted to a very limited victory. The lessons learned from these actions, however, would lead to future successes. CIW gained at least three important insights from these early efforts. First, individual farmworkers do gain power through collective action. That was certain. Second, it had also become apparent that the strike was a very limited weapon. Since workers were poor and could not last more than a few days without income, growers had a huge advantage in the event of a strike. Additionally, the minimal dues of about $2 a year that workers paid to CIW did not provide the organization enough resources to finance a strike. The CIW began receiving contributions from philanthropic organizations in the late 1990s, but certainly not enough to support a sustained work stoppage.[34] Third, by 2001, farmworkers knew that directing job actions against the growers would never work. Growers, after all, are at the mercy of large tomato buyers who use their monopolistic power to drive the price of tomatoes down. Taco Bell and McDonald's, to name just two, have sufficient purchasing power to set the price they will pay for tomatoes. Failure to accept their price could leave a grower with a harvest no one would buy. Put more bluntly, a small handful of billion dollar companies that purchase the bulk of tomatoes have the power to set the price growers must accept or risk going out of business. The monopolistic purchasing power of the giant companies forces growers to keep labor costs down, since labor is about the only production cost farmers have the power to control. Once the farmworkers recognized the power of big buyers over the growers, it became obvious that fighting the growers, as

Greg Asbed suggested, is like banging your head against the wall until it hurt. The CIW needed to change its approach.[35]

CIW members responded to their inability to move forward by discussing and analyzing the root causes of their poverty. They again began with the basic question, why did their wages remain low? Their discussions identified a number of factors. Foremost is the big imbalance in power. Although organized, their limited ability to strike illustrated their lack of power over the growers. The law prohibited them from forming a union, and the migrant nature of the labor force along with the multiple languages spoken by pickers presented numerable obstacles to organizing. The CIW is an organization that involves the farmworkers in all decisions, so it wasn't surprising that a worker's question led to the new course the farmworkers would take. The epiphany of change originated with the obvious question: "If Taco Bell can drive the price of tomatoes down, can't they also drive them up?"[36] Further discussions suggested that pressuring Taco Bell might be the answer. After all, tomato growers didn't sell directly to consumers. They sold at a price set by the big buyers such as Taco Bell. This dynamic meant that the pressure on growers to meet buyers' prices limited the growers' ability to increase wages. But CIW's issues went beyond earning a minimum wage for the pickers. Since CIW sought a livable wage for all, as well as fair and decent treatment of all workers, it was a human rights as well as a workers' rights organization. The role played by big buyers also explains why public campaigns based on appeals to worker and human rights had minimal impact on the growers. Even former President Jimmy Carter's publicized statements in support of the pickers didn't really matter. The growers, as Susan Marquis notes, had no public face and, consequently, were not affected by bad publicity.[37] On the other hand, the big buyers have a public image to maintain. Taco Bell, which has more than 6,000 restaurants in the United States, is a division of YUM BRANDS and part of Tricon Global Restaurants, Inc. In 1999 Tricon's sales revenue approached $22 billion. That same year Taco Bell had sales of $5 billion. Taco Bell sold its products and brand through massive TV advertising. About half the U.S. population watches a Taco Bell commercial on TV every week. This public image, the group concluded, provides a point of vulnerability. Out of these collective insights emerged what one activist characterized as the "boomerang effect." The CIW would take on Taco Bell by turning its buying power and strong public image against them.[38] In other words, CIW decided to leverage their power through consumers. Linking the poverty and abuse of farmworkers to Taco Bell's products could injure the corporation's brand and possibly expand the size of supporting coalitions. If the CIW campaign damaged the corporate brand, Taco Bell and other corporate big buyers could force growers to comply with fundamental principles of worker and human rights—in other words, a code of conduct. As for wages, the program sought a surcharge of one penny per pound on tomatoes that would go to the pickers.[39]

Once it defined the problem and targeted Taco Bell, the farmworkers' group now had to develop strategies and tactics to realize its goals. The first decision by the collective was to do something that labor law prohibits unions from doing. In 2001, to force growers to pay a living wage and treat workers decently, the CIW unleashed its "boomerang strategy" with a national boycott against Taco Bell. This secondary boycott, a practice prohibited by law for unions, was not narrowly focused on improving wages and conditions of Immokalee workers. It was the starting point of a larger "Campaign for Fair Food." The boycott began in April 2001 with just a handful of demonstrators wielding a large papier-mâché tomato to kick off the action in front of a Florida Taco Bell. The organization's modest start eventually evolved into a large national movement. The campaign's broad focus on human rights, fair food, and corporate power as well as worker rights gave CIW an advantage that unions lack and brought support from a wide spectrum of organizations that otherwise would not have participated in the farmworkers' struggle. The emphasis on human rights, for instance, gained the backing of the faith-based community from virtually all religions. The human rights appeal galvanized numerous immigrant and community groups to join the boycott too. The campaign's fair food spin educated consumers on the exploitative process of how food is grown, processed, and delivered. This led a wide spectrum of trade organizations, fair trade groups, and environmentalists to participate in the boycott. The fair food campaign also illuminated the plight of the fast-food workers who sold the produce picked by farmworkers.[40] CIW's appeal to workers' rights gained the endorsement of the American Postal Workers Union (APWU), the UFW, and many union locals across the country. Unions supported the boycott in a number of ways, including providing funds and research to then AFL-CIO President John Sweeney's public backing of the action. The UFW worked closely with CIW, even proposing a merger, which the CIW declined. [41]

In recent years, high school and college students have organized successful anti-sweatshop campaigns. A number of these politically active students participated in CIW's February 2000 march from Fort Myers to Orlando. Participating in the march galvanized students from Florida colleges to become increasingly active in the movement to end what they viewed as "sweatshops in the fields." These students formed the Student Farmworker Alliance (SFA), which soon became a national organization of students that, according to SFA's website, "has been at the forefront of a resurgent farmworker solidarity movement . . . starting with the Taco Bell boycott in 2001."[42] Since 18- to 24-year-olds constitute Taco Bell's primary customer base, broad student support was crucially important to the boycott's success. Like all other coalition members, SFA was an independent, autonomous organization that promoted CIW's interests. For instance, SFA's Boot the Bell campaign managed to keep some twenty-five Taco Bell restaurants from operating in colleges and high schools.[43]

With the backing of early supporters, CIW launched myriad activities designed to build public support and increase consumer pressure on Taco Bell. The Presbyterian Church offered financial support, which relieved the farmworkers from the time-consuming task of fundraising, allowing them to focus primarily on their campaign. In time, the National Council of Churches and Rabbis for Human Rights joined the campaign.[44] Besides circulating Boot the Bell petitions on campuses, in late November 2001, students joined CIW in what was called "Three Days of Action." For three days, students and farmworkers protested outside Taco Bell restaurants in Gainesville, Florida.[45] The coalition inaugurated a series of "Taco Bell Truth Tours," where workers boarded buses to bring their message to cities throughout the United States. The CIW demonstrated at Taco Bell restaurants near colleges and high schools in seventeen cities in fifteen days to increase student support while pressuring Taco Bell. According to one CIW worker, "At the end of the boycott there were around 300 universities and some high schools in solidarity with the workers of Immokalee."[46] Students also conducted alternative Spring breaks that gave them the opportunity to learn more about the farmworkers by actually working with them.

These early actions were just the start. The public activities of CIW and its allies brought much attention to the farmworkers' issues. Through the astute use of the internet, CIW reached out to consumers who generally knew nothing about where their food came from, the plight of the pickers, and the role played by Taco Bell. Within a few years, the CIW's website experienced tremendous growth, occasionally registering nearly 500,000 hits a week.[47] Perhaps the highlight of CIW's publicity campaign occurred during the 2002 World Series at San Francisco's Pacific Bell park. Taco Bell had placed an ad on a float in McCovey Cove where boaters scrambled to retrieve home run balls that reached the bay. Next to the Taco Bell ad, CIW supporters erected a big sign that included the CIW's web address and read, "Taco Bell Exploits Farmworkers." Some eleven million baseball fans saw the sign. Finally, after four years of waging highly publicized hunger strikes, marches, demonstrations at Taco Bell headquarters, postcard campaigns, and getting the public backing of notable celebrities, the fast-food giant yielded. By March of 2005 it had become clear that Taco Bell could not "guarantee its customers that the tomatoes in its tacos weren't picked by slaves."[48] The company had to change its public image. To do so, Taco Bell's YUM BRANDS decided to meet the CIW's two fundamental demands.

First, the company agreed to pay an additional penny-per-pound increase in the price it paid for tomatoes it bought from Florida growers, which would be passed down the supply chain to the workers.[49] This additional penny per pound increased pickers' wages by about 75 percent. The fast-food company also agreed to work with CIW to establish a monitoring process to enforce the "pass-through" payment. Taco Bell would not buy tomatoes from any grower who violated the pass-through. Taco Bell's decision to meet the farmworkers' wage demands marked the first time "that a fast-food leader has agreed to address directly the sub-poverty wages paid to farmworkers in its supply chain."[50]

Second, YUM BRANDS agreed to a code of conduct that required suppliers to adhere to all applicable laws and regulations; it also encouraged tomato growers to provide working conditions similar to those provided by suppliers outside the agricultural industry. This meant farmworkers would have access to drinking water and toilets in the fields. The corporation agreed to cooperate in creating a workable twenty-four-hour complaint system and to allow unannounced inspections of grower's facilities.[51]

Next, the farmworkers set their sights on McDonald's, with its 13,000 restaurants. The fast-food leviathan came to terms with the CIW within two years. In the same period, a number of other events aided the coalition's public activities. U.S. Senate hearings highlighted issues of slavery and other abysmal conditions the pickers often faced.[52] YUM BRANDS extended its contract with CIW to cover all its fast-food eateries, including Kentucky Fried Chicken and Pizza Hut. Burger King signed an agreement, as did Subway. Despite all the buyers agreeing to cooperate with CIW and all the bad publicity from the exposés on slavery in the tomato fields, the growers still refused to negotiate a code of conduct with CIW.

Yielding to increasing pressure from both the CIW and the corporate buyers, Florida's tomato growers finally agreed in November 2010 to negotiate a code of conduct with CIW. The resultant arrangement among farmworkers, buyers, and tomato growers—the CIW's Fair Food Program (FFP)—mandates the penny-per-pound payment and incorporates a human rights code of conduct that includes zero tolerance for sexual assault and forced labor. It also includes worker-to-worker educational sessions conducted by CIW; a worker complaint mechanism; health and safety committees ensuring that farmworkers have a voice in controlling their work environment; and perpetual auditing to ensure that each farm is in compliance with the FFP. Negotiating a code of conduct raises the issues of implementation and monitoring. CIW addressed these issues through the creation of the Fair Food Standards Council (FFSC), an independent agency that focused on the tomato industry.[53] The council's charge was clear: growers who violated the code of conduct would have to correct their violation. If they failed to do so, buyers would not purchase their tomatoes. The FFSC automatically removes from the Fair Food Program any grower who commits acts of slavery or sexual assault. In short, buyers would buy tomatoes only from growers in good standing with the Fair Food Program. The FFP benefits the workers by giving growers an incentive to adhere to the code and penalizing them if they fail to do so.[54]

The CIW's power grows as the number of participating corporations increases. By the end of 2018, about 90 percent of Florida-grown tomatoes were covered by the FFP. The four major fast-food companies (YUM BRANDS, McDonald's, Burger King, Subway) and the three largest food service providers (Compass Group, Whole Foods, Trader Joe's), along with several major supermarkets (Walmart, Fresh Foods, Whole Foods, Trader Joe's) had joined the Fair Food Program. The Immokalee workers are now diversifying into produce other than tomatoes. They are also expanding geographically, bringing their network into North and South Carolina, Virginia, Maryland, and New Jersey.[55] The CIW's efforts have brought workers basic sanitation facilities, a clear definition of what constitutes a thirty-two-pound bucket of tomatoes, a living wage, and numerous other benefits. Importantly, CIW's work has apparently ended slavery and sexual assault in Florida's fields. In fact, a United Nation's official characterized CIW's Fair Food Program as "an international benchmark in [the] fight against modern-day slavery."[56]

When the Coalition of Immokalee Workers was formed in 1993, Florida' tomato pickers were impoverished, abused, and sometimes enslaved. But that's no longer the case. As Susan Marquis observes, CIW's efforts over a quarter-century have "transformed the tomato fields from the worst agricultural situation in the United States to the best."[57] CIW's approach may provide a model for future worker center actions. Dairy farmers in Vermont and workers in Bangladesh are already emulating the Coalition's model of socially responsible change. There's much to be learned by the ability of the CIW to achieve its many victories in a right-to-work state. In fact, the organization's non-union status played a major role in its success. First, CIW forced giant corporate buyers of tomatoes to accept their Fair Food Program by waging a secondary boycott against them. The farmworkers, after all, were employed by growers, not the corporate buyers. The secondary boycott, an action prohibited by unions under Taft Hartley, gave the coalition tremendous leverage over the corporations. Reaction to CIW's methods is sometimes very hostile. Conservative and other right-wing groups are appalled at CIW's approach and the success it brings them. A report by the U.S. Chamber of Commerce claims that CIW, along with other worker centers, "engage in conduct—including protests and secondary boycotts—that would likely be unlawful under the National Labor Relations Act if done by traditional labor unions." Therefore, the report concludes, "federal agencies should no longer allow these groups to receive special treatment under the law."[58] Encouraged by the election of Donald Trump to the presidency, in November of 2017 the anti-labor Center for Union Facts (CUF) filed an official complaint with the Internal Revenue Service claiming that the CIW should lose its tax exempt status because "it is a labor union . . . and does not qualify for exemption."[59] *LaborPain*, the joint blog of CUF and the conservative Enterprise Freedom Action Committee, put the anti-labor criticism of the CIW more bluntly. In their view, CIW is "really tantamount to a shakedown operation"[60] that doesn't deserve tax exempt status as a charity. Attempts to weaponize labor law in order to strip the CIW of its power are sure to continue. This anti-labor attitude is, perhaps, best expressed in the remarks of one frustrated right-wing critic on the website of Francis Rooney, Florida's ultraconservative member of Congress. He complained that the Coalition of Immokalee Workers evade the law and "intimidate companies to increase wages and comply with their other demands"[61] How do you evade a law that excludes you, he asks? The right-wing criticism of CIW's efforts is a testament to their success.

Second, as a human rights and anti-corporate organization, CIW was able to build a broad-based coalition of organizations, some of which are not fans of unions. This large coalition kept the pressure on the fast-food companies and contributed significantly to CIW's success. It is also worth considering whether those anti-union corporations that agreed to the Fair Food Program would have responded to the CIW if it were a union. Some observers believe the companies agreed with CIW's FFP as a means to contain a movement for worker's rights in the fast-food industry. In other words, the agreement with CIW keeps unions out.[62]

Third, unlike most unions, which are hierarchically structured, the CIW is a collective with a relatively flat organizational chart. The CIW's motto, "we are all leaders," clearly reflects the principle of participatory democracy. This means that members themselves develop the organization's strategies and tactics. The practice of collective participation in formulating CIW's policies gives members the ownership and commitment necessary to conduct long-term struggles. CIW's requirement that all staff must work in the fields and receive the same pay as other farmworkers is a practice long absent in most labor unions and another example of the organization's commitment to internal democracy. Finally, CIW takes leadership development seriously. It does not merely hand down information from leadership, as many unions do. Instead, CIW has a serious leadership development program that attempts to implement and make real the "we are all leaders" principle. Compare this approach, as Elly Leary does, to the United Farm Workers, a hierarchically structured union led by a charismatic leader.[63] This is not to suggest that CIW is at odds with organized labor. Unions, in fact, have contributed to CIW in a number of important ways. But CIW's success stems from the fact that it is not a union, and its structure and many of its practices are quite different from most institutions of organized labor.

Despite its record of achievements, CIW and all other worker centers face a similar problem: CIW depends on other organizations for financial support. Without its own source of revenue, it is vulnerable and its existence precarious. Adding to future threats is the fact that legal protections for farmworkers remain minimal, and all the workers' gains derive from CIW's ability to convince buyers to purchase tomatoes only from growers who participate in the FFP. Wendy's has long refused to join the FFP. CIW's ongoing campaign to bring Wendy's into the FFP exposes a possible weakness in CIW's basic operating strategy. Wendy's buys its tomatoes from Mexico, claiming that Mexican tomatoes are both better and cheaper. The availability of cheaper goods across the border raises important questions about the future of the Fair Food Program. Will American consumers even notice the exploitation of Mexican farmworkers? And given intensifying hostility toward Latino immigrants, if consumers do notice, will they care? In this climate, what's to prevent the fast-food companies currently in FFP from following Wendy's lead?

New York's Farmworkers Try To Unionize

New York's farmworkers use many of the same tactics and methods that worked so well for the Immokalee workers. The struggle for change in New York began in 1989 when a coalition of religious, community, and labor organizations initiated the Justice for Farmworkers Campaign (JFW). The JFW program aimed at developing a statewide educational and legislative movement that would give farmworkers the same rights enjoyed by all other New Yorkers: the right to bargain collectively. The coalition of more than one hundred organizations is spearheaded by the Rural and Migrant Ministry (RMM), a not-for-profit advocacy organization committed to social change, in addition to charity and social services. Headed by Richard Witt, an energetic and caring Episcopal minister, the RMM's "Accompaniment Program" recognizes and respects the farmworkers' independence. The Ministry assists the farmworkers and the rural poor, but it does not tell them what to do. Instead, mirroring the practices of the CIW, it asks, "What do you want?" and helps the workers analyze ways to realize their goals. The farmworkers set their own agenda and the RMM contributes by recruiting allies and helping in other ways in the struggle for justice and equality. Under Reverend Witt's guidance, RMM has played the leading role in the campaign by publicizing the farmworkers' plight, garnering public support, and advocating for legislation that addresses their needs. In the 1930s, New York Representative Vito Marcantonio observed that the NLRA's exclusion of domestics and farmworkers from the NLRA guaranteed "a continuance of virtual slavery until the day of revolt."[64] When the Farm Workers Fair Labor Practices Act became law in 2019, the coalition celebrated its success in righting the wrong of eighty years ago. Along with other benefits, this law gives farmworkers the right to form a union to improve their working and living conditions.[65]

The road to this success was not straightforward. One might even say it was a long and winding road. Since the CIW originated in Florida, a right-to-work state in the Deep South, the right to bargain collectively was not a real option. Unlike the Immokalee workers, New York farmworkers sought legislative solutions, with the ultimate goal of gaining the right to unionize. New York is a pro-union state, with 22.3 percent of its labor force organized. When it comes to union density, New York is second only to Hawaii's 23.1 percent.[66] With this high level of union density, New York farmworkers expected and received strong support from existing unions. The United Food and Commercial Workers (UFCW) provided significant funding for the campaign, as did the New York State United Teachers (NYSUT) by furnishing meeting space, membership participation at rallies, financial support, and, most importantly, political backing. Led by Executive Vice President Alan Lubin, one of organized labor's most experienced and effective political operatives, NYSUT played a major lobbying role in the coalition's efforts. NYSUT's political activities illuminate the fact that high union density is also accompanied by significant political power for unions, a fact not lost on state legislators. The JFW Campaign received a boost in 2010 when the political efforts of a coalition that included the farmworkers and a number of labor unions helped domestic workers gain passage of the Domestic Workers Bill of Rights. The Domestic Bill of Rights is the first law of its kind in the country that provides basic benefits for domestic workers, another group excluded by the New Deal's protective legislation.[67] Although the 2010 law did not give domestics the right to collective bargaining, it gave hope to farmworkers that they, too, could eventually make legislative progress.

The structure and diversity of New York's agricultural industry also contributed to the decision to take legislative action. New York farms are generally small and, with the exception of some dairy producers, they primarily sell their goods to small buyers and directly to consumers at the state's nearly 650 farmers markets.[68] Brian O'Shaugnessey, the retired director of the New York State Labor and Religion Coalition, said that the campaign had looked at ways to emulate the CIW model, but the industry wasn't sufficiently concentrated to find a buyer or producer to target.[69] In short, there is no equivalent of Taco Bell to boycott in New York. As an editorial in the *Albany Times Union* observed, the farmworkers' struggle is not a battle between "low-wage, low skill workers against wealthy corporate farming interests."[70] Indeed, according to the Cornell Small Farms Program 2019 report, some 90 percent of the state's farms have less than $350,000 in annual sales. The New York Farm Bureau likes to promote the image of the small New York farmer by reminding the public that 98 percent of the state's farms are family owned and the average net income for each farm in 2017 was just $42,875.[71]

Unlike vegetable, fruit, and flower growers, New York's dairy industry is becoming increasingly concentrated and could become a target of a secondary boycott.[72] In 1997, only twenty-one farms in the entire state had at least 1,000 cows, but by 2012 that number had grown to 103 farms. Several had estimated revenues approaching $2.5 million, and one had estimated sales of $5 million annually.[73] Most of the state's dairy farmers sell their milk to dairy cooperatives. The cooperatives, in turn, either market their own brands or sell to corporations, primarily those Greek yogurt makers that have made New York a leading producer of the product. Big-brand companies such as Chobani depend on these cooperatives for their milk.[74] This suggests that the CIW model might have worked in New York's dairy sector. But, according to the RMM's Richard Witt, the coalition lacked the resources to effectively implement such a campaign. Besides, separating dairy workers from other farmworkers would divide and weaken the coalition and reduce prospects for other agricultural workers to gain the right to organize.

The decision to represent all farmworkers is another distinguishing feature of New York's Justice for Farmworkers Campaign. The CIW represents only tomato pickers, but the New York farmworkers' movement is inclusive. The Campaign for Justice represents all of the state's more than 56,000 agricultural workers.[75] New York's agricultural industry is as occupationally diverse as it is large. In 2014, the state's agriculture was a $5.05 billion industry. New York ranks third in dairy production, which accounts for about 26,000 jobs. It's the second largest producer of apples in the country and the leading vegetable and fruit producer in the eastern United States. In addition to picking apples and grapes and working in the state's many muck farms, New York's farmworkers are employed in greenhouses where flowers are grown; they work on sod farms and in the state's growing number of wineries; they toil in food-processing plants; and they labor in all aspects of the poultry industry, including specialized farms in the Hudson Valley that produce duck liver paté.[76] There's great occupational diversity among New York's farmworkers, but like the Immokalee workers, many live under abysmal conditions. Governor Andrew Cuomo's Task Force to Combat Worker Exploitation in 2016 best summarizes the conditions of the state's farmworkers. The Task Force Report cited some 491 enforcement and compliance cases in the state's agricultural industry. These cases included wage theft, sexual harassment, and poor housing.[77]

The experience of Lazaro, a dairy worker, provides a typical example of what New York's farmworkers face every day. Lazaro worked on a small central New York dairy farm. For seven days a week he labored between nine and twelve hours a day, milking cows, cleaning the barn, and caring for calves. For this he was paid a flat amount of $500 weekly. Given the number of weekly hours he worked, Lazaro's compensation fell below the minimum wage. But like so many other migrant farmworkers Lazaro was afraid of losing his job, so he didn't complain. Then one day during his daily routine work of pushing cows, he encountered two bulls. Lazaro had no real training on how to calm bulls down or how to behave around them. He tried to hide, but a bull charged and tossed him through the air. When he landed face down, he lost some teeth and seriously damaged his eye, almost losing it. His injuries prevented him from working, and he was not paid for the time he lost. Instead his boss fired him, claiming he was no longer physically capable of performing his job. Doctors who treated Lazaro at the hospital told him to see eye and bone specialists, but that was impossible. Lazaro couldn't afford it. With no family in the United States to help, no income, and unaware of his eligibility for workers compensation, Lazaro moved in with a friend.

Lazaro's story was reported in a study jointly sponsored by the Worker Justice Center of New York (WJCNY) and the Workers' Center of Central New York (WCCNY).[78] Lazaro's experience is a microcosm of what other studies and reports confirm as struggles many farmworkers face every day.[79] In a nutshell, they are underpaid, work in dangerous conditions, are ineligible for overtime pay, and by law are not entitled to a day off. But thanks to the successful efforts of the Justice for Farmworkers Campaign, New York's farmworkers are now entitled to receive the state's hourly minimum wage, which in 2020 amounted to $12 on Long Island and $11.10 upstate.[80] Unfortunately, as in Lazaro's case, many do not receive the legal minimum. This constitutes wage theft, a prevalent practice familiar to farmworkers. Farmworkers also do not get overtime pay. That is not wage theft—it's legal. Wage theft takes different forms. Working for less than minimum wage is just one example. Far too often, owners and bosses withhold their workers' final check. Some coerce their workers to participate in unpaid training, and others fail to reimburse workers for essential personal safety equipment. One study found that 28 percent of immigrant farmworkers in New York experienced some form of wage theft. Many others suspected they were victimized but weren't certain.[81] Farmworkers tolerate this abuse for a number of reasons. Language barriers make communicating between workers and their bosses difficult, and many are simply unaware of their rights. In fact, one study found that more than half the workers surveyed were ignorant of their legal rights.[82] The fear of getting fired or being reported to ICE as an illegal immigrant also keeps workers from complaining about their insufficient earnings.[83] Since about half of the state's farmworkers are here illegally, aggressive anti-immigrant policies put in place by the Trump administration gave farm bosses increased leverage over their workers[84] as well as more tools to use against labor activists.[85]

Low pay, long hours, and wage theft barely scratch the surface of the farmworkers' plight. Prior to passage of the 2019 law, New York farmworkers were not legally entitled to a day off. They risked getting fired for taking a sick day, and almost certainly would not get paid for the days they missed. Agricultural work is dirty, strenuous, and dangerous. Nationally, the farmworker fatality rate is the same as that of workers in the mining industry.[86] These already dangerous working conditions are exacerbated by the fact that the vast majority of New York's farmworkers are not protected by the Occupational Health and Safety Administration (OSHA). OSHA exempts small farms from coverage, and almost 90 percent of New York's farms are classified as small.[87] Since 1990, according to a *Times-Union* report, 375 farmworkers were killed on the job, a fatality rate triple that of the state's second most dangerous occupation, construction.[88] Two-thirds of all dairy workers surveyed in New York reported being injured at least once, and sixty-nine were killed on the job between 2006 and 2016.[89] As one dairy worker so lucidly put it, "You can get another worker for less than it costs to replace a cow."[90]

Female farmworkers are especially vulnerable to sexual harassment. According to California Rural Legal Assistance, Inc., 80 percent of all women farmworkers are subject to sexual harassment on the job.[91] Bosses, some workers claim, sometimes take a woman to an isolated area and assault her. Many do not report the harassment for fear of losing their job. One woman agricultural worker in New York, for instance, discussed the vulnerability of female farmworkers: "They are forced to go with the boss . . . They can't say no because they are afraid."[92] The threat of deportation also keeps women agricultural workers from reporting the harassment. "We have to endure sexual abuse," one said. "If we report it, the police will ask you 'do you have documents?' "[93] Cramped living conditions also increase the possibilities for sexual harassment. On Long Island potato and nursery farms, for example, women and men are forced to share bedrooms. Fabiola Ortiz, a doctoral student studying dairy workers in New York, observes that on some farms "women find themselves living with six other guys they don't even know."[94]

Overcrowding is just one problem with farmworker housing. Farmworkers usually get free housing on or near the farm, making it convenient for both the worker and farmer. The worker has no commute; the farmer has the worker at his disposal twenty-four hours a day, a necessity in the dairy industry where cows must be milked several times a day. The quality of this housing varies across the state but is sometimes far below normal living standards. For instance, authorities in Owasco County issued a cease and desist order to one farmer for providing housing permeated with the stench of urine and manure. Additionally, the bedrooms were furnished with stained mattresses and the ceilings so low it was difficult for most people to stand.[95] This may be an extreme example, but it certainly is not unique. In one survey a majority of farmworkers complained of bug infestation, and almost a third reported structural issues, poor bathrooms, lack of potable water, insufficient heating, and broken stoves. Practically speaking, farmworkers are trapped in these living conditions because most can't afford to rent off-site. Additionally, even though undocumented farmworkers became eligible for a driver's license when the Green Light Law was enacted in 2019, most can't afford a car anyway.[96]

Living in crowded substandard housing made farmworkers more susceptible to the Covid-19 pandemic. In fact, during the summer of 2020, 176 workers living in congested housing on a single farm in New York contracted Covid-19. Another New York farm with similar housing conditions reported eighty-two workers had become ill with the virus.[97] At the beginning of the pandemic, the national Center for Disease Control (CDC) guidelines categorized farmworkers as "essential workers," but farmworkers found themselves at the end of the line for getting masks, gloves, testing, and vaccinations. The 2020 Coronavirus Aid, Relief, and Economic Security (CARES) Act and subsequent relief packages explicitly denied benefits to undocumented workers, including thousands of New York farmworkers.

The RMM focuses foremost on political advocacy, but it also knows that the hungry must be fed. That's why the Ministry has worked with the farmworkers to alleviate the harsh conditions they face on and off the job. Guided by the premise that rural workers must have a seat at the table where decisions affecting their lives are made, the RMM helps workers develop the leadership skills essential to building independent organizations that improve the quality of their lives. This educational process has achieved some positive results, including the creation of a Head-Start / Child Care center for children of farmworkers, two worker education centers, and several high school youth empowerment programs that have a 95 percent college matriculation rate.[98]

The political face of the RMM spearheaded the formation of the JFW when, in 1989, then Governor Mario Cuomo recommended the creation of a task force to examine the feasibility of collective bargaining rights for farmworkers. Encouraged by the governor's proposal and his previous veto of legislation exempting farmworkers from a pesticide notification law, the RMM and other farmworker advocacy groups joined forces to create JFW.[99] Under the leadership of the RMM, the JFW developed a long-range plan to achieve political change. Initially a faith-based organization, the coalition decided to wage its campaign on moral grounds. The abysmal and inhumane treatment of farmworkers was just wrong, they argued, as they worked assiduously to expose the horrendous living and working conditions of the farmworkers. The JFW also sought to enlarge and strengthen the coalition. Operating on the premise that small victories provide the foundation for larger successes, the JFW sought small political victories that helped farmworkers and simultaneously increased the visibility and credibility of the campaign. RMM activist Brian O'Shaugnessey recalls how the coalition's activism grew over time. Initially, advocates consulted with Farmworkers' Legal Services, met occasionally with editorial boards, and scheduled public meetings to publicize the issues.[100] According to O'Shaugnessey, this changed in 1992 after the coalition exposed serious sanitation code violations at farmworker camps. This exposé generated much publicity and brought new support for the workers. The coalition's persistent efforts did not go unnoticed. In 1994, the state senate held hearings on farmworkers and a year later released a report in support of giving them the right to unionize. That same year the JFW initiated its Farmworker Day in Albany (FDA), an annual rally day at the state capital.[101]

The expanding coalition's visibility and political influence brought the desired "little" but significant victories that serve as building blocks for their long-term goal of winning the right to form a union. In 1996, all New York farmworkers gained access to potable drinking water in the fields. Two years later, the state legislature mandated the availability of portable toilets and handwashing facilities. In 1999, following a rally in New York City in which New York State AFL-CIO President Dennis

Hughes spoke, more unions joined the coalition. That same year the legislature did away with the farmworker's sub-minimum wage, tying it to the state minimum wage, an immediate raise of 21 percent.[102] The Farm Bureau subsequently unsuccessfully fought to reinstate the sub-minimum wage.

The following year marked the first time the Democratic-controlled Assembly passed the Farmworkers Fair Labor Practices Act, a bill granting the right to collective bargaining, overtime pay, and a guaranteed day of rest.[103] The bill was not brought to the floor of the senate, however, and died in the Senate Labor Committee. Encouraged by the Assembly's actions, the JFW coalition intensified its activities. Thanks to the UFCW, the RMM has an accessible website that along with an ever-growing email list elicits donations and promotes the coalition's many activities. JFW's demonstrations, protests, fasts, public meetings, and marches all brought increasing public support in the form of favorable media commentaries and editorials. In 2003, the coalition's activities reached new heights when over 1,000 supporters greeted FDA with two eleven-day marches to the state capitol, one beginning in New York City, the other just outside of Rochester. The marches were well publicized and even received favorable coverage in the *New York Times*.[104] Still, for the fourth consecutive year, the assembly passed the bill only to watch it die in the senate.

The coalition's legislative and public relations victories triggered retaliation. The coalition's van was vandalized beyond repair outside of Rochester; farmers prevented their workers from taking time off to lobby; and the Farm Bureau used its fiscal and structural power to convince members of the Republican-dominated Senate that passage of the bill would destroy the state's multibillion dollar agricultural industry. The Bureau also filed complaints alleging lobbying and ethical violations. Although the complaints were ultimately rejected, their purpose was to generate negative press against the coalition.[105] The structure of the state's agricultural industry gives the famers another political edge. Not only are there almost as many farms as farmworkers, but the farmers are permanent residents who vote, as opposed to most farmworkers who are either undocumented or seasonal workers, oftentimes both, and cannot vote.[106]

While the scenario of the bill passing the Assembly only to die in the Senate continued, the JFW campaign to educate the public and pressure legislators was virtually nonstop. In 2006, the Labor Religion Coalition assisted in the creation of the Workers' Center of Central New York, another grassroots organization seeking economic justice for farmworkers.[107] Additional pressure was put on the legislature. Robert Kennedy's daughter, Kerry Kennedy, attended an Albany rally and urged both chambers of the legislature to support the farmworkers. Her hard-hitting Thanksgiving commentary in the *New York Daily News* in support of the farmworkers garnered more attention and support for the campaign.[108] Testifying in an eight-hour hearing that March before the Senate Agriculture Committee, Kennedy upset the farm lobby by reporting allegations of sexual abuse of female workers. These allegations were backed by majority leader Espada, but skeptical opponents asked why the incidents were not reported to authorities. The controversy once again brought the plight of the farmworkers before the public. In June, farmworker advocates demonstrated at the Capital in favor of the proposed law. Legislative supporters from both the Assembly and Senate addressed the crowd. Finally, in August 2010, the Senate, with a one-person Democratic Party majority, was ready to vote on the bill. But the path to the vote was somewhat complicated. Since the Agriculture Committee in April had voted it down, the proposed law was presumed dead. But miracles do happen, and on August 3 a slightly modified version of the bill emerged from the Labor Committee for a floor vote.[109] A brief two hours of heated debate clarified the opposing positions. Supporters, mainly Democrats, relied on moral appeals. Senator Schneiderman, for example, reminded his colleagues "that we are talking about fundamental rights owed to every man and woman in this state." Although New York's agricultural industry was prospering, the bill's opponents, mostly Republicans, focused on what they believed to be the bill's economic impact on the upstate economy. Senator Catharine Young's criticism was typical: "I can't think of a worse bill to bring up at this time that hurts New York state economy so badly." When the votes were cast, five Democrats voted with the Republican minority to defeat the bill by three votes.[110] Farm Bureau President Dean Norton hailed the vote as a great victory and promised to defeat the bill again should it ever reappear. The coalition's Richard Witt reassured discouraged onlookers and legislators that "we're not going away."[111]

The claim that passage of the bill would wreak economic havoc on farmers and the upstate economy was always questionable at best. The New York State Civil Liberties Union, a key supporter of the coalition, issued a memorandum in support of the legislation that cited state and federal data undercutting such claims. For instance, according to the United States Department of Agriculture, cash receipts from the state's agriculture exports tripled between 2000 and 2016, growing from $500 million to $1.5 billion. The memo also noted the almost $26 million in government aid a dairy company received for agreeing to open a yogurt plant in Batavia. There were more examples, but none mattered. The vote on the bill was based on political power, not facts. The coalition fell short.[112]

The close vote attracted additional public attention, but hopes for the bill's passage in the next session were dampened in November 2010 when the Republican Party recaptured control of the Senate. These pro–Farm Bureau Republicans held their majority until the 2018 election. During the eight-year interim they gained the support of a small group of Democrats—the Independent Democratic Caucus (IDC)—who broke party ranks to caucus with them. Despite this ominous political setting and the passage of years without significant legislative gains, the JFW kept Witt's promise: it did not go away. The coalition received a jolt of favorable publicity in 2013 when an RMM activist and former farmworker, Librada Paz, became one of only three Americans to receive the prestigious Robert F. Kennedy Human Rights award. In 2016, the JFW organized another 200-mile march to Albany. Farmworkers, students, and advocates all participated in the fifteen-day march, which originated outside Senate Majority Leader Flannigan's office on Long Island. Receiving widespread media coverage on a daily basis, the caravan continued north, passing through three senate districts on its way to the Capital. On reaching the Capital, the marchers were joined by others in a large rally that preceded a well-attended press conference.[113] Their efforts failed as once again the bill died in the Senate committee.

While JFW continued to wage its legislative campaign, a new front opened in the campaign for the right to unionize when Crispin Hernandez, a central New York dairy worker, contested the legality of the state's prohibition against collective bargaining. After calling a meeting of co-workers to discuss a way to protest their miserable job conditions, Hernandez and a co-worker were fired. Enter the American Civil Liberties Union. With the backing of the Workers' Center of Central New York and the Justice Center of New York, in May of 2016, the ACLU brought the case to state court, arguing that the exclusion of farmworkers was unconstitutional. The legal basis for their position was Article I, Section 17 of the state's constitution: "Employees shall have the right to organize and bargain collectively." This provision, the ACLU contended, overrides the state law that conforms to the section of the NLRA that excludes farmworkers and domestics from having the right to organize.

Governor Andrew Cuomo almost immediately announced his support for the ACLU's position.[114]

The governor's decision not to defend the state law ordinarily would have given the dairy worker and the ACLU an automatic win. But after the New York Farm Bureau intervened to defend the law, the case went to the State Supreme Court. In January 2018, Judge Richard McNally ruled against the farmworkers, stating that it is up to the legislature, not the courts, to change labor laws.[115]The ACLU appealed the lower court's ruling. Finally, in May 2019, in what one legal observer described as "a step forward for some of the most vulnerable workers in our communities," the appellate division by a 4-to-1 margin declared the exclusionary law unconstitutional. Both Governor Cuomo and state Attorney General Letitia James applauded the ruling, with Cuomo stating that "farmworkers never should have been denied the same basic rights as other workers. . . ." The Farm Bureau's president, Steve Fisher, responded by criticizing the court's decision, which he claimed would undercut the viability of the state's agricultural industry and force New Yorkers to rely "on food brought in from out of state, or worse yet, out of the country." The Bureau promised "to appeal the court's ill-conceived ruling."[116]

Fisher was most concerned about the Farm Workers' Fair Labor Practices Act. The bill was gaining supporters, and Fisher feared that the legislature may now pass it. As usual, the proposed law had already passed the State Assembly with little trouble. The bill's prospects for passing improved when most of the IDC members lost their primaries and Democrats gained a solid majority in the State Senate in November of 2018. The bill's sponsor, Brooklyn Senator Jessica Ramos, who chairs the Senate's Labor Committee, joined with Jan Metzger, Chair of the Agriculture Committee, to hold three public hearings throughout the state. Testimony at the hearings showed that opponents of the bill were most concerned with the prospect of paying overtime and the possibility of a strike at harvest time. Travis Torrey of the large 15,000-acre Torrey Farms expressed his concern about paying workers for overtime. His farm, he noted, hires about 300 seasonal employees who work seventy to eighty hours during harvest time. Paying overtime would be cost prohibitive. Hiring more workers and cutting back on hours to forty or so would be the alternative to paying overtime. This alternative also prompted some farmworkers to testify against the bill. Migrant farmworkers generally want to earn as much as they can before returning home. An overtime provision could reduce their hours and their pay.[117]

During the last week of the legislative session, after hours of negoti-ations over the previous weekend into the early hours of Monday morn-ing, legislators reached an agreement on a bill giving farmworkers the equality they had been denied for eighty years. Passed by both houses two days later, on June 19, the final day of the legislative session, the bill grants farmworkers the right to collective bargaining, provides disability insurance, a day of rest, and overtime after sixty hours, with a pathway to forty.[118]

Now that farmworkers have the legal right to form a union doesn't necessarily mean they will do so. The UFCW previously waged an unsuc-cessful organizing campaign, but that was without the legal protections now in place. Still, the problems of organizing farmworkers could prove insurmountable. Many are undocumented seasonal immigrants who speak little or no English and who return to their home countries at the end of the season. Despite their newly acquired legal protections, workers are still likely to fear reprisals if they support a union. Scholar/activist Margaret Gray describes the difficulties organizers face in tracking down and talking to workers who are exhausted after picking crops for hours in the hot sun. Gray also notes that organizers frequently encounter resistance from the farmers or supervisors. Threats of violence and other forms of harassment are not uncommon. In a *New York Times* opinion piece, Miriam Pawel notes that in the forty-two years since the passage of California's Agricultural Labor Relations Act in 1975, only about 1 percent of California's farmworkers are in unions and, she claims, their wages and working conditions have barely improved. New York's farmworkers finally won the right to unionize, but Miriam Pawel suggests that their victory is just a promise that requires "effective grassroots organizing in the fields."[119]

Questions also arise concerning union representation. Will one union represent all the diverse occupations in the agricultural industry? If so, which union? Or will different agricultural sectors have different unions? Given organized labors' need to bolster membership numbers, will union organizing campaigns be undercut by jurisdictional battles? Time will provide answers to these questions. Meanwhile, New York farm-workers have a level of stability and security that Immokalee workers lack. Unlike the Immokalee workers, who depend on social justice to leverage private corporations, New York's farmworkers have a state-backed guaran-tee of overtime pay after sixty hours. They also have a legally mandated day of rest, something no boss can take away without consequences; and they are now eligible for unemployment insurance, paid family leave, and workers' compensation benefits—all major victories.[120] Importantly, since these benefits were gained through legislation, it will take an act of legislation to take them away, not merely the arbitrary and capricious decision of some corporate CEO. New York's farmworkers will continue to work with coalitions, but having their gains backed by law reduces their reliance on outside political and fiscal support. If the New York farmworkers overcome the many difficulties they face and unionize, they will generate their own union income and achieve greater independence and autonomy.

The Immokalee model illustrates what workers can achieve outside the union movement. And New York farmworkers have shown how to build on that model in a pro-union state. Perhaps the most valuable aspect of the Fair Labor Practice Act is the legal protections New York's farmworkers now have, whether they unionize or not. These protections, along with the gains won through their work with coalitions, have improved their working and living conditions. For New York's farmworkers unionization may turn out to be more of a promise than a reality, but they can still enjoy the benefits gained by coalition building.

Chapter 4

Worker Centers in Focus

Every day, Jesse spends twelve to fourteen hours in her car driving Uber riders through the streets of Los Angeles, trying to earn enough to pay her bills. She doesn't have much time to spend with her kids, hardly ever has meals with them, but tells them she'll catch up. She never does. When Jesse gets home after a long day on the road, she's done in. She used to make about $1,400 a week. But since Uber slashed its rates, she's fortunate to earn $1,000. "I'm working myself to death . . . And I'm losing my hair," she says. In late March 2019, Jesse joined hundreds of other frustrated drivers in a twenty-five-hour strike organized by Rideshare Drivers United (RDU), a virtual worker center that wants to end the exploitation of rideshare drivers by Uber, Lyft, and other Silicon Valley firms.[1]

Worker centers have been crucial to gains made by the Immokalee workers and New York's farmworkers, but these are just two of many exploited groups of workers, including rideshare drivers, who have turned to worker centers. As union membership continues to drop, worker centers and the worker center movement continue to grow and rack up success after success. Worker centers inspired the Fight for $15 movement that raised the salaries of tens of thousands of low-wage earners. They have empowered fast-food workers, nannies, restaurant employees, taxi drivers, teachers, domestics, warehouse workers and countless other low-wage workers.

To appreciate the growing importance of worker centers in the labor movement, it makes sense to understand where they came from, what they are, and how they relate to traditional unions. Are they partners or competitors? What is their legal standing? And how, in the growing gig economy, do people such as rideshare drivers who work in isolation and don't even report to a brick and mortar facility create functioning worker centers that don't exist in a physical space? Finally, how is the business sector responding as worker centers change the dynamics of the labor movement?

Worker Centers:
Labor's Hope or a Passing Phase?

Not too many years ago most people had never heard of worker centers, let alone understood what they do and how they do it. In the early 1990s only five or so worker centers were in operation. Today that number exceeds two hundred and continues to grow at a rapid pace. This growth needs to be understood in the context of the decline of labor unions along with the simultaneous rise in immigrant populations, as labor scholar Janice Fine points out.[2] Large numbers of these immigrants became part of the American underclass economy, where wages are low and workers' rights and job security are nonexistent. Facing hostile and abusive employers, antiquated labor laws, and unions' reluctance to invest in organizing campaigns, these exploited workers formed new organizations outside the union movement to promote their interests—worker centers.[3]

Worker centers are rooted in a tradition that began in the late nineteenth century when vulnerable workers, including many European immigrants, formed their own protective organizations. They established fraternal and mutual aid organizations and settlement houses and worked closely with local political machines and religious institutions in an effort to promote their interests. These early organizations declined in significance with the rise of organized labor and passage of legislation restricting immigration, particularly the Johnson-Reed Act of 1924.[4] The passage of the Hart-Cellar Act of 1965 removed the quota system, leading to an influx of millions of new immigrants, the bulk of whom came from Latin America. These new immigrants arrived in the states just as globalization was restructuring the U.S. economy, with low-wage, non-union work in the growing service sector replacing millions of well-paying union jobs in manufacturing. Organized labor's subsequent loss of political and social clout made it ever more difficult for working people to resist the corporate onslaught. According to the U.S. Bureau of Labor Statistics, over thirty-one million Americans lived in poverty by the turn of the millennium. This number includes more than 6.4 million working poor, three-fifths of whom worked full-time jobs.[5] Trapped in low-paying, dead-end jobs without union representation, workers began creating their own advocacy organizations in the form of worker centers.

Most centers are community-based nonprofit organizations, which aren't governed by labor laws. Centers are legally distinguishable from unions in that, unlike unions, they do not bargain collectively with their employers. According to one legal scholar, case law clearly suggests that as long as worker centers do not engage "in a 'bilateral mechanism' which enables employees and a particular employer to go back and forth on issues relating to employees' wages and working conditions," they are not subject to the NLRA's restrictions on labor unions.[6] They are free to protest and picket without restriction and can even conduct secondary boycotts, as seen in the case of the Immokalee workers. In short, worker center activists have greater latitude than union members. As labor historian Jefferson Crowie describes them, "Worker centers are part of a broad scramble of how to improve things for workers outside the traditional union/collective bargaining context. They've become little laboratories of experimentation."[7] The centers provide a host of services. English classes are useful to non–English speaking immigrants. Centers refer workers to available health care organizations, and advise them of available social services. Legal assistance and education training on worker rights are among the most important services offered by worker centers. As the previous chapter noted, the CIW basically took off after a trained farmworker questioned the authority of his boss. Legal aid is an effective way of addressing wage theft, a common practice among employers of low-wage workers. Janice Fine reports that "centers have annually recovered . . . between $100,000 and $200,000 in back wages—and some have gotten more."[8] But centers do more than provide services. They also organize workers to build sustainable organizations that rely on direct collective action to realize the members' goals.

Since a dedicated and organized membership is the foundation for change through direct action, centers can function effectively only if they develop a cadre of highly skilled and committed activists. This is why, unlike unions, increasing membership numbers is not necessarily a goal. Again, as Fine points out, "most centers view membership as a privilege that is not automatic but must be earned."[9] Like the Immokalee workers' experience, centers require workers to participate in educational programs to gain a better understanding of the issues they face and how they might resolve them. These educational programs often begin with "know your rights" training, but the long-range goal of educational programs is to produce an ideologically committed cadre of active members. Given the obligations expected of members, the cadre of rank-and-file members is usually small.[10]

The internal workings of the centers differ from unions in a number of other ways too. First, worker centers emphasize the role of internal democracy. Decisions aren't made in a hierarchical order or by powerful allies; members themselves must decide what they want, why they want it, and how they plan to realize their goals. This emphasis on democratic decision making is closely connected to a center's educational program. Internal democracy and the development of "active consciousness" are part of the same piece. Both pieces play an essential role in leadership development, something centers take seriously, and organizing. Second, worker centers don't attempt to negotiate contracts for workers at single work sites. Instead, they rely on direct action aimed at key institutions or individuals to achieve wage gains and better working and living conditions for an entire sector. Their actions may organize around economic issues, as in the case of the Immokalee workers who targeted big corporate buyers of tomatoes.[11]

As in the experience of New York's farmworkers, the Fight for $15, the Domestic Workers United, and others, centers often direct their activities at government institutions and public policy makers. Public policy advocacy frequently pressures government agencies to improve enforcement of existing laws and regulations, or, as the New York experience illustrates, to pass new laws that improve wages and working conditions. It's also worth noting that worker centers usually form alliances with other community groups, particularly faith-based institutions such as Catholic Charities and the Rural & Migrant Ministry. In fact, the Economic Policy Institute study of worker centers conducted by Fine revealed that the vast majority of the centers in the study cited the faith community as crucial to their work.[12] Working with their allies, the centers often undertake boycotts, picketing, marches, slowdowns, strikes, and just about anything else that shines a public light on the larger political, social, and economic issues behind the personal troubles of individual workers.[13]

Since the vast majority of worker center members earn low wages, dues are not a significant source of revenue. Consequently, most centers have small budgets and even smaller staffs. They also must depend on outside sources for financial help. Because most centers are organized as not-for-profits, they are legally able to receive foundation grants, assistance from community and religious institutions, and, of course, direct aid from unions. A U.S. Chamber of Commerce study, for example, found that between 2013 and 2016 worker centers received over $50 million in direct aid from foundations.[14] The Chamber also reports that unions are major contributors to worker centers, particularly the Service Employees International Union (SEIU). SEIU spent $3.1 million alone on Jobs With Justice (JWJ) between 2013 and 2016.[15] Other major union contributors to JWJ during this time span include the Communication Workers of America ($824K), the United Food and Commercial Workers (UFCW) ($739K), and the AFL-CIO ($507K). The AFL-CIO also provides the lion's share of financial assistance to Working America, an AFL-CIO non-union affiliate that engages non-unionized workers to promote labor's political interests.

The dependence of worker centers on funding from outside organizations has far-reaching implications. In his article "Who Should Fund Alt-labor?," former union organizer Josh Eidelson explores the question of "who should pay the bills?"[16] This issue is significant for a number of reasons. Karen Nussbaum, founder and director of Working America, sees financial dependence as incompatible with internal democracy. "Worker organizations that aren't self-sustaining can't be democratic," she claims. Others reinforce Nussbaum's view. City University professor Hector Cordero-Guzman, a former officer at the Ford Foundation, expressed concern that foundations' fiscal influence could easily shape the policy decisions made by organizations receiving such funds. Other activists agree.[17]

In the past, unions frequently viewed worker centers as competitors. But that changed in August of 2006 when the AFL-CIO agreed to form a partnership with the National Day Laborer Organizing Network (NDLON), an extremely democratic worker center dedicated to improving the lives of day laborers, migrants, and low-wage workers. Shortly after, Change to Win formed a similar partnership with NDLON. The relationship between NDLON and organized labor opened the door for increased cooperation between unions and worker centers.[18] In 2011, the National Taxi Worker Alliance, an organization of independent contractors not covered by the Fair Labor Standards Act and lacking the right to bargain collectively, became an affiliate of the AFL-CIO. This marked the first time an organization of independent contractors achieved union affiliation.[19] Guided by the motto of the 2013 AFL-CIO convention—"Dream, Innovate, Act"—President Trumka introduced his "New Strategic Initiative," a multi-phase program to build an effective working-class political movement. Recognizing the need to increase labor's political clout despite declining membership numbers, Trumka called for more partnerships with worker centers, which he viewed as a crucial part of a new working-class movement.[20] The convention supported their president's call by electing Bhairavi Desai, director of New York City's Taxi Workers Alliance, to the executive council. The Alliance does not negotiate collective bargaining agreements, concentrating instead on putting political pressure on New York City's Taxi and Limousine Commission, the government agency that sets rates and rules for taxi drivers.[21] The Taxi Workers Alliance was further integrated into the new working-class movement when the steelworkers coughed up funds to assist them in their national organizing efforts.

The AFL-CIO's commitment to coalition building and partnering with worker centers received many accolades. *Labor Notes'* Steve Early describes the positive media coverage and enthusiastic response of convention attendees to the organization's New Strategic Initiative, which one union leader happily described as "the most radical restructuring of labor since the AFL and CIO merged nearly sixty years ago."[22] The American Federation of Teachers' Randi Weingarten clearly stated the importance of the new program to all workers when she chanted "community is the new density" to conventioneers.[23] But organized labor's embrace of worker centers was not universal. Amidst all the talk and hoopla celebrating the perceived rebirth of organized labor, critics spoke out. Steve Early decried the convention's lack of focus on the need to develop strategies to defend and enhance the interests of existing members. Reminding everyone of the squeeze on current union members, Early concluded that the formation of coalitions is old hat and insufficient to address the issues members face every day on the job. Cribbing an old Yogi Berra-ism, Early asked, is it "Déjà vu all over again?"[24] Firefighters President Harold Schaitberger protested that "our responsibility is to represent workers' interest on workers' issues," and warned that alliances with progressive groups would likely make the AFL-CIO gain the moniker of "the American Federation of Progressive and Liberal Organizations."[25]

Anti-labor forces made their view of worker centers crystal clear by dubbing them UFOs—Union Front Organizations. Their concern with the centers' increasing success was heightened with the release of the AFL-CIO's interim report to council members prior to the 2013 convention. The report, which suggested that organized labor should "open its rolls to other workers outside a collective bargaining context," appeared almost simultaneously with stepped up attacks on worker centers.[26] Glenn Spencer of the U.S. Chamber of Commerce's Workforce Freedom Initiative expressed concerns about the relationship between unions and worker centers by observing, "Judging from Trumka's remarks, organized labor sees a lot of potential in this model."[27] But anti-union forces don't merely complain about worker centers, they take actions to neutralize their effectiveness. For example, in a July 2013 letter, the Republican chair of the House Committee on Education and Workforce, John Kline, along with a Republican colleague from Tennessee, Phil Roe, asked Tom Perez, the new labor secretary, for a determination on the legal status of working centers. Their goal was to get an official ruling declaring that worker centers fall under the requirements of the Labor-Management Reporting and Disclosure Act (LMRDA). If centers are designated as labor organizations, they would have to submit detailed financial reports to the Department of Labor that would be available to the public. Additionally, they would also have to conform to the LMRDA's rules on internal governance and organizational structure. The Secretary of Labor ignored the inquiry.

Republican attacks on worker centers continued through the duration of the Obama administration. John Kline (R-MN), the former Chair of the House Labor and Workforce Committee, for instance, spent four years investigating Obama's Labor Department treatment of prominent worker centers, even though the Obama position was "consistent with the position taken by the Bush Administration" that worker centers are not unions.[28] The election of Donald Trump in 2016 foreshadowed new attacks on worker centers. In a November of 2017 hearing before the House Education and Workforce Committee, Trump's new labor secretary, Alex Acosta, announced that the Department of Labor (DOL) was prepared to prescribe new regulations on worker centers. Two months later, the Republican chair of the House Committee on Education and the Workforce requested the DOL to investigate several worker centers in order to determine if they were "front groups controlled by big labor special interests."[29] The letter of request specifically focused on the financing of the centers and implicitly complained of the Obama administration's failure to follow up on a previous request by the House Committee on Education and the Workforce.

Acosta responded to the growing concerns anti-labor groups had with the centers by assigning Nathan Mehrens, a former president of the anti-union, anti-big government Americans for Limited Government (ALG), to investigate the question of whether worker centers are actually union front organizations.[30] Mehrens has a long history of animus toward worker centers. As president of ALG, he wrote an article in 2015 with the provocative title "Big Labor's Tax Deductible Organizing Scam" that called for removing the tax exempt status of some worker centers. Some worker centers, he claimed, deal directly with employers, which he believed qualifies them as labor organizations not eligible for tax exemption under subsection 501 I(3) of the Internal Revenue Code. Mehrens also questioned the legality of the tactics used by some centers. Reminding his readers that illegal activities remove the 501c(3) status of organizations, Mehrens accused centers of a list of tactics he viewed as illegal, including trespassing and blocking entrances to worksites.[31]

Hailed as a positive sign by the Chamber of Commerce, Mehrens launched an investigation of a Minneapolis worker center—Centro de Trabajadores en Lucha—that forced Macy's, Target, and other big retailers to hire unionized janitorial services.[32] This investigation gave a green light to other anti-union groups to go after a wide range of worker centers, including the Coalition of Immokalee Workers, which the Trump administration put under closer scrutiny. Despite its clamor, the Trump administration was slow to follow through. It did not appoint a director of Office of Labor Management Standards (OMLB), the office charged with administering and enforcing the Labor Management Reporting Disclosure Act (LMRDA), until July of 2018. The investigation certainly did not get off to a fast start and as of this writing no definitive actions have been taken against worker centers. The absence of visible action, however, does not necessarily signify that the centers are not under the gun. It is OMLS policy not to reveal whether an investigation is actually taking place.

If anti-labor groups succeed in having worker centers designated as labor unions, the centers could no longer wage secondary boycotts or employ secondary picketing. They would also be prohibited from taking contributions from foundations, a major source of their income, and individuals could not claim a charitable tax deduction on any contributions made to the centers.[33] Reclassification of worker centers as unions would also require centers to meet burdensome reporting requirements in accordance with the LMRDA's regulations, and would place restrictions on the organization's internal structure, its election procedures, and its methods of governance. This ongoing debate regarding the nature of the relationship between worker centers and unions has primarily focused on the restrictions worker centers could face if they are designated as unions, a goal of the anti-labor political right. What is often missing from these discussions is the frequently overlooked and forgotten protections that Section 7 of the NLRA may provide worker centers.[34]

Worker center participants tend to view the NLRA as a weapon anti-labor interests want to use against them. But as a number of scholars point out, the law also provides protections for non-union workers. Section 7 of the NLRA guarantees "the right to self-organization, to form, join or assist labor organizations, to bargain collectively . . . and to engage in other concerted activities for . . . mutual aid and protection."[35] If an individual employee acts in concert with one or more other workers or singly attempts to begin a group complaint or action in the interests of employment, the section 8(a)1 protections of the NLRA kick in. Section 8(a)1 renders any interference with the rights granted in Section 7 as an unfair labor practice. In other words, management cannot threaten or punish workers who complain as an individual or as part of a larger group, even if they are not in a union or trying to organize one. This rule was clearly established in the 1962 case of *NLRB v. Washington Aluminum Company*. In that case, the U.S. Supreme Court ruled that four non-union employees who were dismissed for walking off the job to protest working in cold weather were protected by Section 7. Therefore, the court ruled, their firing was an unfair labor practice.[36] The NLRA's protections of non-union workers are not absolute. Workers who take illegal action or commit egregious behavior unrelated to their employment are not protected.

Another of the NLRA's protections for non-union groups is the defense it offers against state defamation lawsuits. During strikes and other labor disputes workers may publicly criticize their employers in any number of ways, including oral statements directly to the media and handbills listing their grievances in unflattering terms. Not surprisingly, employers have initiated state defamation lawsuits that claim the workers' statements are false and slanderous. Obviously, the threat of defamation suits has a chilling effect on employee behavior. Supreme Court decisions, however, have upheld the NLRA's free speech protections as expressed in Section 8(c) of the NLRA. In the 1966 case of *Lynn v. United Plant Guard Workers*, the Court ruled that false injurious statements made with malice are subject to libel suits, but defamatory statements made during labor disputes fall under the jurisdiction of the NLRA in order to protect the free discussion established by that law.[37] While the Supreme Court has yet to rule whether worker centers are protected from libel suits under the Lynn ruling, Kati L. Griffith is among those scholars who believe the NLRA's defamation defense should apply to worker centers. As labor law scholar Cynthia Estlund puts it, the NLRA "protects speech about unionization or other forms of employee representation, discussion of work related grievances and petitioning for redress."[38]

Despite the NLRA's protections, worker centers are not taking advantage of them. Estlund, for instance, observed that her casual inquiries indicate that Section 7 protections for non-union workers are not well known to most law students and even to many lawyers practicing labor law. "The NLRA," she contends, "is widely regarded as a world unto itself, one that deals strictly with unions and collective bargaining."[39] Griffith's 2015 study identified just seven worker centers that helped workers file a total of twelve NLRB charges.[40] Her analysis of worker centers' scarce reliance on the NLRA supports Estlund's more casual observations. Griffith found that since many centers lack stable funding and legal staffs, they may be unfamiliar with the option of seeking relief under the NLRA. There's also the possibility, she notes, that centers may avoid turning to NLRA protections out of concern about tying up their limited funds in fighting an employer's countersuit. Centers also have access to other legal avenues, including Title VII of the Civil Rights Act and the FLSA. Of course, as noted in earlier chapters, many occupations employing hundreds of thousands of workers are completely exempted from NLRA coverage. Think domestics, farmworkers, and the rising numbers of workers defined as independent contractors who make up the bulk of the gig economy.

The steady and continuing decline of union membership has left more and more workers without any real job protections. Low wages, bad working conditions, and lack of job security are the negative consequences of organized labor's decline. But worker centers are now filling the vacuum created by the absence of unions. These centers do not negotiate traditional labor agreements with a single employer. Instead, they may be understood as part of a loosely structured social movement that defines the struggle of low-wage, mostly immigrant workers, in moral terms. Worker centers, as Janice Fine notes, may also be viewed as labor market institutions that achieve the bulk of their victories through direct action and the filing of lawsuits.[41] However understood, worker centers are playing an increasingly important role in the development and formation of a new labor movement. The rise of centers has caught the attention of the U.S. Chamber of Commerce, which is sufficiently concerned that the worker center movement is gaining momentum and sophistication and is helping unions "find entry into facilities where workers have previously declined to embrace unions."[42] The AFL-CIO's willingness to embrace worker centers and its characterization of them as part of the pre–New Deal working-class movement has fueled the fears of the Chamber and other anti-labor counterparts. A reality check indicates that the suddenly frightened Chamber spent over a billion dollars lobbying government during a fifteen-year period ending in 2012, leading the nonprofit Public Citizen group to ask, "Why is the elephant so scared of the mouse?" The successes of California's gig economy workers, a segment of labor that Chamber allies thought could never be organized, suggest that the elephant's fears are not unfounded.[43]

California's Gig Workers Struggle to Get Real Jobs

A growing body of literature documents the success of worker centers in various low-wage occupations. David Rolf's *The Fight for $15* and Janice Fine's *Worker Centers: Organizing Communities at the Edge of the Dream* are among the best. Rolf's book surveys the national struggle for a $15 an hour minimum wage that began in 2012 and has spread to virtually every large city in the United States. Fine's excellent study looks at several successful struggles as she analyzes the history, future prospects, and challenges facing worker centers. These seminal books focus mainly on traditional worker centers, but a changing economy presents new challenges for workers in the growing gig sector. Originally used by musicians, the word "gig" has now become a blanket term to describe any kind of nonpermanent job: temps, freelancers, contract worker, day laborers, they're all looking for their next gig.

Emily Guendelsberger's *On the Clock*, Louis Hyman's *Temp*, and Sarah Kessler's *Gigged* are among the works that examine the effects of the changing economy in the workplace. These changes include the rise of temporary jobs and the lack of job security, a dearth of social interaction among workers, and permanent speedups monitored by apps. Employers wrap these dismal conditions in a glossy Horatio Alger myth that plucky individual initiative and hard work will produce fabulous financial rewards—as long as they do what their app overseers tell them to do. These studies chronicle the working conditions in this new economy that keep workers fragmented, much to their employers' benefit, but they don't address in any detail what workers are doing in response.

McDonald's workers have been trying to unionize for years without success, but with the help of SEIU and the Fight for $15 movement, they have won legislation in four states that raised the minimum wage to $15 an hour.[44] Amazon warehouse workers across the country are also trying to unionize. These are gig workers who have an app for a boss, but they have the advantage of reporting to a real brick-and-mortar facility. In contrast, for a huge number of gig workers, the workplace is wherever they are—a Starbucks, a public library, their kitchen table, their car. This expanding world of the virtual workplace is the new frontier of the labor movement. Talk about fragmented. In this virtual workplace individual workers don't even know who else is a member of their community. The rise of the technology that supports this gig explosion in the first place also gives gig workers the tools to take collective action. A case in point is California's rideshare drivers.

The False Promises of Virtual Gig Work

Workers of the world no longer need to unite. Instead, they "just need to think outside the boss."[45] Such is the vision of those who proclaim that this new virtual gig economy is just what the modern worker wants. The rise of the virtual workplace gives individual workers the freedom to do their own thing. Forget about a common workplace—gig work is all about you, just you. The gig economy supposedly gives today's workers an unparalleled flexibility that means goodbye to the outdated 9-to-5 work day. Since gig workers set their own schedules, their work revolves around them, and they, not some boss, get to choose what work they want to do and when they want to do it. Want to play with the kiddies in the afternoon and do the work that interests you later that night? No problem. But it gets even better. Commuting to work is no longer a necessity, saving gig workers time and money. Working in isolation also cuts down on exposure to germs that cause sickness and lost productivity. As one pundit puts it, "getting sick is less common for the savvy freelancer." Since nirvana, at least for employers, is attainable in the isolated individualism of gig work, it's no surprise that the gig economy is growing. In 2016, about one-third of the workforce consisted of freelancers of one kind or another. But some projections indicated that about 43 percent of the country's workers would be employed in the gig economy within the next few years.[46] Heaven has surely come to earth thanks to the opportunities offered by gig work. Or has it?

California's gig workers, led by Uber and Lyft drivers, are more likely to believe their jobs are located somewhere deep inside Dante's circles of hell rather than in the heavenly utopia that made their jobs sound so attractive in the first place. A key to understanding the rise of gig work is the simple fact that it basically owes its existence to a restructured economy in which giant corporations make billions for their CEOs and stockholders by eliminating permanent decent-paying jobs. Several studies reveal an inverse relationship between a job-producing economy and the increase in the number of gig workers. One such investigation by JP Morgan Chase and Company concludes that if the traditional labor market grows, workers will abandon gig jobs. The option of regular employment outside gig work is also likely to make it increasingly difficult to recruit workers for the gig economy, a factor that may limit future growth in the gig sector.[47] A 2018 Economic Policy Institute study backs these findings and concludes that the number of gig workers is overstated in that if a person employed elsewhere does even one hour of gig work a month, that person is counted as a gig worker too.[48] Louis Hyman puts the relationship between an economy that produces traditional jobs and gig work in crystal-clear terms when he reminds us that a generation ago "teenagers who needed extra money delivered pizza . . . by the time Uber came around, however, adults and teenagers were delivering pizza."[49] In other words, an economy that was losing decent-paying, steady jobs pressured adults to take any job they could to make a living, including jobs once the domain of high school kids. Again, Hyman clearly puts it, "The choice [is]. . . not between driving for Uber or working on a unionized assembly line. It is between Uber and slinging lattes."[50] The difference between delivering pizza for Pizza Hut, Dominoes or, better yet, working at a full-time union job is that the delivery person and the factory worker get a W-2 form and may receive some benefits. Uber or Lyft drivers get a 1099 form and nothing else except the ability to deduct the depreciation of their vehicle.

Uber doesn't supply cars. Instead it offers two apps, one for drivers and one for customers. Customers merely have to "tap a button, get a ride." Once the customer taps Uber's magic button, the company contacts a nearby driver who soon afterward picks up the rider. Uber receives the fare, takes a commission of about 33 percent, and pays drivers weekly.[51]

Lyft works in a similar fashion. The almost immediate appearance of the driver may seem like magic to the rider, but it's always a mystery to the driver, who isn't told where the rider wants to go until after the ride begins. One driver who works the Los Angeles Airport complained that he had to take some passengers to distant parts of California and even to Las Vegas. These time-consuming trips kill the flexibility in flex time, and the trip home is "off the clock."[52]

Claiming that their apps are the basis of their business, ride-hail companies identify themselves as technology rather than transportation companies. This classification allows drivers to pick up riders without having to purchase expensive medallions that traditional cabs are required to have. More importantly, the claim that ride-hail firms are a technology industry allows the companies to exploit their drivers as independent contractors. Drivers pay all transportation expenses. In addition to using their own cars, they buy the gas and pay for repairs, insurance, licensing, and all other expenses necessary to keep their cars on the road. For those many drivers who can't afford to buy or rent a car, Uber follows the old old-fashioned company store model of exploitation by providing loans or leases that it collects directly from their earnings. Should drivers fall behind in their payments, Uber repossesses the car through its subsidiary Xchange Leasing.[53] Calling their drivers independent contractors liberates the companies from legally mandated responsibilities companies owe to traditionally classified employees. Drivers do not get health insurance, sick or leave time, vacation days, disability insurance, or workers compensation. They're only paid when they are actually driving a customer. In other words, they are not paid for downtime between rides, coffee breaks, meals, or jury duty.[54] As independent contractors, they are not protected by traditional anti-discrimination laws, they are prohibited from unionizing, and they can be fired at will.[55] Since drivers work without any direct contact with a boss, driver evaluation is conducted solely through Uber apps. Drivers use their app to rate passengers on a scale of one to five, just as passengers use their app to rate drivers. The ratings provide algorithms that determine rewards and punishments, including firing, or, to use the gig economy's Orwellian term, "deactivation." Workers who get bad ratings or turn down riders may be "deactivated" without notice. When the company shuts off its app, the driver instantly joins the ranks of the unemployed.[56] The rideshare business model exploits not only drivers but also taxpayers in the states where these companies operate. Since drivers are not employees, companies don't have to pay payroll taxes. For instance, in California, rideshare companies save about $7 billion a year that should be going to the state.[57] Now do the math for all the other states allowing rideshare operations.

Uber was formed in 2009 in San Francisco following the Great Recession. Four years later it faced competition from Lyft, then a new rideshare company also based in San Francisco. Today both Uber and Lyft have evolved into behemoth corporations. Uber, the larger of the two, operates in 300 cities in fifty-eight countries and employs about three million drivers. Drivers initially enjoyed the flexibility of gig work, with most of them working part-time to earn a few extra bucks. The pay really wasn't too bad at first. But later on as more people took to ridesharing work, wages began to plummet. Nationally, between 2010 and 2014 the number of Uber drivers alone grew by 69 percent. As the number of drivers grew, drivers found it increasingly more difficult to maintain earnings. Rideshare companies took advantage of the abundant labor force by increasing their commissions and slashing mileage rates. Recall the story of Jesse, who spends twelve to fourteen hours a day behind the wheel in Los Angeles. That's over sixty hours a week. She used to earn $1,400 a week but now considers it a good week if she pulls in $1,000.[58] Her experience is not at all unique in the state with the second highest cost of living in the United States.[59]

Working more and earning less has increased drivers' hostility toward Uber and Lyft. Squeezed by growing competition for work, declining wages, and the rising costs of maintaining their cars, drivers began to challenge their classification as independent contractors. They also objected to Uber's pay system. Complaining that it was vague and difficult to follow, many drivers felt cheated. Drivers found Uber's policy on the reimbursement of tips particularly irksome. Uber's advertisements said the fare included gratuities, a directive to riders that they need not tip the driver. But drivers complained about not getting tips and not knowing how much the company actually owed them. Drivers began a series of protests in front of Uber's headquarters and other publicly visible locations. Their actions were often spontaneous and uncoordinated, but they caught the attention of the public. Finally, in August of 2013, several angry drivers in conjunction with an activist pro-labor attorney filed a lawsuit in the U.S. District Court in the Northern District of California. The suit addressed Uber's policy on gratuities and, importantly, sought to convert the driver's classification from independent contractor to employee.

Drivers Turn to the Courts

The class action lawsuit filed by four Uber drivers against the company was one of several filed against Uber and Lyft. In this case, as in others, the drivers sought full reimbursement for all gratuities due them and, most importantly, a correction of the company's misclassification of drivers as independent contractors. If the drivers won the litigation they would be eligible to bargain collectively, a goal held by many, including their activist counsel, Shannon Liss-Riordan. The drivers contended that "without drivers, Uber's business would not exist." In fact, Uber didn't even own the vehicles that provided the company's revenue. Furthermore, their argument continued, since drivers "are graded, and subject to termination, based on their failure to adhere to requirements Uber imposes on them," they should be Uber employees. The suit then requested that Uber reimburse the drivers for the expenses incurred in the performance of their jobs.[60]

Uber responded by hiring a high-powered attorney who had successfully defended Walmart before the U.S. Supreme Court in a massive employment class action case. The company based its defense on the drivers' flexibility and the premise that they enjoy being their own boss. The company also now included mandatory arbitration provisions in the drivers' employment contracts to shield Uber from class action employment lawsuits. Uber nevertheless suffered a series of legal setbacks. In March of 2015, the federal district court in San Francisco rejected Uber's motion for a summary judgment, which meant that the case would proceed to trial before a jury. In December, the court held that the arbitration agreements were not enforceable, thereby bringing all drivers who signed those agreements under the umbrella of the class action suit. This meant that almost all of the 160,000 current and former Uber drivers were now included in the litigation.[61] U.S District Justice Edward Chen also ruled that drivers could seek partial reimbursement for use of their smart phones, as well as mileage reimbursement for car expenses based on IRS mileage rates. This was in addition to an earlier ruling that drivers could recover tip compensation.[62]

The drivers' lawsuit gained some momentum in June of 2015 when the California Office of the Labor Commissioner reversed its 2012 determination that drivers were independent contractors. Responding to a complaint filed by a former Uber driver, Barbara Ann Berwick, the office ruled that Uber drivers are employees, not independent contractors. The commissioner's office concluded that "Uber exercises tremendous control over the drivers, requiring them to pass background checks and accept a given percentage of ride requests." Uber was ordered to pay the driver over $4,000 for past expenses.[63] Not surprisingly, Uber appealed. The labor commissioner's ruling came on the heels of a $227 million settlement by FedEx for a similar suit. The settlement came after a federal appeals court decision in Oakland concluded that since FedEx actually controlled the way drivers did their jobs, it had improperly classified its drivers as independent contractors. These rulings prompted one Los Angeles journalist to predict that under California law Uber and similar gig companies are "cruising for a bruising."[64]

But Uber had only begun to fight. The rideshare company went on the offensive just two days after Judge Chen's ruling by sending all of its more than 400,000 U.S. drivers a twenty-one-page legal document that barred them from participating in future class action suits. Uber instructed drivers to sign the agreement if they wanted to pick up any more riders. The agreement had an opt-out provision, but most drivers didn't take advantage of it. As one driver remarked, "many Uber drivers speak English as a second language and would have a lot of trouble deciphering a 21-page PDF." Another driver who had a degree from the University of California at Berkeley explained he didn't have much "interest in reading 10-point type on a cell phone."[65]

Uber's imposition of mandatory arbitration clauses on drivers' contracts has become a common practice these days, thanks largely to a series of U.S. Supreme Court decisions. The Court's chipping away at class action lawsuits culminated in the case of *Epic Systems v. Lewis*. In this case, the Court determined that despite language in Section 7 of the NLRA that allows workers to take collective action against their employers "for the purpose of collective bargaining *and other mutual activities*," mandatory arbitration provisions are legal (emphasis added).[66] Lead attorney for the drivers, Shannon Liss-Riordan, a workers rights advocate who had previously taken on Starbucks, American Airlines, FedEx, and other large corporations, views the Supreme Court's backing of mandatory arbitration provisions as an important hammer in the corporate toolbox to evade the law at the expense of workers. She finds "it reprehensible that the Supreme Court has allowed all these companies that are blatantly breaking the law to protect themselves."[67] Known as "Sledge-Hammer Shannon," the hard-punching attorney believed Uber had again overstepped the limits of the law by trying to bury the opt-out clause in a lengthy document filled with legalese and fine print. She argued before Judge Chen that Uber "should not be able to curtail liability . . . on the 14th page of an email on an iPhone."[68] The Judge ruled in her favor and allowed the drivers to file a class action suit. Uber appealed.

The rideshare drivers long and winding road toward justice continued the following April (2016) when the U.S. Court of Appeals for the Ninth Circuit said it would hear Uber's appeal in June. The appellate court's decision to take the case raised the possibility in Liss-Riordan's mind that the appeals court could reverse Judge Chen's ruling, leaving the drivers with nothing. Consequently, she began to negotiate a settlement with Uber. A little more than two weeks later, Uber and the drivers reached a tentative agreement. Uber agreed to pay $100 million to drivers in California and Massachusetts, since the litigation was also filed on behalf of Massachusetts' drivers. It placed limits on Uber's firing practices, established an appeals process for terminated drivers, prevented the company from deactivating drivers for low pick-up rates, and advised customers that tips were not included in the fare. As part of the settlement Uber agreed to provide assistance in the creation of "drivers associations" in both California and Massachusetts. Significantly, the settlement failed to reclassify drivers as employees. Their status quo as freelancers in the gig world remained

The Guardian declared the settlement a victory for Uber, stating that "the proposed settlement is a victory for Uber's business model."[69] The *New York Times* agreed with the *Guardian's* assessment, as did other media outlets. Many drivers also viewed the settlement as a sellout by their attorney, who would make millions on the deal, even though she cut her fees by $10 million. Edward Escobar, head of the recently created Alliance for Independent Workers, called the settlement money a pittance as he and other drivers carried signs that read "Fire Shannon."[70] Attorneys with other class action suits against Uber chimed in, with one claiming that Liss-Riordan "stuck a knife in the back of every Uber driver in the country."[71] After claiming that the settlement's acceptance of drivers as independent contractors "could have slowed down the process for everyone else" who fought the misclassification of drivers, Bhairavi Desai, head of the New York Taxi Workers Alliance, helped some 200 Uber drivers mount a formal protest against the proposed agreement.[72] In May, Escobar enlisted the support of Veena Dubal, an activist labor attorney, who filed suit on behalf of a group of drivers opposed to the settlement. Driver criticism of the agreement gained credence in August when Judge Chen rejected the proposed settlement, ruling that it was "not fair, adequate, and reasonable."[73] Escobar claims Chen's rejection of the settlement was due in part to the public pressure generated by the Alliance.[74]

Days after the Uber settlement was announced, a U.S. District Judge in San Francisco rejected a proposed settlement between Lyft and its drivers, also negotiated by Liss-Riordan. This proposal basically mirrored the Uber settlement, but since Lyft was a smaller company with fewer drivers, the monetary reward was just $12.25 million. Claiming that Lyft had "short-changed" the drivers, the judge announced that the agreement "does not fall within the range of reasonableness."[75] Lyft had originally presented the drivers' attorneys with outdated figures that understated expense reimbursements due them. The original amount, according to Lyft, was $64 million. Subsequent updated numbers revealed the amount to be almost twice as much, some $126 million. In mid-May a final settlement was reached when Lyft agreed to pay $27 million. Still, drivers were not reclassified as employees.[76]

In September of 2018, Liss-Riordan's concern that the Court of Appeals might reverse Chen's ruling became a reality. The appeals court decided that the mandatory arbitration provisions were enforceable, which meant that drivers covered by an arbitration agreement had to pursue their claims through individual arbitrations, not a class action suit. The following March, the more than 13,000 drivers not covered by arbitration provisions received a share of a $20 million settlement negotiated by Liss-Riordan. Companies prefer mandatory arbitration over class action lawsuits primarily because most aggrieved workers do not use the procedure. By now, however, drivers had begun organizing with the help of the Alliance for Independent Workers (AIW), the teamster-backed California App-Based Drivers Association (CABDA), and other emerging virtual worker groups. Drivers also identified each other by using these new social media platforms that kept the community of drivers updated on their struggle.[77] Additionally, as they met at staging lots at airports, gas stations, coffee shops, and other likely locations where they would run into colleagues, drivers encouraged other drivers to file for arbitration. Activist attorneys used the media as well as the new worker centers to publicize the importance of seeking arbitration. Law firms, according to AIW's Escobar, played the major role in getting drivers to file for arbitration. "Law firms got on it like ambulance chasers," he said.[78] All these efforts paid off when about 60,000 drivers agreed to pursue arbitration just days before Uber was to go public. "What we are doing against many companies is we're taking them at their word and bombarding them with thousands of arbitration demands," explained Liss-Riordan.[79] The sheer numbers of drivers who accepted arbitration was not only surprising, it threatened to overwhelm the company. Some experts claimed that resolving the case would become part of Uber's everyday business and could cost upward of $600 million.[80] The filing of arbitrations en masse was a clear sign of drivers' increasing ability to organize and take effective collective action. California's rideshare drivers were becoming an effective political force.

From the Courts to the Streets

Organizing a group of gig workers is not an easy task. It's even more difficult to organize gig workers in California's rideshare economy. The drivers' work itself is very atomistic and socially isolating. A large majority work part-time, often just to make a few extra bucks, and don't necessarily regard rideshare driving as their "real" occupation. And how do organizers reach drivers who are geographically dispersed all across the huge state of California? Then there are the challenges of communicating with the many immigrant drivers who have a limited command of English. The filing of a spate of lawsuits against Uber and Lyft raised drivers' hopes and engaged them in the struggle for reclassification from independent contractors to employees. The legal victories, however limited in the eyes of some, sent a positive message that change was possible. Drivers' participation in the legal actions awakened many to the need of organizing and contributed to the formation of new workers' organizations and structures of communication.

As these legal struggles unfolded, informal, uncoordinated drivers' actions evolved into the creation of several virtual worker centers. In 2014, for instance, drivers in southern California who relied on gig company apps for riders formed the California App-Based Drivers Association. "The company's manifest indifference to the plight of the drivers" led to the formation of the group, according to Lofti Ben Yeder, a member of its seven-person leadership council.[81] After Uber refused to meet with the group's leadership, the drivers formed an alliance with Teamsters Local 986 for organizational and political support. Two years later, drivers led by Uber worker Edward Escobar formed another virtual worker center, the Alliance for Independent Workers. This newly created advocacy organization was open to all gig workers, not just drivers. In Escobar's view, the organization was part of a larger workers' movement well beyond rideshare drivers. Not surprisingly, the large portion of drivers among gig workers and within Escobar's Alliance made drivers the major force within the organization. In fact, among the Alliance's members was Douglas O'Connor, a plaintiff in the original 2013 case against Uber. Echoing the mantra of other worker centers, Escobar expresses the egalitarian spirit of worker centers. "We're all leaders," he says, insisting that the Alliance is a team effort. The organization initially worked with labor unions, including the teamsters and, later on, SEIU, an organization Escobar respects for its efforts in the Fight for $15 movement. But the Alliance distanced itself from unions primarily because members believed most union organizers had little or no experience as drivers and didn't understand the issues rideshare workers faced.[82]

As part of a larger social-political movement, the Alliance, according to Escobar, is focused on issues that go beyond the immediate interests of drivers. Uber and Lyft, Escobar insists, are waging corporate attacks on public transportation in San Francisco and throughout the United States with the ultimate goal of privatizing it. Escobar paints a grim picture of the problems his Alliance faces. Lower fares, he claims, already make Uber and Lyft desirable alternatives to public transportation. Uber's founder and former leader, Travis Kalnick, stated the company's long-term objective of getting rid of that "other dude in the car," meaning, of course, the driver.[83] Ride-hail companies could reduce fares and still make substantial dollars if they deployed driverless cars. Plummeting fares would shift more riders to Uber from the public transportation system, leading to more traffic congestion and dirtier air. To support his point, Escobar notes that ridership in San Francisco's public transit system has dropped by 13 percent since the formation of Lyft and Uber. The national threat of driverless cars and privatization to public transportation led the Alliance to partner with Drivers United, the national organization of gig drivers.[84]

In January of 2016 Uber again cut fares in cities across the United States. Once again, Lyft followed suit. San Francisco drivers took a 10 percent cut, while New Yorkers took a 14 percent hit. These rate cuts galvanized a number of drivers to take actions on Super Bowl Sunday. On the Monday before the big game New York drivers demonstrated, holding signs in dozens of different languages, and waged a strike with limited success. On that same day in San Francisco a caravan of about one hundred cars tied up traffic by driving from San Francisco's Candlestick Park to the city's International Airport and then on to Uber headquarters. Organized by a group calling itself Uber Drivers United, the caravan "spanned about two or three blocks of cars, four lanes across."[85] Upon reaching Uber's headquarters, the demonstrators promised to take more actions on Super Bowl Sunday.

Although news accounts reported a record number of drivers backed taking some form of direct action, drivers lacked the organizational ability to wage an effective campaign. There was still no large worker center with the resources and ability to coordinate drivers' activities. Drivers would have sporadic meetings at airports' staging lots while waiting for riders, but otherwise they remained dispersed, uncoordinated and relatively unorganized. Without centralized coordination, communications among them were spotty at best. Some drivers heard about scheduled actions by reading flyers, others through word of mouth. Still others depended on on-line forums and social media communications for information. When it came to communications among workers, it was still on the "catch as catch can" level. Many didn't even know about the actions. Bad communications were only part of the problem. Drivers didn't agree on what actions to take. Some wanted a boycott, others opted for another driver caravan. As drivers discussed tactics, Uber made an offer that some just couldn't refuse. The ride-hail company offered drivers a guaranteed $40/hour fare two hours before and after the game. One driver told BuzzFeed news that he "came here to make a buck, not make a point."[86] Despite the growing numbers of drivers participating in the action, the boycott had little impact on Uber.

The following fall the Alliance for Independent Workers joined Drivers United in a national protest organized by the Fight for $15 movement. According to news reports, the demonstrations targeted twenty airports and major cities throughout the United States.[87] Protestors turned out in large numbers, leading Escobar to observe that while drivers are usually not coordinated or unified, their partnership with the Fight for $15 movement was an exception. As Escobar surveyed the large number of gig participants, he told an SEIU organizer that "we are the future of work."[88] The mass actions generated much publicity and caught the attention of many, but it failed to achieve the goal of showing Uber and Lyft their ultimate dependence on the drivers. Nevertheless, it was a good rehearsal for future demonstrations and protests.

Uber and Lyft drivers continued to wage job actions and other forms of protests. Their efforts brought growing public attention to their plight, but neither Uber nor Lyft took steps to address their concerns. In August of 2017 more than 100 drivers protested at Los Angeles International Airport (LAX). Demanding a mileage reimbursement increase of about one dollar, the drivers shouted down cars with Lyft or Uber stickers, urging them to "join us or turn off your app."[89] The fact that other drivers still picked up riders is indicative of the limited success protesting drivers faced. Communications were still far from perfect, as many drivers who carried passengers didn't even know there was a job action going on. Yet, however slow, change was coming. Driver frustration with constantly declining earnings was increasing. Protests had become commonplace; groups of drivers began using new forms of communication, such as Viber; and, most importantly, a growing number of drivers wanted to create an effective, democratically run workers organization. In autumn 2017, Los Angeles–area rideshare drivers, encouraged by the strike efforts at LAX, decided the time had come to establish their own drivers' organization, Rideshare Drivers United, an association, they claimed, to be *for* the drivers and *by* the drivers.

To give drivers a more effective voice in determining their working conditions, Rideshare Drivers United had to develop better ways for supporters to communicate with each other. As the Rideshare Drivers United new website put it, "Tech companies count on us not knowing or talking to each other." To overcome this social isolation, a driver and a software developer combined forces to design an easy-to-use software program to organize drivers: organizers call every driver who contacted Rideshare United on Facebook and ask if they would participate in a ten- to fifteen-minute telephone interview. The names of those who agree to the interview, along with their availability, is entered into the software and given to an organizer who makes the contact. After the call, the organizer gives the information provided by the new contact to team members, who evaluate where that new contact fits into the software's four categories of interest, ranging from "disengaged" to "potential core" or "future leader?" The organizer who does the interview becomes the new contact's sponsor.[90] Within the first six months of its existence, the software helped the organization recruit some 3,000 members.

In April 2018, the drivers received an unexpected boost from a ruling by the California Supreme Court. In the case of *Dynamex Operations West, Inc. v. Superior Court of Los Angeles*, the court ruled in favor of delivery drivers who the company had converted from employees to independent contractors. In its ruling the court established what became known as the "ABC" test that classifies workers as independent contractors only if the person (a) is free from control and direction in the performance of work; (b) performs work outside the hiring company's usual course of business; and (c) customarily earns a living doing that kind of work independently of whatever company they happen to be doing a job for at a particular time.[91] The *Dynamex* decision appeared to pave the way for reclassification of Uber and Lyft drivers, as well as other gig workers.[92] Lyft and Uber responded by claiming that the decision applied only to Dynamex workers, not to Uber and Lyft drivers.

The Dynamex decision initiated what would eventually become intense political battles between the ride-hailing companies, their supporters, and the drivers. Shortly after the ruling, gig businesses throughout the state reacted to the decision. Fully aware of the potential costs the decision would impose on the gig industry, the Chamber of Commerce created a political coalition—I'm the Independent Coalition—to resist the possible reclassification of workers. The coalition's members included Handy, Lyft, Uber, Instacart, the California Restaurant Association, the California Retailers Association, and the Internet Association, an organization involving Amazon, Google, LinkedIn, and Facebook. The newly formed politically powerful advocacy group immediately launched a lobbying campaign aimed at neutralizing the consequences of the Dynamex decision.[93]

The Dynamex decision also encouraged drivers and their supporters to take action. First, within weeks after the court ruling, Lorena Gonzalez, a member of the California state assembly, introduced a bill—AB5—that codified the Dynamex decision. If passed, AB5 would allow gig drivers to be classified as employees. Edward Escobar, who collaborated with Gonzalez to draft the bill, described it as a "game-changer." Not surprisingly, Escobar expected serious pushback from Uber, Lyft, Instacart, and DoorDash as the proposed law worked its way through the state legislative process. Second, rideshare drivers in the Bay Area emulated their counterparts in Los Angeles by creating another workers group, Gig Workers Rising.

Gig Workers Rising is an advocacy group consisting of app workers who drive for Uber and Lyft, do on-demand deliveries with Door-Dash, Instacart, or GrubHub, and platform workers who find assignments through TaskRabbit, Handy, SitterCity, Wag, or Care.com. Backed by Working Partnerships USA, a grassroots community organizing group, Gig Workers Rising also received financial support from both Working Partnerships USA and the Teamsters. Unions play an important role in the establishment of gig worker organizations. In addition to assisting Gig Workers Rising financially, SEIU created the Mobile Workers' Alliance. Despite the availability of all these newly created organizations, the vast majority of the hundreds of thousands of drivers and other gig workers in California did not join these organizations. Nevertheless, the new app-driven worker centers gave both members and nonmembers a voice in their ongoing struggle to improve wages and working conditions.

In March of 2018, Uber and Lyft, both bleeding profits and in anticipation of going public, responded to increasing investor pressures to cut labor costs by slashing mileage rates from eighty to sixty cents per mile in Los Angeles and Orange County.[94] Upset drivers almost immediately began urging their colleagues to participate in a twenty-five-hour strike against Uber and Lyft. News reports suggest that this repeat of the 2017 strike at LAX included many who participated in that earlier action. Only this time the strike was led by Rideshare Drivers United. Some of the organization's drivers conceded that the previous boycott's lack of strategy, cohesiveness, and agreement on demands resulted in low driver participation. To remedy these issues, Nicole Moore, a leader of the new organization, argued that more drivers would participate if the focus was mainly on salaries, an achievable goal.[95] Moore agreed that the reclassification of drivers to employee status was an essential long-term objective, but "drivers need gas in the car . . . so we can pay our rent and put food on the table for our family."[96] In light of the millions the companies' bosses earned, low wages for drivers was likely to garner public support. Rideshare Drivers United sought the restoration of the recent 25 percent wage cut and a guaranteed minimum salary of $28 per hour. Despite the narrow focus, the strike's effectiveness was minimal as drivers continued to drop off riders at LAX.[97] Nevertheless, media coverage of the strike exposed Uber's treatment of its drivers and brought their ever-worsening economic condition to public attention.

The demonstrations, strikes, and protests did little to improve wages and working conditions. Lyft and Uber did offer drivers a method of earning more through bonuses based on passenger ratings and the type and frequency of their rides, but most drivers found the bonus proposal insufficient.[98] By now it was becoming clear to the many drivers who wanted to continue their struggle that they had organizations to support them. Just prior to Uber's IPO offering of over $80 billion, rideshare drivers across the state, led by Gig Workers Rising and Rideshare Drivers United, participated in an international action. Members of Gig Workers

Rising demonstrated in front of Uber headquarters. Also as part of this international action, about 200 to 300 drivers shut off their apps from noon to midnight in a coordinated national protest aimed at rush-hour riders. In the Los Angeles area, Rideshare Drivers United organized a twenty-four-hour strike and held rallies in key locations, including local Uber offices, as they demanded a minimum wage equal to that of the New York City Taxi Alliance, a 10 percent commission cap on driver's earnings, a driver representative on the boards of Uber and Lyft, and a speedy and more equitable appeals process for deactivated drivers.[99] Nicole More of Rideshare Drivers United claimed that as many as 4,300 drivers joined the job action.[100] Commenting on what was then viewed as the largest internationally coordinated action against ride-hailing companies, one academic observer noted that "the groups organizing the strikes are playing the role traditionally played by unions."[101]

The international protest received a lot of media coverage, as did the almost simultaneous passage of groundbreaking legislation by the California Assembly. At the end of May 2019, AB5 cleared the state Assembly and moved to the Senate for further action. Apparently concerned that the bill would sail through California's Democratic-controlled Senate, NLRB General Counsel Peter B. Robb, a Trump appointee with a long record of representing business interests, issued a memorandum stating that Uber drivers are independent contractors, not employees. The ruling was a significant victory for Uber, a company caught in a squeeze between drivers complaining of extraordinarily low wages and a profit and loss statement revealing about $2 billion in losses. Although powerless to do anything about it, Obama's former NLRB chair disagreed with the ruling, opining that driver's independence is "completely circumscribed by the company's control of price."[102]

As AB5 worked its way through the Senate's committee system, Uber, Lyft, and pro-business groups lobbied behind the scenes to "carve out" or exempt drivers from the proposed law. These lobbying efforts were not confined to California. A report by the National Employment Law Project found that Uber and other gig sector companies, along with politically powerful corporations and far-right groups such as the American Legislative Exchange (ALEC), were working on a state and national level to "pass policies that lock gig workers who find work via their tech platforms into independent contractor status, stripping them of basic labor rights and protections." The groups' lobbying efforts also aimed at the avoidance of payroll taxes.[103] In 2018 their anti-worker lobbying campaign produced significant results when seven states passed laws "excusing" gig companies from payroll taxes and excluding their workers from basic labor protections. California had now become their biggest target.

While Lyft and Uber lobbyists worked the legislature with their corporate allies to weaken AB5 and gain exemptions for drivers, the companies also waged an aggressive public relations campaign to keep drivers classified as independent contractors. In June 2019, the heads of Uber and Lyft wrote an op-ed piece in the *San Francisco Chronicle* acknowledging the tough reality drivers face. Conceding that "a change to the employment classification of rideshare drivers would pose a risk to our business," they offered a compromise that included some worker benefits, a minimum salary that kicks in only when there's a passenger in the car, and the establishment of a drivers association. Drivers had everything to gain through this compromise, the CEOs argued, for without the compromise, drivers would lose the flexibility they love and demand.[104] Uber followed up on the op-ed article by sending emails and in-app messages to drivers urging them to oppose AB5. They told the drivers to "tell lawmakers to protect driver flexibility."[105] The company also offered to pay up to $100 and provide a free lunch to drivers who demonstrated against the bill in Sacramento. Most drivers rejected the company's proposed compromise and reminded their co-workers that AB5 had nothing to do with flexibility. The ride-hail companies' unspoken threat was they would have to recoup their new labor costs by significantly reducing the number of drivers and assigning them to straight shift work. Workers United tweeted that drivers do not support their executives and invited drivers to attend a press conference in front of Uber's headquarters.[106] In an opinion piece in the *San Francisco Chronicle*, Lyft driver and organizer Lauren Swiger found the companies' willingness to compromise a sign of drivers' growing momentum. "They mean our organizing is powerful and effective," she proclaimed.[107] AB5 also received a boost when the city of San Francisco, responding to a request from SEIU and Teamster locals, held hearings on "worker rights in the gig economy."[108]

In July, as the Senate held public hearings, hundreds of drivers flooded Sacramento, some in support of AB5, others in opposition to the bill. Members of Rideshare Drivers United drove through the night in a caravan of cars to lobby and participate in the rally. Others, including members and supporters of Gig Workers Rising and the SEIU backed Mobile Workers Alliance, arrived by car or bus. Almost all took directions and talking points from a seasoned SEIU lobbyist, who emphasized the importance of relating the details of their lives to the senators. Driver support for AB5 was not unanimous. A group sponsored by the Independent Coalition, an organiza-tion of drivers who supported management's proposed compromise, rallied against AB5. Many of these drivers, who feared the loss of flexible hours, had received in-app communications from the company inviting them to rally for flexibility at the state house. While Uber's communication played on the drivers' fear of losing flexible hours, it neglected to remind them that the proposed law would make them eligible for a whole range of employ-ment benefits they now lacked. Nevertheless, opponents of the bill came out in large numbers, with one report claiming they outnumbered the bill's supporters.[109] The large number of drivers protesting AB5 did not augur well for passage of the bill. It also revealed the extreme difficulty drivers faced in organizing tens of thousands of workers with apparently different interests. The bulk of the drivers worked part-time and wanted to make a few extra dollars when they could. The 20 percent or so full-time drivers wished to be treated as traditional employees.

As negotiations continued in the Senate, more than fifty industries received exemptions from AB5. The Senate's exemption of health care professionals, hair stylists, barbers, freelance writers, and a spate of other non-gig workers encouraged gig companies and their corporate allies to step up the political pressure. Their efforts brought some results, including a favorable July editorial by the influential Los Angeles Times. The editorial characterized AB5 as "overkill" and supported a compromise by suggest-ing that, "Rather than expanding the definition of who is an employee, a better approach would be to give more wage and labor protections to independent contractors."[110]

An additional cloud was cast over the likelihood of AB5's passage when a split between organized labor and the rideshare drivers appeared likely. The possible breakup of the informal coalition was triggered by a New York Times report that SEIU was holding secret meetings with Uber and Lyft to discuss the companies' proposed compromise. Rideshare Driv-ers United responded by rejecting any so-called "back room" compromise, making it clear that they would not work with a union that would limit their rights as employees. After a large California local, the United Health Care Workers West, threatened to publicly oppose any compromise, SEIU leaders restated SEIU's position to fully support AB5.[111] Subsequently, the California Building and Construction Trades Council advised Governor Newsom in writing that the labor affiliate and its full membership, includ-ing the teamsters union, opposed any exemptions for the gig companies,

along with any attempt to create a third category of employees as suggested in the proposed compromise. It now appeared that a legislative
compromise of any kind was dead on arrival.[112]

In late August, as AB5 was moving through the various Senate committees, Gig Workers Rising and the Mobile Workers Alliance organized a
drivers' caravan in support of the legislation. Backed by SEIU and other
unions, the three-day caravan originated in Los Angeles, stopped for protests in San Francisco, and culminated at the state capitol in Sacramento
on August 26. The drivers were greeted in San Francisco by presidential
candidate Pete Buttigieg, the fourth Democratic presidential candidate
to publicly support them. In his statement to the workers, Buttigieg proclaimed, "If you're working a gig, that means you ought to be protected as
a worker."[113] On Friday, August 30, the bill cleared another hurdle when
it passed the Senate appropriations committee, guaranteeing its passage
on the Senate floor. The following Monday—Labor Day—Governor Gavin
Newsom, announced his backing of the legislation, reversing his previous
support of a compromise. After the bill cleared the Senate in a partisan
vote, the governor characterized it as "landmark legislation" and signed
it into law. The next step, he said, was to provide ways for the drivers to
form a union. Lorena Gonzalez, author of the bill, proclaimed, "California
is now setting the global standard for worker protections for other states
to follow."[114] A *New York Times* editorial applauded the passage of the law
and concurred with Gonzalez by stating "other states should follow close
behind."[115] AB5 took effect January 1, 2020. To no one's surprise, the gig
companies announced they would not implement the law. Still insisting
that drivers are not the core of their business, they challenged AB5 in the
courts while drivers struggled to make a decent living.

With corporate earnings still declining, the ride-hail companies
insisted they could not afford the cost of reclassifying their workers. However, Uber, Lyft, and DoorDash could afford to spend $30 million each
in support of a ballot initiative that would let voters decide the issue. To
gain support of their ballot initiative, California Proposition 22, which,
if passed, would legally maintain the drivers' status as independent contractors, the companies threatened to stop operating in California until
the issue was decided in the November election. The promise to cease
operations was a false one, but the rideshare companies poured tens of
millions into a public relations campaign in support of Proposition 22.[116]
They also emailed petitions to their more than one million riders claiming
that AB5 makes ride-hail service unreliable and asking for their sup-

port. Backers of AB5 characterized the petitions as a "misinformation campaign."[117] Uber and Lyft outspent unions by a margin of more than ten to one in a record-setting $200 million public relations campaign to convince voters to approve Proposition 22, which they did. In November, Proposition 22 passed with almost 60 percent.

Prop 22 exempts gig drivers from the state's AB5 law and saves the gig companies billions by not having to pay Social Security, Medicare, unemployment insurance, and other benefits regular employees receive. Prop 22 obliges companies to pay drivers 120 percent of the state minimum wage, but only while they are providing rides, not for the time drivers are sanitizing their cars or waiting for a rider or making a 200-mile return trip. Drivers will also receive a stipend toward health insurance, provided they work at least fifteen hours a week. Some drivers cheered the passage of Prop 22, but most wanted the protections AB5 would have given them. As reported in *Bloomberg Businessweek*, RDU organizer Nicole Moore summed it up: "We got smashed. . . . If we compromise employment rights, we're going to have a whole lot of people, including ourselves, who are second-class."[118]

After AB5: What's Next?

Nationally, AB5 represents a major breakthrough for gig workers in the United States. It built on an ongoing national struggle to remedy the outrageous exploitation that gig workers face on the job every day. As one writer for *The Nation* observed, it may be "the first legislation that directly attacks the exploitative labor structure of Uber, Lyft and the other Silicon Valley moguls."[119] New York City, for instance, has taken important steps over the past several years to protect its crippled Yellow Taxi industry. The City placed a cap on the number of ride-hailing vehicles allowed on the streets and subsequently on the number of empty vehicles permitted to cruise Manhattan. This came after the City provided a $17.22 hour minimum salary to ride-hail drivers. Other cities regulated ride-hail companies by taking action to prevent wage theft and other forms of exploitation. California's AB5 went much further. AB5 struck at the heart of exploitation by undercutting the classification that shifts the costs of doing business onto the drivers while putting the profits in the pockets of the owners and managers.

However groundbreaking AB5 was, as a model, its sweeping approach creates complex and troublesome obstacles to its implementation. Consider the situation in California prior to the passage of Prop 22. First, while the law reclassified the drivers as employees, the companies did not implement it. Shannon Liss-Riordan filed a class action suit on behalf of Uber drivers seeking an injunction to force the companies to comply. But the litigation faced at least one significant problem: the bulk of drivers for both Uber and Lyft signed on to private arbitration when they were hired and the ride-hail companies are sure to seek enforcement of these agreements, even though some drivers claimed the arbitration does not apply to them because the Federal Arbitration Act provides exclusions for transportation workers. This litigation was certain to be a long, time-consuming process, whatever the outcome.[120]

Litigation was one avenue for winning the gains AB5 promised, but the passage of Prop 22 has made litigation moot, at least for drivers. Organizing is another. But what kind of organizing has always been the jugular question. Whether drivers can exercise their right to form a union under the auspices of NLRB is problematic. The chief counsel for the Trump NLRB issued a memorandum in May 2019 stating that the drivers are independent contractors. The federal PRO Act would give independent contractors the right to organize, but as of this writing it hasn't passed in the U.S. Senate. Should the PRO Act fail to become law, California legislators could still pass legislation giving gig workers the right to unionize, but even if they could unionize, there is little or no consensus on what approach to take. Some drivers want a large statewide union that any of the 300,000 drivers could join. Others prefer smaller, regional unions. Following the passage of Prop 22, Lyft, Uber, and the SEIU expressed support for some form of industry-wide sectoral bargaining.[121] Some drivers, such as members of the Independent Workers Alliance, prefer not to unionize at all. They would rather work for Uber as real independent contractors who set their own rates. Escobar explains this arrangement: the rider makes a request with details of the ride—destination, pickup time, acceptable range of mileage rates—and the Uber app filters the request to all drivers who have presets to accept those request parameters. The first driver who accepts the terms gets the rider.[122]

A third option is for gig drivers to create what Janelle Orsi characterizes as their own "free-lance owned cooperative." After all, drivers, not the rideshare companies, own and maintain the cars. Roads and other infrastructure essential to their work are part of the public domain. The drivers just need to organize and develop their own rideshare app.[123] As interesting as this idea sounds, it's a bit unrealistic. In addition to the issue of organizing enough drivers—80 percent of whom work part-time—to buy into the idea, there are the technical challenges. Denise Cheng, a graduate student of labor issues, claims that it's "not so much the number of people who want to do that, it would be the talent to do it." In other words, the software system essential to the establishment and maintenance of a workers' co-op is extraordinarily complex. Finding engineers who would want to take on this task at a workers co-op, Cheng concludes, would be very difficult.[124] Cheng's analysis, already several years old, does not mean that the formation of a drivers' cooperative is technically impossible, but to do so presents a huge challenge. In fact, over the past few years, drivers in New York City and several other locations have tried to develop their own apps that would give them a stake in their own rideshare company, but so far nothing has come of their efforts.[125]

In September 2019, Governor Newsom announced that he would be calling a meeting of labor, business, and legislative leaders to determine how to grant drivers the right to collective bargaining without necessarily forming a union; in other words, the resulting agreement would probably emulate the New York City model of the Independent Drivers Guild (IDG), a worker center backed by Uber and supported by the machinist union that has improved the working conditions of the City's gig drivers.[126] In California the ride-hail companies are willing to assist drivers in creating a statewide drivers' association. The establishment of a drivers' organization, combined with legislation giving drivers the right to negotiate a statewide agreement is apparently at the core of any compromise. But the new association of drivers would be a statewide worker center, not an independent union. Should a compromise materialize, many drivers who support the formation of independent unions are likely to oppose it. After all, how independent can an organization created in part by the "boss" be? In fact, Uber was accused of illegal action—that is, establishing a company union—when it promoted the creation of New York's IDG. Uber got off the hook with the NLRB ruling that IDG is not a union since the drivers are independent contractors. As neither a company union nor a labor union, nevertheless, the IDG has achieved much for its drivers. IDG doesn't have collective bargaining rights but in becoming a significant force in New York City's political arena it has gained many benefits for drivers through City regulations and laws. In any case, the companies expect a compromise to reflect the proposal they previously made.[127]

The fate of AB5 thwarted the high expectations of drivers. But its initial passage was a victory for the drivers who organized and fought for relief from increasingly deteriorating terms and conditions of employment. Drivers of diverse backgrounds and nationalities, including large numbers of immigrants, banded together to form effective organizations that struggled successfully to gain passage of AB5. After the bill passed both houses of the legislature, drivers expressed their newfound power when Edward Escobar confidently remarked that if the governor didn't sign the bill, drivers would vote him out of office.[128] Despite their physical isolation, drivers managed to organize and take to the streets, brought their plight public, and put some political hurt on the gig companies. With the political, fiscal, and organizing assistance of unions and support from the public, the drivers became an effective force that fought successfully for legislation that could shape the future of gig work across the nation. Indeed, New York's gig workers are already demanding legislation similar to California's AB5.

Amid all these legal and political battles, the pandemic hit Uber, Lyft, and other rideshare gig drivers hard. As long as people need to eat, farmworkers will have jobs, pandemic or not. That's not the case with gig rideshare drivers. As the virus spread, people stayed home, and the rideshare business plummeted. Business at Uber fell by 80 percent, and Lyft did no better. Layoffs became the order of the day. Passenger demand for Lyft and Uber fell by 60 and 80 percent, respectively, resulting in thousands of layoffs. Uber cut 14 percent of its total labor force; not to be outdone, Lyft followed suit by laying off 17 percent of its global workforce.[129] When eventually business began to pick up, rideshare drivers faced serious health risks every time they took a fare. The responsibility for implementing new safety precautions fell to the drivers themselves as they paid out of their own pockets for extra masks for passengers and sanitizers to clean their cars after each ride. Despite these precautions, many fell ill, and some died.[130] Because Prop 22 exempted rideshare drivers from AB5, workers still lack unemployment insurance and other benefits that employees enjoy, including paid sick leave. Gig workers received the checks and some limited unemployment benefits provided by the CARES Act and subsequent Covid relief packages, but it was no panacea. Like other low-wage workers, gig drivers continue to lack the economic safety net they need.

The Immokalee worker center model for taking direct collective action may have been regarded as an outlier two decades ago, but this model is now replacing traditional unionism as the heart of the new labor movement. California's gig drivers achieved much through the activities of their virtual worker centers. Whether or not they become part of organized labor remains to be seen. But that's almost beside the point. Their willingness to take on the Big Gig companies through collective action illuminates the increasingly obvious fact that a new labor movement is emerging in the United States. Now, legislative action, not collective bargaining, is the tool of redress, and the role of organized labor is to give these new labor warriors whatever support they need.

Chapter 5

Freelancers Union

Backward to the Future?

For the past fourteen or so years Alice has worked as a freelance writer. Recently she was hired at the last minute to do a quick edit on a book manuscript about Ebola. The contractor, who said he was a doctor, claimed to have done a lot of research on the outbreak of the disease. When Alice completed the work and turned in her invoice, the doctor claimed he had lost or misplaced his wallet. Alice contacted him several times in the following days to collect her pay, but after making excuses for a few days, he stopped answering her calls. He just disappeared. Alice never received payment and eventually concluded the contractor was a fraud who had lied about being a doctor.[1]

Alice is part of the new fifty-million-plus gig workers' surge that reflects the changing structural nature of work in the United States. As a freelance writer, Alice no longer toils at a steady 9-to-5 job, which once defined what most of us think of as work. Rather, as a contract worker, she has the benefit of a flexible schedule. Alice can work when she pleases and where she pleases: at home, at a coffee shop, a library, or anywhere else. Many freelancers view a routine 9-to-5 job as oppressive. Alice's liberation, of course, comes at a price: she is sometimes not paid for her work. But that's not unusual. Nearly three of five freelancers have similar experiences.[2] In fact, on average, freelancers lose about 13 percent of their annual income through nonpayment.[3] Needless to say, like all other gig workers, Alice has little financial security and survives from job to job. No job, no pay. What about health care? As one gig worker so lucidly put it, "Let's hope I don't get sick."[4] People like Alice, who account for a growing segment of the country's workforce, don't get the benefits and

117

other protections regular employees receive. And they are not protected by existing labor laws. The changing structure of the economy has shifted much of the risks companies traditionally took onto the backs of these precarious workers. Sara Horowitz, founder of the Freelancers Union, characterizes these changes as the new Industrial Revolution.[5]

Previous chapters examined the political and social struggles waged by the Immokalee workers, New York's farmworkers, and California's gig workers to gain the protections and benefits of traditional employees. The Immokalee workers organized, formed coalitions, and took to the streets to force the giant corporate buyers of produce to participate in programs that provide a livable wage and other significant protections. New York's farmworkers and California's gig workers also organized and took to the streets, but, unlike their Immokalee counterparts, they used their collective power to pressure state legislatures to enact laws giving them the basic rights of employees. In all these cases, workers chose to confront the changing nature of work through collective struggle and direct action, a path that has proved difficult and thus far produced mixed results.

In contrast, the Freelancers Union, a worker's center with almost 500,000 members, accepts the changing structure of the workforce as inevitable. Rather than fight a losing battle trying to stop the changes, the Freelancers Union embraces the changes and works to ensure "that these new workers have the support and opportunity they need to thrive."[6] Having accepted the inevitability of the structural changes in the labor force, the organization is not leading a struggle to reclassify independent contractors as employees. Instead, it aims at providing freelancers with benefits and services found in traditional employment.[7] Horowitz justifies this position by noting that unions in the early twentieth century didn't attempt to stop the transformation from an agricultural to an industrial society. Instead, they focused on addressing the issues workers faced in the new industrial economy such as low wages and horrific working conditions.[8] This view raises a series of fundamental questions: Exactly what is the Freelancers Union and what, if anything, is unique about it? What are the intellectual foundations of Horowitz's approach? Absent a challenge to the corporate hegemony driving our economy, can the Freelancers Union actually provide the new precariat with the support they need to thrive and prosper on the job? If so, how can this be done without collective bargaining? What has the Freelancers Union achieved, and what are its long-term prospects for success? Finally, does the organization's strategy play into the hands of corporate power and the anti-labor political right, as some suggest?[9]

What Is The Freelancers Union?

A graduate of SUNY Buffalo law school and a former union organizer, Sara Horowitz worked long hours practicing law in Manhattan. Unfortunately for Sara, her employer had classified her as a contract worker. Consequently, she was denied the usual benefits regular employees receive. Significantly, she received no health insurance through her workplace and had to pay for the costly coverage out of her own pocket. As an independent contractor, she wasn't entitled to unemployment and disability insurance, or a spate of other employment benefits. After exploring her options and discovering that government policies did not address her employment situation, she realized that independent workers had to organize if they were to successfully promote their interests. "I kept thinking," she said, "if you want to build the next union movement, what will . . . get it moving?" The answer, she concluded, was health insurance.[10] More than anything else, independent workers needed affordable insurance. The former union organizer began by creating Working Today in 1995, the first organization of its kind to advocate for independent contractors. After several years of slow membership growth, Horowitz dropped her cautious approach to recruiting members and rebranded the organization as the Freelancers Union.

The mission of the Freelancers Union is to promote "the interests of independent workers through advocacy, education and services."[11] The Freelancers Union is not a union in the traditional use of the word. It does no collective bargaining, it doesn't organize strikes or picket lines, and it does not represent workers in a single company or industry. It doesn't collect dues, either, as membership in the Freelancers Union is free. The organization receives grants to initiate new entrepreneurial service projects, but basically supports itself by selling these services to members at reduced costs. It reinvests all its profits into new programs that further benefit the members. More on this later. The Freelancers Union is an inherent part of a new labor movement outside traditional unions. In the words of its founder, it's "a nonprofit social purpose organization" that's "a trade association of sorts for independent workers."[12] Perhaps the organization is best understood through the lens of Martha King, who sees it as an amalgamation of the practices of labor unions, professional associations, and worker centers.[13] So why does the Freelancers organization call itself a union? In an interview with Richard Greenwald, Horowitz claimed the word "union" was chosen because it worked well in focus groups.[14] The union concept also works well in a world of work increasingly populated by independent workers or, as Guy Standing dubs them, the precariat.[15] Today the Freelancers Union's claims to have nearly 500,000 members, and Horowitz expects to reach the one million mark within a few years.[16] Members work in occupations running the gamut from artists, editors, and graphic designers to Uber drivers and website developers and just about everything in between. Despite this diverse range of occupations, members are fused together through the common experience of unpaid work, sporadic earnings, no benefits, little or no job security and relatively few government protections. Freelancers can experience great stress from this economic insecurity. Add to these financial pressures the social isolation of their work, and it's no wonder that a disproportionate number of freelancers suffer from some form of depression. Indeed, Horowitz observes, "You work with coal miners and you learn . . . about black lung. You work with freelancers and you learn about depression."[17] The isolated, insecure freelancer of today is far removed from William Whyte's description of the secure, conformist organization man of the 1950s.[18]

Membership in the Freelancers Union is growing rapidly in part because it is free. Members don't pay dues or any other fee, but they do receive free e-newsletters and discounts on some services and products. While they lack collective bargaining rights, they benefit from the organization's political action programs and have the opportunity to interact with other freelancers, an option many isolated workers find attractive. Designated as a 501(c)4 organization by the IRS, the Freelancers Union lobbies and conducts political advocacy campaigns. Its members who, Horowitz claims, need to "stand up together to be counted,"[19] apparently keep their eyes on the ballot box, as they vote in greater numbers than average citizens. But in Horowitz's view, political action can't stop the forces of change that have generated what she calls "Middle-Class Poverty." She knows that government has a primary role in building a social safety net, but decades of political inaction on the part of both political parties clearly suggest that government is currently not the answer. "Our work policies are stuck in the 1950s," she says.[20] Freelance work simply can't sustain a middle class without a better support system, Horowitz believes. The Freelancers Union hopes to fill the vacuum by providing the foundation for new institutions of social change.[21] It plans to do this by approaching the future with an eye set on the past. More specifically, rather than depend on government, the Freelancers Union is trying to effect change by building on the model of social unionism of the 1910s and 1920s in which workers helped other "workers to transform the economy together."[22] Horowitz dubs this approach the "New Mutualism."

The New Mutualism and Its Historical Roots

Horowitz believes that at this moment public policy isn't the primary answer to the plight of freelancers. The underlying idea of the new mutualism is DIY—do it yourself. The new mutualism emphasizes the role of individuals but also believes that individuals can't do it alone. They need to connect with other workers to stay on top of their professions, find new jobs, collaborate on projects, and maintain mental health after working alone for hours and hours at a time. Connecting with others through the Freelancers Union also creates a sense of community that is essential to support the organization's new mutualism. "Do it yourself" is really do it ourselves. In Horowitz's words:

> This big idea of connectivity is what we call the new mutualism. New mutualism is a community of people with shared interests, the realization that we are much stronger as a group than as individuals, and the understanding that we can form our own cooperative model to meet our needs—while still maintaining our independence and individuality. What binds us is the shared need for protections, supports, and a voice for the independent worker . . . We must join together and use the resources and power that exist in our group to get health insurance, retirement, education, and training.[23]

The Freelancers' new mutualism is not really new. It is rooted in the long history of the formation of cooperatives and other voluntary institutions in the United States. Horowitz clearly expresses her commitment to this voluntarism by pursuing an updated version of the social unionism developed by Sidney Hillman's work in the 1920s with his union, the Amalgamated Clothing Workers of America (ACWA), in response to economic and political conditions not unlike those that unions face today: "We need to go back to Hillman's vision and look beyond the current valley of union decline."[24] For a clear understanding of the Freelancers Union's new mutualism, it is essential to clarify Hillman's vision of social unionism and the context in which it emerged.

Fed up with the anti-labor policies of the industry and refusing to take pay cuts, more than 40,000 Chicago garment workers, including those who belonged to a weakened United Garment Workers (UGW), walked off their jobs in 1910. The international union attempted to settle the strike, but rank-and-file workers rejected it and continued the walkout, eventually winning some concessions. At its 1914 convention the UGW attempted to disenfranchise its more militant locals. Those locals quit the UGW and formed their own labor organization, the Amalgamated Clothing Workers of America (ACWA). The new union drafted Sidney Hillman to become its first president.[25]

Upon its formation, the ACWA was not recognized by the AFL and was constantly harassed by the UGW. Nevertheless, the new union benefited from factory contracts with the federal government's Board of Control and Labor Standards for Army Clothing during World War I. That changed after the war when companies in most industries sought to reestablish their control over the workforce. Led by a general strike in Seattle, in 1919 more than four million workers subsequently walked out. In an attempt to organize, some 350,000 steelworkers, mostly immigrants, went on strike, as did 400,000 coal miners. These massive immigrant-backed strikes shut down the country's basic industries, stoking management's fears that the strikes were the start of a revolutionary conspiracy. Motivated by xenophobia and the Red Scare following the Russian revolution and communist uprisings in Europe, national and state governments waged war on the strikers, eventually breaking the walkouts and virtually destroying the union movement. The ACWA endured a lengthy lockout in New York City, but unlike unions in steel, coal, and multiple other industries, it emerged from the attacks stronger than ever. In contrast, throughout the 1920s and into the 1930s, most unions were barely surviving and, much like today, they hemorrhaged members. Union density plummeted. Even after the excesses of xenophobia and the Red Scare subsided, government didn't pretend to be a friend of organized labor.[26] Silent Cal Coolidge's famous quote "The business of America is business" clarified that government's role was to assist the Robber Barons of the time in their pursuit of profits.

Sidney Hillman's social unionism is an historical spinoff of America's long experience with cooperative and utopian ventures, ranging from Ben Franklin's 1752 mutual fire insurance company to Robert Owen's short-lived nineteenth-century New Harmony experiment in Indiana, the late nineteenth-century cooperative ventures of the Knights of Labor, and dozens of others, including contemporary Utopian communities such as Missouri's East Wind Community.[27] Hillman dismissed the inevitability of class struggle and the need for revolutionary actions. Instead, he operated on the assumption that all classes could work together for common ends. Although criticized by the left for its lack of revolutionary fervor, Hillman's pragmatic approach challenged the power of industrial capitalism during the anti-union era prior to the New Deal. Proclaiming that "the Cooperative Movement will bring a large measure of democracy and human happiness into industry,"[28] Hillman confronted corporate hegemony by using a portion of members' dues payments to invest in a series of cooperative business ventures that benefited the union's members, including a union bank, an insurance company, and affordable housing for the union's members, all ventures still thriving today.

Under Hillman's leadership, in 1924 the ACWA established the Amalgamated Bank with the purpose of providing working families access to the same banking services enjoyed by the wealthy. The Amalgamated Bank was the first bank to provide unsecured personal loans, the first to offer free checking accounts, and the first to establish a foreign-exchanges transfer service allowing immigrants to send money to relatives overseas.[29] In addition to providing services to union members, the bank helped stabilize the competitive clothing industry by giving loans and providing other services to companies on the verge of closing. These loans often saved union jobs, made some money for the bank, and increased the ACWA's power both within the labor movement and in the political arena. Even today, years after its founding, the bank proudly describes its charge in glowing terms: "We don't just have a mission; we're on a mission: to be America's socially responsible bank."[30] The union subsequently undertook other business ventures, including the formation of the Amalgamated Life Insurance Company, which provided affordable insurance to working people.

Addressing the need for decent housing, the ACWA also provided affordable housing to more than 2,500 union families by sponsoring co-operative apartments in the Bronx and the lower East Side of Manhattan.[31] In addition to providing decent, affordable homes, the co-operative housing units offered a series of programs running the gamut from citizenship classes to activities that helped create a sense of community outside the workplace. The co-operative housing ventures were so successful that other unions emulated them. By the 1960s, the AFL-CIO joined in by establishing the Housing Investment Trust (HIT), which today has over $4.5 billion in assets available to assist in the development of low-cost housing.[32]

The ACWA's decision to establish banks, insurance companies, medical centers, and other ventures not only greatly benefited its members, it also gave the union financial stability and sustainability. The rent money and profits from the businesses built capital, paid off the union's loans, and allowed it to borrow additional funds to invest in even more worker-friendly projects. Sara Horowitz describes this innovative approach as "a virtuous cycle."[33]

Looking to the past to determine future actions, Horowitz has a contemporary vision of this "virtuous cycle" that makes the Freelancers Union's new mutualism work. In concrete terms, the principles of connectivity, community, and DIY focus on larger collective goals that benefit the membership while sustaining the organization. These larger collective ends are determined by the membership and may include "building banks, insurance companies, day care centers . . . and even dreaming up new 21st-century institutions, like union-owned urban farms."[34] These new cooperative institutions are market oriented but funded by foundations, government, and social purpose businesses rather than profit-seeking venture capitalists. By creating such institutions, the dues-free Freelancers Union attains sustainability. It also gains financial and political independence from the corporate and governmental sectors, as well as from other unions. Sustainability and financial independence distinguish the Freelancers Union from other worker centers. It also provides the foundation for the organization's advocacy operations. Indeed, as workers collectively transform the economy through the creation of sustainable cooperative business enterprises, the political clout of the Freelancers Union increases, putting it in a stronger position to advocate more effectively in the governmental arena.

The Makeover Takes Off

To achieve its goals, the organization needed to increase its membership base. The quest for members placed a premium on the institution's branding. How potential members view the organization was crucial to its development. In the early years of Working Today, growth came slowly. The organization initially focused on job security issues, but also recognized the importance of health care to those many freelance workers not covered by company benefits. To provide affordable health insurance, Working Today attempted to use the collective power of independent workers, as Horowitz then dubbed them, to negotiate lower health insurance premiums in a group plan. But after six years, fewer than 2,000 independent workers had signed on to the plan. The group's bargaining power was limited by the reality that it bought only about $1.2 million in health insurance every year. In 2002, Horowitz hired Cultural Group Strategy (CGS), the marketing company that had previously branded Ben & Jerry's, to determine how her organization could improve its public image and increase its membership. After conducting extensive research, CGS recommended that Working Today change both its name and its business model. As noted earlier in this chapter, these far-reaching recommendations essentially rebranded the organization and paved the way for rapid growth in both organization membership and participation in the health insurance program.

CGS first found that Working Today did indeed address a major economic need stemming from labor market dislocations, but it also discovered that Horowitz's branding of the organization was overly cautious. Fearing that prospective participants would not take Working Today seriously, Horowitz, according to CGS, "stripped out the ideological foundations of her innovative service—the labor activism"[35] and marketed her enterprise in much the same way as large insurance companies. Even the name "Working Today," along with its tagline "Benefitting the way you work," mirrored the efforts of large insurers. Horowitz's initial approach, which emphasized the independent workers' professionalism, was just not working. CGS claimed the ineffectiveness of the approach came from Horowitz's failure to fully recognize the unique characteristics of her target audience. This audience, CGS discovered, consisted of many young, free-spirited types who mistrusted the corporate sector and felt that health insurance companies were not trustworthy. The marketing firm also learned that these independent workers who worked alone from job to job had a collective desire for group solidarity based on their bohemian, left-leaning worldview.[36] These findings provided the basis for a rebranding of Working Today.

The goal of bringing more independent workers under the umbrella of Working Today was predicated on the creation of a rallying call around how society should treat workers. More concretely, the organization's recruitment strategy promoted the idea that health care was a human right for everyone. In so doing, the emphasis was as much on social change and egalitarianism as on health insurance. Since CGS's research indicated that the name "Working Today" did not resonate with potential participants, the organization was renamed the Freelancers Union. The term "freelancer" replaced the former usage of "independent worker" because it enabled the artsy, bohemian types to distinguish themselves from corporate consultants and similar professional workers. The decision to use the word "union" in the rebranding appealed both to the targeted audience's desire for solidarity and to what CGS characterized as their rebellious spirit. After the rebranding, Working Today became the research and policy arm of the new organization now called the Freelancers Union. To further promote the rebranded organization, the marketing company developed a new logo that hearkened back to the designs of early twentieth-century unions. The logo looked like a union badge: two outer rings with the name of the organization between the rings. Inside the circle was the date of the union's founding and, to represent the collectivity that freelancers belonged to, a beehive. Three bees appear on top of the beehive to represent the independent individual within the larger organic whole, or more explicitly, as Horowitz so clearly states it, "a community of individuals where the well-being of all and the well-being of each are one."[37]

The rebranding was followed by a low-cost advertising campaign designed to gain the support of activists who lacked health care. Ads with headlines such as "Health Insurance vs. Paying Rent" and "Your primary care physician should not be a website" intended to address the frustrations of the many isolated freelancers who could not afford health insurance and felt disconnected from larger social groups. All the initial ads ended with the tagline, "Welcome to Middle-Class Poverty." This was a way of invoking the structural changes in the labor force and challenging the conventional wisdom that the new economy was bringing middle-class prosperity.[38] These ads were later supported by other ads emphasizing creativity and change. Since the bulk of Freelancers Union's members are New Yorkers, it relied heavily on subway ads such as "Re-Examine, Re-Think, Re-Invent" that appealed to creativity. Its slogans "85,000 Members Make for a Damn Squeaky Wheel" and "Organize and Mobilize" focus on its commitment to change.[39]

The rebrand also brought a significant shift in priorities to the Freelancers Union's website. Rather than focusing on health insurance, the site now emphasized joining the organization. The strategy of recruiting members into the organization prior to selling them health insurance attracted a larger pool of prospective buyers and created an effective sale funnel for the renamed enterprise. Within the first five months after the rebranding, health insurance membership tripled from 2,000 to 6,000, and revenues for 2003 jumped by 619 percent to $7.6 million. Six years after the rebranding, the Freelancers Union had 93,000 members in its group insurance program.[40] This success was achieved in part by commercializing the organization's ideology, as expressed by its appeal to "join the union of broke middle-class workers who can't afford health insurance."[41] Today the Freelancers Union is prospering as a self-sustaining organization engaged in the new mutualism.

By 2019, the Freelancers Union claimed more than 490,000 members and have its sights set on a million. Its members reside throughout the United States, but are heavily concentrated in New York, New Jersey, and California. According to its website, the organization's members are engaged in an almost infinite line of freelance work "from graphic designers and contractors, to entrepreneurs and moonlighters."[42] The occupations of members are quite diverse, but as observers note, the Freelancers Union caters to workers who are generally young, educated, and better paid than other members of the working class.[43] The "Sixth Annual Freelancing in America" study backs this observation with its finding that "skilled services are the most common type of freelance work."[44] A 2012 internal survey of members by industry overwhelmingly supports this premise. The survey suggests that more than 70 percent of Freelancers Union's members are engaged in professional or semi-professional service work. Film and television employs 10 percent of the union's members, with another 5 percent in advertising. The fields of journalism, visual arts, graphic design, education and training, information technology, fashion, and health care are not far behind at 4 percent each. In contrast to what the general public may think, less than 1 percent of the members work in the transportation industry, which, of course includes Uber and Lyft drivers.[45]

What Workers in the Creative Economy Want

Many members of the Freelancers Union are skilled professionals who earn a median hourly rate of $28, more than about 70 percent of all workers in the economy.[46] Unfortunately, they lack job security and their hours of work are often unpredictable and not guaranteed. It's worth repeating that as independent workers they do not receive such benefits as health insurance, paid sick and vacation days, pensions, and other perks. Despite a decent hourly wage, the vast majority of these freelancers are among the most exploited people in the workforce, which is one reason they joined the Freelancers Union in the first place. Freelance workers also tend to be young and marginally more diverse than the general workforce. A study by Upwork, a forum for businesses seeking freelancers, found that younger, rather than older, people are more likely to freelance. About 53 percent of generation Z workers freelance, as do some 40 percent of millennials, while only 29 percent of Boomers engage in freelancing. According to freelance writer Adam Warner, 84 percent of all freelancers are under the age of forty.[47]

Despite Horowitz's vision that the Freelancers Union will achieve change primarily outside the political arena, the many young, skilled professionals belonging to the Freelancers Union increases the likelihood that the organization could soon become an important political player, as young people are becoming the country's largest voting bloc. In the 2018 off-year elections, for instance, people aged eighteen to fifty-three accounted for more votes than the rest of the electorate combined. Not only is the population of young people growing thanks to naturalizations exceeding deaths, their voter turnout has also increased. In fact, turnout rates increased the most for Millennials, nearly doubling from 22 percent in 2014 to 42 percent in 2018.[48] The finding of the Freelancing in America study that freelancers by a 19-point margin are more likely to vote than non-freelancers reveals the organization's significant political potential. What is the likely direction of this political participation? Public opinion polls indicate that both Generation Z and Millennials are tilted somewhat to the left in the American political spectrum. The PEW Research Center, for example, found that both lean toward the Democratic Party and support a more activist government by wide margins over other generations. Generation Z and the Millennials were also the most critical of President Trump's job performance and, more than other generations, support the notion that increasing ethnic and racial diversity is a social good.[49] But they are also practical and dedicated to pursuing their interests as freelancers. Some 72 percent said they would cross party lines to support candidates who backed freelancers' rights.[50] Freelancers' commitment to political action and the dominance of members in Generation Z and

Millennials places the Freelancers Union in a strong position to use its increasing political clout to effect social and political change. The Sixth Annual Freelancing in America Study, a survey of over 6,000 freelancers, asked, "What factors should politicians most focus on to encourage more freelancers to move to their city/state?"[51]

Continual increases in the annual cost of the plans make the availability of affordable health insurance freelancers' top priority, even though 83 percent of full-time freelancers somehow managed to get health insurance. The majority are covered through Medicaid, Medicare, a spouse's or parent's policy, or an employer's plan, but 47 percent of full-time freelancers purchased their own plan. Since independent contractors do not have employer-funded pension plans, it's not surprising that tax incentives making it possible to save for retirement ranked second behind affordable health coverage. Follow-up polling of freelancers revealed that 46 percent are willing to move to a city that gives them tax breaks.[52] Not getting paid on time or not getting paid the full amount or even getting stiffed for the work, as in the case of Alice, ranks third among problems that freelancers want government to address. When they are not paid they are likely to rely on credit cards and incur debt from exorbitantly high interest rates. According to a Freelancers Union study, nonpayment costs the average freelancer about 13% of their annual income.[53] Rent control and affordable housing programs ranked fourth among urban freelancers, who more and more are priced out of big-city real estate markets. Finally, training and obtaining the resources necessary to build a successful freelance career rank as priority number five. Over a six-month period, 65 percent of skilled freelancers and 54 percent of all freelancers participated in some sort of training. Only 40 percent of non-freelancers received training. More than 80 percent want more training on the business skills they need to prosper. These skills include how to hire, supervise, and develop staff; the basics of project and financial management; and knowing what is needed in an employment contract to protect a freelancer's interest. Virtually all freelancers want more education and training on the soft skills they need for success.[54] Since a majority list the cost of training as an important obstacle, it's not surprising that they look to government for assistance.

Missing from the list of priorities is a desire for legislation similar to California's AB5 that would reclassify freelancers as employees, thus giving them government protections and employee benefits they now lack. New York, New Jersey, and other states are considering such legislation, but rank-and-file demand for this legislation is not even among their top five political goals. In fact, in New York and New Jersey, rank-and-file freelancers formed oppositional groups and joined with the Freelancers Union to monitor the proposed legislation. One activist from #fightfor-freelancersNewYork, Halley Bondy, proclaimed that the bill "as written could put a lot of freelancers out of work, many of whom are working mothers."[55] Opposition to a general reclassification bill should not be sur-prising given that the majority of the union's members are skilled pro-fessionals whom a reclassification law might hurt. Consider, for instance, the impact of California's AB5 on freelance journalists. AB5 allows free-lance writers to keep their status as independent contractors until they have written thirty-five articles for the same company. After that, the law assumes the company will hire the writer. Unfortunately, it isn't likely to happen. Rather than taking on the costs and responsibilities of hiring a new employee, the company simply seeks new writers from all over the country, leaving its author of thirty-five previous articles looking for work. But the reluctance of Freelancers Union members to opt for reclas-sification goes beyond their conditions of employment. Most freelancers choose freelancing primarily because they like its flexibility. According to a report conducted by Upwork and the Freelancers Union, 51 percent like freelancing so much that they wouldn't take a traditional job no matter how much it paid.[56] The Union is aware of its members' attitudes toward reclassification and has even launched a survey to gain more information on members' attitudes on this issue. In the meantime, the organization says it "supports efforts to combat misclassification where it exists," but opposes any laws that threaten the livelihood of those who choose free-lancing as a career.[57]

In addition to determining freelancers' political concerns, the Sixth Annual Report also identifies their overall basic concerns, which, unsur-prisingly, are all linked to finances, particularly income predictability and savings.[58] There is some overlap between freelancers' political priorities and the issues they find most concerning. Having sufficient savings for retirement (76%) and enough money to get through periods without work (75%) are the two uppermost concerns for freelancers. Issues tied for third include unpredictable income, earning a fair salary, and access to affordable health care. Trepidation over high tax rates (70%) ranks fourth, followed by fear of an economic downturn (65%). Other concerns include incurring debt (65%), finding work (63%), competition from other free-lancers (57%), as well as large businesses (55%), and access to loans

(63%). The Freelancers Union and Upwork have diligently identified the political and economic concerns of Freelancers Union's members. Now the two primary questions become: (1) How has the Freelancers Union addressed these issues? (2) What degree of success, if any, has the organization attained?

The New Mutualism in Action: Insurance for Freelancers

The Freelancers Union promises to promote the interests of freelance workers through benefits, policy advocacy, and community, and they've done a great deal in each of these areas, particularly in helping to provide the much-needed benefits that freelancers lacked. As noted previously, Horowitz believed that the availability of affordable health insurance is the key to rebuilding the labor movement. Accordingly, within a few years of its founding, Working Today joined with twenty-three other organizations to form an affordable group health insurance network, which also offered disability and life insurance. The union's participation in the group insurance project did not come easily. Under New York law, Working Today was not eligible to purchase group insurance. The organization didn't employ the people it wanted to cover, its members performed an array of diverse services, and it wasn't a traditional union.[59] But as Martha King observes, Horowitz successfully persuaded the New York State Insurance Commission that Working Today met the state's legal criteria required of organizations participating in reduced-rate group insurance programs.[60] A United Hospital Fund report subsequently characterized the agreement between the Freelancers Union and the state insurance department as "an unusual arrangement."[61] Nevertheless, in 2001 Freelancers Union's members had access to health insurance below the private market rate, and the union had a steady stream of income. Members could also buy dental and vision coverage at discounted rates.[62]

In November 2008, Horowitz announced that the Freelancers Union was going into the health insurance business. Assisted by foundations, including the Ford and Rockefeller Foundations, the Freelancers Union dropped a previous arrangement with Empire Blue Cross Blue Shield and launched the Freelance Insurance Company (FIC) with the promise of better coverage and lower premiums. Available only to members in New York, the plan took some members by surprise and initially generated a good deal of criticism. Dissenters even formed their own website (upsetfu. blogspot.com) and wrote an open letter to Horowitz complaining that she had failed to consult with union members, had justified changing the health plan by nebulous promises of future benefits, had failed to negotiate with the previous provider, and did not provide comparison between the former plan and the new.[63] Horowitz responded that "anything new you start is going to be messy." Besides, she continued, "This is a long-term proposition." Now that the Freelancers Union has its own insurance company, it has much greater control over costs, especially since it no longer must pay a fee to outside insurance providers. At least one freelancer concurred, happily announcing that she was saving almost $1,000 monthly with Freelancers Union's new plan.[64] Many others apparently agreed, too. Within the first several weeks of the announcement, about 8,000 members joined the plan.

In 2011, the FIC was certified as a B corporation by B Lab for meeting high standards of social and environmental performance, accountability, and transparency. Despite receiving the honor associated with a B corporation certification, the FIC was not without problems. One was the open hostility of some outside the organization who opposed any challenges to private health care systems. An article by Richard Pollack in the conservative *Washington Examiner* expresses that hostility while also revealing a number of substantive problems with the FIC. Pollack presented data backing his assertion that low consumer ratings may have contributed to the company's decision to eventually cease operations. In 2013, for instance, New York's Department of Financial Services ranked the FIC third from last among forty-five commercial carriers in terms of consumer complaints. The FIC also faced 176 grievances that year and had to reverse its previous decisions about coverage in forty-eight cases, a 27 percent reversal rate.[65] Yet, despite these data, by 2014 the FIC had approximately 25,000 members enrolled in health insurance coverage. It was apparently doing something right.

With the creation of the FIC, the Freelancers Union had met its goal of providing affordable insurance coverage to contract workers. But then came the Affordable Care Act (ACA). Following the passage of the Affordable Care Act, federal regulators gave the FIC a one-year waiver to meet the new rules and regulations prescribed by the ACA. On September 30, 2014, the FIC announced it was shutting down. By providing access to affordable health care, Obamacare fulfilled the function performed by the FIC, rendering moot the issue of complying with the costly regulations of the Affordable Care Act. Now instead of offering its own insurance, the Freelancers Union instituted two new programs. First, it established a National Benefits Platform (NBP) that connects freelancers throughout the United States to vetted insurance benefits, including health, disability, retirement, life, dental, and liability.[66] Closing the FIC did not have an impact on the organization's membership growth. Indeed, purchasing health insurance through Freelancers Union's NBP connects an individual to a wide network of other benefits, as well as to similarly situated, likeminded colleagues. It also provides the Freelancers Union with a steady stream of revenue. The Freelancers Union's second health care innovation is its participation in the Consumer Operated and Oriented Plans (CO-OP) program. The ACA sought to increase competition and consumer choice among health plans by establishing the CO-OP program. The CO-OP program offers health coverage through health insurance exchanges in small markets. With the assistance of $340 million in federal funding, the Freelancers Union in 2014 launched three consumer driven CO-OPs in New Jersey, New York, and Oregon. The CO-OPs are independent from the Freelancers Union, with their own boards of directors and management teams.[67] With medical practices in Brooklyn and Manhattan, the Freelancers Union now had its own clinics operating under ACA guidelines.[68]

Conservative opponents of the ACA contested the very concept of CO-OPs and cut funding to the program several years running as part of a campaign they waged to illustrate their claim that CO-OP programs wasted taxpayers' money. An important aspect of their political crusade was to attack the Freelancers Union for receiving a $340 million award from the Centers for Medicare and Medicaid Services to create the health insurance CO-OPs. Republican-led subcommittees of the House Oversight and Government Reform Committee held joint hearings to investigate the issuance of federal loans to create CO-OPs. The Freelancers Union was one of only two organizations brought before the House to defend its participation in the CO-OP program. Critics had three basic complaints. First, they claimed that the Freelancers Union was ineligible to receive any CO-OP funding because of its relationship with its for-profit insurance company, the FIC. Second, they attacked the Freelancers Union for successfully lobbying regulators to promulgate rules allowing it to participate in the CO-OP program. Finally, Republican opponents of Obamacare accused the Freelancers Union of reaping millions in profits from the CO-OPs in the program.[69]

Although the Freelancers Union's decision to close the FIC eventually undercut much of the first critique, Horowitz testified in detail on the Freelancers Union's qualifications to participate in the CO-OP process. After reminding House members of Freelancers Union's commitment to transparency throughout the entire process, from the application stage through providing benefits, Horowitz argued that the Freelancers Union's experience in creating and effectively operating its own health insurance company made it the most qualified organization to sponsor CO-OPs. Responding to the charge of unfair political influence, Horowitz restated her premise that the Freelancers Union is not a partisan institution, but one that "advocates on both sides of the aisle . . . and works to achieve social goals, not to make political statements."[70] She might have added that lobbying is an expression of free speech and an inherent part of American democracy, as affirmed by the Supreme Court's decision in *Citizens United*. As for the charge that the Freelancers Union was raking in millions of tax dollars, Horowitz responded that "developing sustainable programs to benefit independent workers is core to who we are and what we do," but, she concluded, the CO-OPs are independent entities and the Freelancers Union's role as a sponsor is finished.[71]

Over time the Freelancers Union addressed other less politically controversial insurance needs of its members. In 2009, it established a retirement plan for freelancers, and the following year created Health Partners, a mental health provider network. In 2018, the Freelancers Union took a major step forward in teaming with Silicon Valley's Sequoia Capital to form Trupo, a company partially owned by the Freelancers Union that provides disability insurance for freelancers too sick or injured to work. Since most short-term disability plans are available only through employers, and some plans require applicants to produce a W-2 form, something freelancers simply don't have, Trupo fills an important niche in freelancer insurance coverage. "If freelancers can't work, they lose out on critical income," observes Caitlin Pearce, who replaced Horowitz as executive director of the Freelancers Union in November 2017. A survey by Prudential Insurance found that only 5 percent of freelance workers had short-term disability coverage, as opposed to 42 percent of traditional full-time employees. With Trupo, freelancers will pay $20 to $50 a month to receive 50 percent of their monthly income for up to twelve weeks, providing they can prove they are too sick or injured to work.[72] Keith Mestrich, CEO of Amalgamated Bank, applauded the collective action upon which Trupo was founded. Saying "all benefit when they come together for a common good," Mestrich concluded that "through Trupo, freelancers are creating their own safety net that will provide income stabilization in the event they're unable to work."[73]

Freelancers Union: A Rising Political Force?

The Freelancers Union provides benefits primarily through an entrepreneurial approach tied to the marketplace. As one observer so eloquently put it, the Freelancers Union's entrepreneurial approach "would make anyone who believes in private enterprise proud."[74] The Freelancers Union—not government—creates and operates the social purpose organizations directly or indirectly. It then puts profits back into the organization to further promote the interests of freelance workers. This is in keeping with Horowitz's dictum of DIY, the underlying principle of the new mutualism. But while the Freelancers Union sees itself as part of a larger social as opposed to political movement, it still relies heavily on political advocacy to realize its goals. In fact, the Freelancers Union has political action committees (PACs) at both the state and federal levels to advocate for its members' interests. Consider, for example, the Freelancers Union's political efforts to provide health insurance. Without convincing state insurance commission regulators to modify regulations, the union could not have offered group insurance or subsequently establish its own health insurance company. On the national level, the Freelancers Union's advocacy led to public hearings on Obamacare's CO-OP programs. A primary focus of these inquiries was the Freelancers Union's exercise of its political influence to get $340 million from the federal government. Change comes, Horowitz insists, when freelancers make their case to political leaders.[75]

The Freelancers Union did make the freelancers' case to gain several important policy victories. On the federal level it convinced the General Accounting Office to include contingent workers in its 2006 survey on Employment Arrangements and convinced the U.S. Bureau of Labor Statistics to restore funds for the Contingent Worker Supplement of the Population Survey.[76] Locally, the Union responded to members' concern for tax relief by successfully advocating for changes in New York City's Unincorporated Business Tax (UBT). New York's UBT charged a tax on the profits of those unincorporated private partnerships that service the corporate sector. The idea was to tax these legal, financial, and accounting firms in the same way corporations are taxed. When the UBT was enacted in 1966, the number of freelance workers was small. Although freelancers are not corporate service businesses, they had to pay the UBT as well as a personal New York City income tax. In other words, they were taxed twice on the same income. By 2009, the Freelancers Union had about 70,000 members in New York City, many of whom packed two public City Council hearings on the issue. In early June dozens more traveled to Albany to lobby state legislators for tax reform. Their efforts paid off. The legislature saved freelancers up to $3,400 a year by eliminating the UBT tax on independent workers earning up to $100,000 annually. The tax reform also provided a tax credit for freelancers earning as much as $150,000.[77]

In March of that same year then-NYC Mayor Bloomberg took action in support of the Freelancers Union's political agenda. Stating that "freelancers lack any safety net to fall back on during hard times," Bloomberg proposed a federal unemployment benefit for freelancers. The Freelancers Union proposed an Unemployment Protection Fund that would require the state or federal government to provide matching funds for money freelancers put into a designated fund. Unfortunately, despite the mayor's support, the fund has yet to come to fruition.[78]

The year 2016 proved to be a good one for New York's freelancers. That year the New York State legislature enacted a family leave law that allowed freelancers for a very small percentage of their income to buy paid leave for illness, births, and other family-related events.[79] A major victory came when the New York City Council passed the Freelance Isn't Free Act. The first law of its kind in the United States took effect in 2017. The Freelance Isn't Free Act—a long-term goal of the Freelancers Union—gives independent contractors "the legal right to written contracts, timely payment, and freedom from retaliation." An estimated half-million New York freelancers should benefit from the law, according to a study by New York's Department of Finance. Workers can now file complaints with the city's Department of Consumer Affairs (DCA), which will assist freelancers in pursuing their claims. "By requiring hiring parties to issue written contracts, we can better ensure that workers are paid on time and in full," explained DCA Commissioner Lorelei Salas.[80] This important win for freelancers was achieved only after extensive political efforts by freelancers and their organization.

Getting their stories told was the first phase of the political "Get Paid, Not Played" campaign. Aware that many freelancers were reluctant to publicly share their stories for fear of losing work, the Freelancers Union set up a website called *The World's Longest Invoice* for workers to tell their stories about getting stiffed.[81] Initially, the responses were slow in coming, but after the first handful of stories appeared, other freelancers began to respond. The stories poured in. About a year after creating the website, freelancers submitted claims of $15.8 million in unpaid invoices. With the stories in hand as weapons for change, members of the Freelancers Union took to the streets to conduct a number of actions. Hundreds of freelancers participated in actions at Brooklyn Borough Hall, a rally at City Hall, and a panel at Civic Hall on a special day of action and legislative hearings. This, claims the Freelancers Union's Laura Murphy, demonstrated to lawmakers that the freelance community is an active one, "not just one that waits for change to happen."[82] After lobbying City Council members in each of the city's fifty-one council districts, freelancers turned to social media to build awareness of their issue and circulated a petition that garnered over 10,000 signatures. They also made astute use of the media, appearing before TV cameras to tell their stories, talking to newspaper reporters, and seeking out interested news outlets to spread their message. In recognition of the important role played by the Freelancers Union, council member Brad Lander thanked the Freelancers Union "for their leadership in passing this first-of-its-kind legislation."[83]

A year later, DCA issued a report on the effectiveness of the new law. The report revealed that 264 freelancers had filed complaints, 98 percent of which involved late or nonpayment violations. DCA helped them recover $254,866 in lost income. The report also found that freelancers who had lodged complaints were highly satisfied with the support they received from DCA. Not only did 90 percent of freelancers recover the full amount owed, but 98 percent recovered their wages without going to court. The willingness of contractors to pay without going to court is a function of a provision in the law that penalizes contractors if they lose their case in civil court. The Freelancers Union is currently working with friends in Congress to enact similar national legislation.

The Freelancers Union's lobbying efforts, particularly in New York City, continue to bear fruit. Like many other workers, freelancers are sometimes subject to sexual harassment and discrimination. A Freelancers Union's investigation discovered that about 75 percent of discrimination or harassment violations against freelancers are not reported. In fact, most freelancers have no place to report violations. The Freelancers Union used its growing political clout to address these issues. Advocating for legislation that would protect freelancers in NYC and backed by the testimony of freelancers, in 2019 the Freelancers Union convinced the New York City Council to enact legislation that expanded the anti-discrimination protections of New York's Human Rights Law to cover freelancers. "We have finally achieved the goal of making NYC a sanctuary for freelancers against crimes of harassment and discrimination," said Nina Irizarry, a freelancer who testified about the harassment she experienced.[84]

Providing Information and Building Community

Freelancers are interested not only in insurance and financial security. The Freelancers Union addresses those ecoomic needs in myriad other ways. In 2006, the organization established its Web Portal, a website that provides an online gateway to available benefits for freelancers such as health insurance, tax information, and networking advice. It connects members to each other and to new clients.[85] Several years later, the organization attempted to address the issue of clients who fail to pay by creating the Clients Score Card. By participating in the scorecard rating, freelancers provide the Freelancers Union with a body of information that allows other freelancers to evaluate prospective clients. Did the client pay? Did they pay the market rate? Were there any hassles?[86] That same year, 2011, the Freelancers Union addressed another important concern of freelancers—what constitutes a good contract—by establishing Contract Creator. The Contract Creator website gives freelancers the opportunity to build a standardized client contract step by step and responds to questions the freelancer may have on the subject. The contract provided by the Freelancers Union is based on the requirements of the Freelance Isn't Free Act to ensure clients and freelancers comply with the law.[87]

Knowing how important detailed information about freelancing is to freelancers and in response to complaints concerning the absence of a manual on freelancing, in 2012 Horowitz, with Sciarra Poynter, wrote *The Freelancers Bible*. This 474-page tome provides freelancers with everything they need to know to achieve success. The book provides detailed information ranging from the many challenges and issues new freelancers face to complex tax matters that working freelancers are sure to confront. In the words of one reviewer, the book "offers viable and creative solutions to problems even seasoned freelancers face."[88]

Two years after the publication of *The Freelancers Bible*, the Free-lancers Union joined with the American Federation of Teachers, Lyft, and several other organizations to create the National Benefits Platform (NBP). The new NBP program enables freelancers to conduct searches by zip code for benefits available to freelancers in the area. These benefits include a wide range of insurance options such as dental, disability, life, liability, and health insurance, as well as 401k plans.[89] That same year, the Freelancers Union initiated its Sparks program, an educational and networking program. Sparks chapters in over twenty cities and growing throughout the United States hold monthly meetings where freelancers connect to learn from each other and to share ideas. They explore topics of importance to freelancers, such as how to get paid, how to do your taxes, and so on. The Union also connects freelancers virtually on a monthly topic through its community forum (Hives), which allows freelancers to discuss what works, what doesn't work, and what to do next.

Responses to the *Freelancing in America 2019* survey made clear that many freelancers believe their formal education did not properly equip them for a career in freelancing. Matt Cooper, CEO of Skillshare, summarized freelancers' concerns: "Traditional and training models just don't work. You can't run down to the community college and take a class on the latest version of Adobe that just came out yesterday."[90] His company, Cooper insists, is trying to find ways to connect freelancers to each other so they can learn from each other. In response to these concerns, the Freelancers Union in October of 2018 partnered with the Independent Film Maker's Project and the New York City Mayor's Office of Media and Entertainment to establish the first of its kind freelancer training program in the nation. Located in Brooklyn and called the Freelancers Hub, the new undertaking fills several important needs of New York's freelancers. In addition to providing space for freelancers in media and entertainment fields to gather and network, Hub is the home of Spark for Creatives. The Hub provides a place for freelancers to get information on available benefits, to participate in know-your-rights workshops, and to attend a plethora of other training seminars and workshops, including how to start and sustain a freelance business. Since more than 70 percent of complaints under the Freelance Isn't Free Act come from workers in the entertainment and arts sector, the Hub also provides legal assistance to freelancers on contracts, intellectual property issues, disputes over payment, and other legal matters relevant to freelancers.

So What?

Most freelancers struggle to make ends meet. Nationally, their median hourly rate is about $20 an hour, slightly more than the average hourly median rate of just under $19 per hour for all workers. Since most freelancers have gaps between jobs, the $20 hourly rate doesn't accurately reflect their annual income.[91] Structural changes in the economy continue to undercut the income and standard of living of the many skilled and educated freelancers. "In today's economy, there's a huge chunk of the middle class that's being pushed down into the working class and the working poor and freelancers are the first group that's happening to," Horowitz observes.[92] Labor unions traditionally helped workers address issues of falling wages and other terms and conditions of employment. But organized labor is on the decline, and outdated labor laws hold independent workers back from unionizing anyway. The Freelancers Union has met with some success in trying to fill this gap.

Thanks to its size, the Freelancers Union has become a major political player in New York City and a growing political force on the national level. The organization has used its political clout to provide important legal protections in New York City, where a large percentage of freelancers live and work. The Freelancers Union successfully used its political and collective social power to provide its members access to virtually every kind of insurance they may need. It also gives its members access to a vast array of training programs and other kinds of information essential to their work. The Freelancers Union has taken on the issue of isolation that many freelancers experience by providing web seminars and other virtual forums where workers can meet, discuss, and share ideas. Freelancers in NYC have the additional option of participating in the Freelancers Union's recently created Hubs. These brick-and-mortar Hubs provide work spaces for freelancers and give them the opportunity to meet face to face with others to exchange ideas, network, or just plain socialize. On top of all this, freelancer members are eligible for discounts on a variety of goods ranging from gym membership to car insurance and almost everything in between. Rather than negotiating contracts directly with employers, it provides workers with the tools and support they need to fend for themselves in the face of ongoing changes in the global economy.[93]

Rebecca Smith of the nonprofit National Employment Law Project, an organization that advocates for workers, applauds the Freelancers Union for its success in assisting freelancers. "They have concentrated a lot of their work on delivering benefits to freelancers," she writes.[94] The Freelancers Union undoubtedly provides its members with the assistance and support they need, but questions remain: What are its prospects for growth? Will it organize millions of freelancers into a major political and economic force across the United States? How significant is the Freelancers Union as a player in the new labor movement? More importantly, is this new mutualism even a viable model for the new labor movement?

Pointing to the growth in the Freelancers Union's membership and its success in providing services to members and gaining important political victories in New York, Horowitz and others assert that the Freelancers Union personifies the future of the labor movement. Underlying this belief is the claim that some fifty-seven million U.S. workers, or more than one-third of the entire U.S. workforce, engaged in freelance work during 2018. The proliferation of freelance work has led the Freelancers Union to project a membership of one million within the next few years. Compare these numbers to the 400,000+ active members in the UAW or to the nation's largest industrial union, the United Steelworkers, with about 860,000 active members. Given these numbers, the Freelancers Union appears to be on the verge of becoming a major player in the American labor movement. But do these numbers tell the story the Freelancers Union thinks they tell?

The belief that freelancing work is fast becoming the dominant occupation in America is based on data generated by the Freelancers Union. But independent analyses by the Bureau of Labor Statistics (BLS) and the Economic Policy Institute (EPI) indicate that Freelancers Union's survey results may be grossly overstating the number of freelancers. The Freelancers Union/Upwork survey of 2014 claimed there were fifty-three million freelancers, comprising about 34 percent of the working population. For this same period, BLS identifies 14.8 million independent workers, comprising 10.1 percent of the workforce, and the EPI's Larry Mishel identified only 11.3 million independent workers, representing 7.7 percent of total employment.[95]

Disparities in the number of freelancers in the labor force are a function of who is included in the count. The Freelancers Union/Upwork study includes everyone "engaged in supplemental, temporary, project—or contract-based work, within the past 12 months." The study counted freelancers who employed other freelancers, temporary and permanent part-timers, people who worked short term on a single project, and even some who didn't have any 1099 earnings. This methodology led the EPI to conclude that the Freelancers Union's definition of freelancer stretches "the group beyond recognition."[96] A Gallup survey finds that 28 percent of working people hold multiple jobs, meaning that the Freelancers survey could have counted a single individual multiple times.[97] Author and activist Kim Moody illustrates the inaccuracy of the Union's counting method. Moody held a full-time academic job and was clearly not a freelancer. Yet, book royalties he earned included him in the count as a freelancer.[98] The BLS addresses the question of multiple jobs by including only those whose primary income or primary job is from self-employment, but as Mishel observes, this count includes that category of freelancers who employ other freelancers. In contrast, the EPI reaches its number of 11.3 million by counting only those who "work for themselves and have no paid employees." This, combined with data indicating a decline of 1.8 million independent contractors in the workforce between 2014 and 2015 leads the EPI report to conclude "there is no reason to believe that in the . . . future a large or growing share of people will obtain their main source of income from freelancing or doing gig work."[99]

Careful analysis of the number of freelancers suggests the tsunami of change in the labor force foreseen by Horowitz and others is overstated. The number of freelancers in the economy remains significant, but the Covid-19 pandemic has set the ranks of freelancers in flux. In mid-March 2020, a Freelancers Union survey of its members revealed the devastating effect of the virus on freelancers. Of the more than 5,000 respondents to the survey, 76 percent said they had lost clients, and 65 percent reported difficulty in finding new jobs. Given their loss of income and the closing of childcare facilities, 12 percent had to reduce their workload to care for their children. Significantly, over 90 percent of workers in the "creative" industries such as musicians and performing artists lost their contracts. Almost all freelancers surveyed lost income, with 10 percent losing more than $20,000. The CARES Act helped these freelancers, too, but more than half still needed assistance to pay for food and housing. The Freelancers Union responded by creating the Freelancers Relief Fund to provide immediate help.[100]

On the other hand, despite the economic insecurities associated with freelancing, many newly unemployed people have turned to freelancing in order to pay their bills.[101] An Upwork study finds that some thirty-six million workers performed freelance work in 2020, an increase of over two million from 2019.[102] Although the Upwork study applauds the growth of freelancing, the disappearance of millions of permanent jobs suggests that many are now turning to freelancing out of necessity rather than choice.

The steady growth of freelancing gives credibility to the Freelancers Union's million-member projection in the near future. But what does it mean to be a member of the Freelancers Union? Obviously, members are consumers of the variety of services the organization offers. In fact, the Freelancers Union is so effective at providing services that critics complain the organization is primarily a service-providing non-government organization (NGO).[103] The overall top-down approach in governance taken by the Freelancers Union supports this criticism. Former New York City Council member Rafael Espinal, who in March of 2020 took the helm of the organization, characterized the Union's executive board as mainly advisory, which puts policymaking in the hands of the executive director.[104] Unlike labor unions and many worker centers, the Freelancers Union's executive board is not elected by members. Not only is it not elected by the membership, the board has only one rank-and-file freelancer among its membership, and that member is appointed after undergoing a careful screening process. Compare this hierarchical approach to that of the Immokalee workers.

Freelancers Union members not only consume the organization's services, they also participate in its information and training programs and in its political activities, which are mostly limited to New York City. These training platforms differ greatly from traditional union educational classes. Consider, for example, what it means to be an IBEW electrician. When clients hire an IBEW electrician, they know the worker has gone through an extensive apprenticeship program and is, above all else, a highly skilled electrician. Compare that to the training offered by the Freelancers Union. The Freelancers Union's programs generally focus on issues outside the workers' substantive area of expertise, including how to find new clients, how to prepare taxes, what their legal rights are, and so on. In short, Freelancers Union training programs teach workers not only how to interact with the people who hire them, but also how to compete more effectively with other freelancers, many of whom may also belong to the Freelancers Union. But once hired, freelancers are mostly on their own, unlike people who get hired for jobs covered by union contracts.

The final question focuses on the Freelancers Union's viability as a model for the new labor movement. The Freelancers Union has brought to the public's attention the plight of freelancers and their importance to the economy. The Union provides these freelancers with services they otherwise could not obtain. But unlike the Immokalee workers, New York's farmworkers, those engaged in the Fight for $15 and even Uber and Lyft drivers, the Freelancers Union never directly confronts an employer. Practically speaking, who would it confront since there are as many potential employers as there are freelancers. The underlying assumption of the Freelancers Union is that change in the structure of employment is inevitable. Rather than engaging in political struggle to confront the conditions resulting from this change, the organization addresses symptoms, not causes. The consequences of this approach are far-reaching. First, the new mutualism fails to challenge the corporate power that created the problem in the first place. In offering exploited workers attractive and much-needed first-aid, the Freelancers Union takes the corporate sector off the hook, which could give companies an incentive to increase profits by hiring even fewer workers as traditional employees. Second, the Freelancers Union is founded on and perpetuates the premise that freelancing is liberating. In his *The Age of Acquiescence*, Steve Fraser argues that acceptance of this idea helps keep exploited workers from organizing to pressure government into providing an adequate social safety net.[105] Third, the Freelancers Union's approach plays into the old American narrative of rugged individualism. That is, individual choices, not the system of power, determine our lot in life. To echo C. Wright Mills, the ability to find a job, earn a decent wage, and to live a comfortable life become the personal troubles of individuals, rather than larger social issues begging for political change.[106] Finally, contrary to the fundamental principle of union solidarity, the basic underpinning of the Freelancers Union is individualism as opposed to cooperation. In short, the Freelancers Union is not a model for social or political change. Its new mutualism is rooted in the many failed voluntarist experiments of the past, and even on this level its interpretation of social unionism is incomplete. Hillman was, after all, a union president who became an important advisor to Franklin Roosevelt and an architect of the New Deal. The New Deal and the prosperity it gave generations of American workers grew out of political struggle.

The Freelancers Union is a unique undertaking that has drawn criticism from both sides of the political spectrum. It's under attack from the political right for its collective, nonprofit activities, such as its creation of CO-OPs.[107] The political left criticizes the Freelancers Union because of its apolitical, band-aid approach to changing economic conditions and its unwillingness to engage in political struggle.[108] But the Freelancers Union and its new mutualism isn't about taking direct action to achieve big political change—it's about DIY. Freelancers Union's supporters would respond to critics by saying, open your eyes and look at what we've accomplished. These accomplishments are not without value. The Freelancers Union, like the American Association of Retired People (AARP) and other advocacy organizations, does an effective job in providing services and representing its constituents. But one fact is inescapable: since the Freelancers Union does not confront employers and substitutes the providing of services for political struggle, it is clearly an outlier within the developing new labor movement.

Chapter 6

Taking to the Streets

Albina, twenty-eight, earned $9.05 an hour after working as a part-time cashier at McDonald's for more than ten years. She was among the fifteen million U.S. workers who earned less than $10 an hour, which isn't even $20,800 annually for full-time work. Married to a cook at the same McDonald's, she made about $12,000 a year and relied on food stamps and Medicaid to provide food and medical care for their two young daughters. When the opportunity presented itself, Albina joined the Fight for $15. Now, after participating in nine one-day nationwide strikes and myriad demonstrations and protests, she and her husband each earn $15 an hour. "A few years ago, nobody was talking about raising our wages," she explained. "Now all the talk is, 'We need $15 and a union.' "[1]

On a November day in 2012, a vibrant new labor movement was born when two hundred underpaid fast-food workers from about forty fast-food stores in New York City walked off their jobs and took to the streets. Demanding a wage of $15 an hour and union rights throughout the fast-food industry, they chanted, "Hey, hey, what do you say, we demand fair pay."[2] This new movement—the Fight for $15—started in New York City, but it soon became a tsunami spreading across the country to more than 300 cities and then onto six continents. These protesting workers don't sit at a bargaining table to discuss their terms and conditions of employment with their employers. Instead, they pressure state and local governments to provide them with the benefits and protections of a typical labor contract. Inspired by the energy, determination, and ability of these fast-food activists to garner much public support, low-wage workers in retail and other service industries such as restaurants and bars, health, transportation, warehousing, and home and child care soon joined the crusade. Mary Kay Henry, President of SEIU, compared the growing momentum of the Fight for $15 to labor's struggle for the eight-hour work day: "This fight for $15 is growing way beyond fast food. It's getting to be what the eight-hour day was in the twentieth century."[3]

Bob Dylan's iconic lyrics that "the times they are a-changin'" proved true in 2018 when teachers in conservative, right-to-work states took to the streets. Fed up with state budget cuts that slashed their earnings, took away their professional dignity, and threatened to destroy public education, teachers—the proletariat of the professional class—emulated the strategy of fast-food workers. They held rallies, participated in demonstrations, and even walked off their jobs, leading AFT President Randi Weingarten to observe, "People are now using the legislative process to get things that normally have happened at the bargaining table."[4]

Previous chapters analyzed struggles of exploited workers who were not classified as employees and, as such, lacked basic legal protections and the benefits employees traditionally enjoy. This chapter looks at the struggles of fast-food workers involved in the Fight for $15 and the One Fair Wage movement among full-service restaurant workers who rely on the generosity of customers' tips to make a living. Although the occupations of these service sector groups differ slightly, they have much in common. Unlike the farmworkers and gig workers studied in earlier chapters, these workers are classified as employees and, in theory, receive the protections of existing labor laws. But their earnings are abysmally low; most are vulnerable to various abuses such as wage theft, arbitrary firings, and sexual harassment by employers; and they can't count on the fair and impartial implementation of the law to protect them. That's why they've taken to the streets to build public support for their economic plight. To better understand the rising new labor movement and its future prospects, it's necessary to ask several questions: What are working conditions like in the fast-food and full-service restaurant business? How are workers responding? What have these groups achieved so far, and what are the prospects for additional gains? Do the tactics restaurant and fast-food workers use fit their overall strategy? How does the Fight for $15 approach differ from traditional union organizing drives? What role do unions play in this new direct action movement? And, finally, is unionization the inevitable next step for these workers?

Can't Lose What You Never Had

Prior chapters looked at the decline of unions and the loss of hundreds of thousands of good union jobs. These long-gone jobs provided millions of workers entrée into the middle class. They paid a livable salary, provided decent health care insurance, pensions, paid sick and vacation days, overtime pay, and a host of other benefits, including, of course, the weekend. Many workers to this day mourn the loss of these good jobs. But the more than twelve million restaurant workers are not among the mourners. Their industry isn't unionized and doesn't offer much in the way of good jobs. The financial squeeze on restaurant and fast-food workers is devastating, but they face many other workplace obstacles every day. For instance, look at Fran Marion's day at a Popeyes[5] restaurant in Kansas City. Like other fast-food joints, Popeyes' insistence on "instant" customer service places tremendous pressure on workers who have just three minutes to take an order, cook it, bag it, and deliver it to the patron. That's exhausting work, but it often gets worse. Fran, for instance, occasionally works when the restaurant is on "short shift," which is another way of saying when it is grossly understaffed. Short shift means that Fran must do all the jobs herself. Despite twenty-two years of experience in the fast-food industry, Fran scrambles as she takes the order, cooks it, and delivers it to a satisfied customer. It's only recently that she was permitted to take a short break. For all this, Fran gets paid $9.50 an hour. After completing her shift at Popeyes, Fran works another full-time job from 5 p.m. to 1:30 a.m. as a janitor for $11 an hour. "I have always needed two jobs," Fran said. "You basically need two jobs to survive working on low wages."[6] Forced to work two jobs to put food on the table, Fran, a thirty-seven-year-old single mother, doesn't get to spend much time with her two teenage children. In fact, she goes days at a time without seeing them since the city condemned her rented house and made Fran homeless. Her children now live with a friend while Fran sleeps on another friend's sofa. And like Albina and millions of other fast-food workers, the restaurant does not provide Fran with health insurance, sick pay or vacation pay, or anything else a good union job offers. In fact, in the absence of basic health insurance, Fran has not seen a doctor once in her entire adult life.[7]

Albina and Fran are among the more than twelve million restaurant workers in the United States, including nearly four million who work in fast foods. Job growth in the restaurant and fast-food industry has exploded in recent years, even keeping pace with the surge of employment in the retail industry. Workers in both these sectors are poorly paid, but restaurant workers are slightly worse off. In fact, seven of the ten poorest paying jobs in the country are in or related to the food service industry.[8] It's no wonder the average turnover rate at a fast-food eatery is 150 percent. This rate translates into a store having to replace all workers plus half more every year. The fast-food industry justifies the low pay and tough working conditions by claiming that most workers are teenagers or students trying to make a few extra bucks to pay for a Saturday night out, gas in the car, or nonessential purchases. Recall McDonald's omnipresent TV commercial boasting that "McDonald's is committed to being America's best first job." The facts refute this claim.

Although about 70 percent of the jobs are part-time, the average age of fast-food workers in 2017 was twenty-nine, and slightly more than a quarter were parents working to support their children. Wage discrimination prevails throughout the industry, too. Women, a majority of whom are women of color, comprise about two-thirds of the fast-food labor force but are paid about 60 percent less than their male counterparts. Wages are so low in the industry that 13 percent of all food workers depend on food stamps to feed their families, nearly double the rate of other industries.[9] The average annual gross earnings for a full-time fast-food worker as of January 2020 is $22,046, and that's before payroll tax withholdings. To put this in perspective, consider that the National Employment Law Project estimates it would take over 900 years for a minimum-wage worker to earn as much as the annual earnings of the CEO of YUM BRANDS, the parent company of Taco Bell.[10] McDonald's recognized the financial pressures its workers faced by creating an online personal budget guide to help their employees spend their earnings in a rational and frugal manner. The budget, as William Finnegan observes in *The New Yorker*, had a number of bizarre assumptions that revealed just how out of touch McDonald's really was. For instance, it assumed that employees worked two full-time jobs and could purchase health insurance at the bargain price of twenty dollars a month. The company also provided employees with an equally clueless health advice page. This page suggested that workers should sing to relieve stress and urged them to reduce the risk of a heart attack by taking two annual vacations, unpaid, of course. McDonald's heaped additional insult on its workers by suggesting they could make their meals go farther by breaking the food into smaller pieces.[11]

The fast-food industry is not alone in exploiting its workforce. Workers in full-service restaurants are often paid even less. The federal minimum wage for waitstaff and other restaurant workers is $7.25 an hour, but federal law requires the employer to pay only $2.13 of that, the difference to be made up by tips. The federal requirement of $2.13 an hour is called the sub-minimum wage. Eighteen states pay the sub-minimum, and another twenty-six plus the District of Columbia pay a tipped minimum greater than $2.13 but less than the full minimum wage. If wages and tips fail to reach the $7.25 minimum, the employer must pay the difference, a difficult requirement to enforce.[12] Workers don't always keep an exact account of all tips they received during a given pay period, many are unaware of the law, and some are afraid to ask the boss for the difference. With the passage of the Minimum Wage Increase Act of 1996, the sub-minimum wage, which at the time represented 50 percent of the federal minimum, was frozen at $2.13 and decoupled from the minimum wage. According to a joint study by the Economic Policy Institute and the Center on Wage and Employment Dynamics, today the value of the sub-minimum is just 29.4 percent of the minimum wage.[13] But tipped workers sometimes don't even earn the minimum wage. When a customer pays the bill by credit card, for example, some states, including New York, allow the employer to deduct the credit card fees, usually 3 percent, from the worker's tip.[14] Research conducted by the Restaurant Opportunities Center (ROC), a worker center that organizes restaurant workers and advocates on their behalf, indicates that some restaurant workers don't receive a paycheck at all. The ROC pointed to the experience of one worker, Claudia, who "took home a pay slip but no pay, all her wages having gone to taxes,"[15] which means that she basically lived off cash tips. The Center also noted that workers like Claudia often go hungry and are sometimes desperate for a few bites of leftover food.

Darden Restaurants, which includes Olive Garden, Long Horn Steakhouse, Cheddars Scratch Chicken, Yard House, Capital Grille, Seasons 52, Eddie V's, the Cheesecake Factory, and, until recently, Red Lobster, has found still another way to increase its profits at the expense of its low-paid hourly employees. The largest full-service chain on the globe, Darden pays nearly half of its 140,000 hourly workers by payroll debit card rather than check, a trend that is growing among low-wage employers.[16] The company justifies this form of payment through the reasonable claim that cards provide a convenient way for those workers lacking checking accounts to access their earnings. According to the ROC, the company saves nearly $5 million annually by using this more "convenient" method of payment. Sounds like a win-win game, doesn't it? Unfortunately, Darden's workers have to pay to get access to the money they've earned. An ROC study found that the vast majority of employees had to pay fees of about $1.75 to access their earnings, a $10 fee for a lost card, and a $5 monthly charge for inactive accounts. About a quarter of workers also had to pay a store fee when they made a purchase.[17]

An Economic Policy Institute study reveals that wage theft deprives low-wage workers of more money than all the robberies of banks, gas stations, and convenience stores combined.[18] The lion's share of these wage thefts come from the fast-food and restaurant business. Wage theft occurs when workers are not paid their contractual or legal wage. It's a standard practice throughout the restaurant industry and happens when employers take workers off the clock, fail to pay minimum wage, refuse to give meal breaks or overtime pay, and in the case of tipped workers, when the employer pays the tipped minimum wage for non-tipped work or skims off some tip money.[19] In the fast-food industry a 2014 survey by Hart Research in ten metropolitan areas revealed that almost nine of ten fast-food workers felt victimized by wage theft. The workers' feeling of being robbed are backed by data. In the past several years alone, McDonald's settled wage and hour claims to the tune of almost $8 million. Taco Bell, Wendy's, and others also paid millions to similar claims.[20]

Restaurant workers who rely on tips for the bulk of their pay are extraordinarily vulnerable to wage theft. In 2011, the U.S. Department of Labor issued a regulation affirming the longstanding practice that tips belong to the employee. The rule also prohibited employers from forcing workers to share tips with employees not in the direct line of service who earn the legal minimum wage.[21] Despite these legal protections, employers often screw restaurant tip workers out of pay by requiring them to pool their tips with workers not in the direct line of service. The pool of tip money, then, is taken from service workers earning a sub-minimum wage to supplement the minimum-wage payment of non-tip workers, which the employer is legally obligated to pay in full. Workers often fear retribution by the employer if they complain, so these illegal acts often go unreported and unpunished. The Trump administration attempted to make this form of wage theft legal. A 2017 decision by the Tenth Circuit Court of Appeals ruled that employers in the states covered by the Tenth Circuit Court own the tips, providing workers are paid the legal minimum wage. Trump's DOL jumped upon this ruling by proposing a new regulation that implemented the decision of the Tenth Circuit nationally.[22] This proposed regulation would have allowed an employer to establish tip pools for employees who traditionally don't rely on tips, an effective way to shift some of the payroll burden from the employer to tip-earning service workers. It also would have given employers the legal right to take whatever they consider to be their fair share of the tip money.[23] This latest attempt to hijack tips was stopped in 2018 when Congress amended the

Fair Labor Standards Act to prohibit employers, managers, and supervisors from taking tip money. Then in December 2020, the DOL issued final regulations that conform to this FLSA amendment.[24]

A 2018 *New York Times* editorial calling for the end of the sub-minimum wage in New York commented on the large degree of wage theft and other labor violations in the food industry. The editorial cited the Department of Labor's somewhat shocking estimate that almost 84 percent of the full-service restaurants it investigated between 2010 and 2012 had violated labor standards, including tip violations.[25] Even a cursory glance of data concerning wage theft in the full-service restaurant sector suggests the DOL's findings are not so shocking after all. Wage theft violations are apparently endless and far too numerous to list here. Nevertheless, the reader is sure to gain a good understanding of the depth of the problem by looking at the violations of Darden Restaurants, which owns two thousand or so restaurants. First of all, Darden pays its employees with debit cards, leaving it up to the workers to pay any fees imposed by card issuers. But that practice barely scratched the surface of the company's abusive treatment of its workforce. Over the past fifteen years Darden has settled numerous suits alleging some form of wage theft. According to the Corporate Research Project, in 2005, after workers accused managers of Olive Garden and Red Lobster of shortchanging their paychecks, Darden coughed up a $9.5 million settlement. Three years later it paid another $4 million to settle a wage dispute with bartenders. In 2011, the DOL ruled that Darden did not pay workers for all their hours on the job, forcing the company to pay back wages to some 140 employees at a Texas Olive Garden. Other fines resulted from not paying workers who were on the clock, failing to compensate at time and a half for overtime, and for allegedly retaliating against employees who complained. This list of settlements goes on and on.[26] But the Corporate Research Project's "Good Jobs First" project best summarized the extent of Darden's violations by noting that the food conglomerate paid over $24 million in fines for wage and hour violations between 2000 and 2019.[27]

Restaurant and fast-food workers must put up with more than wage theft and speedups. Racial and gender discrimination sometimes cuts into their earnings. In September 2020, several workers at various Darden restaurants filed complaints with the Equal Employment Opportunity Commission claiming that Darden managers assigned women and workers of color to low-tip sections of the restaurant. "There's a system in place where they're trying to put a certain type of server up front, that being a white male," one complainant said.[28] Scheduling, too, is often an issue for a number of reasons. Sometimes it's simply a matter of employers giving workers too little notice about their work schedule, making it difficult for workers to plan their lives. On other occasions bosses weaponize scheduling to get a more compliant workforce. The New York City Council tried to regulate scheduling in the fast-food industry in 2017. But thanks to litigation initiated by the food industry, the issue is tied up in the courts.[29] Scheduling is sometimes viewed as an inconvenience or sometimes even a weapon in the boss's hands, but other significant issues also plague restaurant workers. Food service workers are prone to injury, violence, and sexual harassment. People may think restaurant work is relatively safe, but that's not the case. A survey of New York City restaurant workers revealed that more than a quarter had suffered burns on the job, more than a third had endured cuts, and almost two-thirds described feeling stiffness or aching in the joints while on the job. Worse yet, for the customer at least, 98 percent of all workers who sneezed or coughed on the food lacked sick days, and 80 percent had no health insurance.[30] Absent paid sick days, workers often come to work when they're ill and transmit their germs to customers. The Center for Disease Control claims that about 70 percent of all non-virus outbreaks, such as stomach flu, are traceable to infected workers.[31] The Covid-19 pandemic has exacerbated the situation. An ABC-6 news report from Columbus, Ohio, captured the dilemma restaurant workers faced when eateries were still fully open in the summer of 2020. Employees who refused to show up for work risked losing unemployment compensation and the extended benefits of the CARES Act. Those who stayed risk their health on a daily basis. As the bartenders being interviewed described it, " 'They said, you need to come to work or you will be kicked off unemployment because we are going to report you. . . . These restaurants that are choosing to stay open and not follow guidelines are putting the community at a high risk.' " Another interviewee reported that at least a half dozen of her co-workers had already tested positive for Covid-19.[32]

"Customer Shoots McDonald's Manager over Frappe Order," blurted a June 2017 New York Post headline. Violence of all varieties has become almost routine in the food service industry. In 2014, the Bureau of Labor Statistics reported fourteen worker homicides at limited service restaurants, another twenty-three in 2016, and fifteen more in 2017. In the full-service sector for 2017, some twenty-one employees were killed. This wave of violence does not include innocent bystanders who died or suffered injuries, nor does it include the death of the perpetrator. These violent killings tell only part of the story. The violent deaths of workers is the most flagrant form of carnage, but the bloodshed continues throughout the industry. The National Employment Law Project issued a report based on 721 reports of violence at McDonald's alone during a three-year period ending in April 2019. Of the 721 violent incidents, 12 percent resulted in death and 39 percent led to injuries to one or more persons. Violence is so pervasive in fast-food outlets that some Wendy's and Burger King stores provide security guards who carry firearms and Tasers. One McDonald's worker describes the omnipresent violence in the fast-food industry in the following terms: "I have witnessed so many fights and robberies," she said. "Once a man hit me on my back with a yellow wet-floor sign because he wanted to use the bathroom that I was cleaning."[33] One McDonald's in Chicago experienced twenty-four crimes in 2017 and another twenty-three in 2018, including a kidnapping, a sexual assault and several other assaults, two robberies, and a weapons violation. The fast-food industry has reacted to the violence by cutting back on late-night hours when most crimes take place, installing CCTV cameras, providing security, and offering safety training. An industry spokesperson defended its remedial efforts, stressing that "paying for safety was never an issue."[34]

If unpredictable scheduling, hazardous work, and the threat of violence aren't enough, restaurant workers also confront sexual harassment on the job, particularly those who rely on tips. A study by the Restaurant Opportunities Center found that almost 90 percent of women restaurant workers who depend on tips experienced some form of sexual harassment or assault while at work. Sexual harassment happens to men as well. Forty-six percent of male workers reported harassment, and 60 percent of transgender employees experienced uninvited sexual behavior or harassing comments. Since these workers depend on tips for their livelihood, they tend to tolerate such behavior. In the full-service sector, customers do most—not all—of the sexual harassing. That's not necessarily the case in fast-food restaurants. In the fast-food sector, where tips play a minimal role, research by the Hart Associates found that 40 percent of female fast-food workers experienced sexual harassment, most often by managers and co-workers. According to *USA Today*, most fast-food managers are young males, often with inadequate training, so harassment of co-workers should come as no surprise. Small wonder that McDonald's workers in ten cities were so angry they walked off their jobs in protest.[35]

Restaurant workers bear the economic, physical, and psychological costs that come with their jobs. But they are not alone in paying the price for low wages and unsettling working conditions. Taxpayers take a major hit as well. Abysmally low wages, irregular working hours, and the virtual absence of benefits force fast-food workers such as Albina to turn to public assistance for support. According to a 2013 report by the Berkeley Center for Labor Research and Education, at 44 percent, restaurant and food service workers have a higher participation rate in public assistance programs than workers in any other industry. When researchers focused on a subset of employees in the restaurant industry—fast-food workers—they discovered that 52 percent of the families of these workers relied on federal public assistance programs, including Medicaid and Children's Health Insurance, Temporary Assistance for Needy Families, the Earned Income Tax Credit, and food stamps. The cost to taxpayers? Seven billion dollars annually.[36] The $7 billion, which does not include additional state spending, is best understood as a hidden subsidy to fast-food companies that make exorbitant profits on the backs of an exploited labor force. And profitable they are. In fiscal 2018 McDonald's earned $5.9 billion on revenue of $21 billion. According to Americans for Tax Fairness, the Trump tax cut was estimated to add another $900 million annually into the corporation's coffers. The massive tax giveaway did not pour into employees' salaries, as Trump had promised, but the salary of Steve Easterbrook, McDonald's CEO, rose 42 percent, bringing his annual earnings to $21.7 million. In an ostensible display of generosity, McDonald's committed $150 million of the tax break over five years to increase educational opportunities for workers through its "Archways to Opportunity" program.[37] The next time you watch a McDonald's TV ad showing lucky Maria receiving tuition money from the company, remember who is paying for it: you, the taxpayer, and exploited, underpaid workers like Maria.

To the Streets!

The Fight for $15 has its roots in a winter 2012 action led by the New York Communities for Change (NYCC), a community-based organization created to resist the economic forces behind racism.[38] Established in 2010, NYCC rose from the ashes of its predecessor organization, the Association of Community Organizers for Reform (ACORN). On that cold February day back in 2012, NYCC joined forces with the United Food and Commercial Workers (UFCW) and the Retail, Wholesale and Department Store Union (RWDSU) to rally around a Brooklyn supermarket. Complete with a marching band and a plethora of politicians, the action protested wage theft and the poor treatment of immigrant workers. Unions funded the action with the goal of organizing workers at a number of small, independent grocery stores.[39] But while unions aimed to organize more workers, NYCC had a larger objective. The community organization sought to organize across industry lines rather than on a store-by-store basis. This sectoral approach, NYCC leaders believed, would work especially well in the fast-food industry. After reaching out to SEIU for support, a new partnership was formed between the community organization and the union that would have national, even international, consequences.[40]

On Black Friday, November 23, 2012, hundreds of Walmart workers in forty-six states walked off their jobs to protest low wages and bad working conditions. On that same day in Chicago, fast-food and retail workers joined the Walmart picket lines and demonstrated at major retailers throughout the city. The Chicago actions came on the heels of the founding convention of a new low-wage workers organization, the Workers Organizing Committee of Chicago, which claimed to have some 200 members in fast-food and retail sectors.[41] Less than a week later, a new labor movement was officially born. In what the New York Times characterized as "the biggest wave of job actions in the history of America's fast-food industry,"[42] hundreds of workers at various fast-foot restaurants in New York City went on strike for the day. The walkout at McDonald's, Burger King, Taco Bell, Wendy's, KFC, Domino's, and Papa John's was anything but spontaneous. SEIU hired the Berlin Rosen public relations firm to promote the campaign. The firm brought SEIU staff, made sure the rally received sufficient news coverage, and even gave workers a "Strike in a Box" toolkit explaining how to conduct a successful strike within the confines of the law.[43] But that wasn't all. For months, a squad of forty NYCC organizers had met with fast-food workers in an effort to form a new union and get a livable wage of $15 an hour. One striker's comments made clear that the organizers were cultivating fertile ground for the job action. "They're not paying us enough to survive," he said.

One-day strikes may not always close a store down, and the short duration won't put a heavy squeeze on the owners, but the approach does attract public attention and keeps strikers from losing their jobs. Although management has the legal right to fire workers who strike for union recognition or higher wages, workers who base their walkout on legitimate claims that management has violated labor law are legally protected. One-day strikes allow a handful of the stores' more militant workers to take job actions without waiting until a majority of their co-workers are ready to join them. As Josh Eidelson observes, this approach has an important educational function. By striking and then returning to work, activists demonstrate to recalcitrant workers that they too can walk off the job without getting fired. This is likely to inspire others to join the fray in the future.[44] Nevertheless, strikers always risk management firing them, legally or not. Minimum-wage workers simply lack the resources to challenge the bosses' actions in court, and seeking redress from the NLRB is both time consuming and unlikely to result in a favorable ruling. Yet sometimes when workers are fired, community activists may save the job. Wendy's fired a participant in the November strike, but almost immediately rehired her after local politicians, clergy, workers, and community groups rallied and occupied the store.[45] Another risk that strikers take is lost wages. Lost wages often mean skipped meals and unpaid bills. Again, unions, in this case the SEIU, came to the rescue by reimbursing the strikers for the day they missed.

SEIU supports the workers' quest for a decent wage primarily because the union's leaders initially viewed fast-food and restaurant workers as fertile ground for organizing. But in taking the cause of these workers to the streets, SEIU transformed traditional organizing into a political movement. In 2011, SEIU's leaders, motivated by what they characterized as the 7 percent problem—the percentage of unionized workers in the private sector—decided the union movement needed to take two drastic, albeit risky, steps. First, SEIU would attempt to change the public debate about the economy by exposing corporate greed and the horrific working conditions most workers toiled under. Second, rather than organize on a shop-by-shop basis, the union would attempt to organize entire industries. SEIU dubbed this campaign the Fight for a Fair Economy (FFE) and committed some $60 million to wage organizing and public educational campaigns in seventeen cities throughout the United States.[46] The vast fast-food industry with its millions of exploited workers provided an ideal target.

SEIU used its financial resources first to give the Fight for $15 movement a kickstart and then to help sustain it. SEIU bankrolled the fast-food workers' struggles through the creation of Fast Food Forward, a coalition that functions as a worker center and coordinates closely with NYCC. In fact, as revealed in its 2012 disclosure filing with the Department of Labor, SEIU helped launch the struggle for a $15 minimum wage by pouring almost $2.5 million into the NYCC's coffers for the purpose of organizing. The union's support gave workers the backing and security they needed to take additional militant actions.

On April 4, 2013—the forty-fifth anniversary of the assassination of Martin Luther King Jr., who died while supporting striking sanitation workers in Memphis—hundreds of New York City fast-food workers again walked off their jobs. Tying the fast-food workers' struggle to the civil rights movement, NYCC's Jonathan Westin noted that the protest represented the "continuation of a civil rights fight against low wages." In 2013, the minimum wage in New York was just $7.25 an hour, which is generally what fast-food workers earn. Supported by clergy, SEIU, FFF, NYCC, and the Black Institute (a progressive think tank that "translates the think into action"), New York City's second fast-food worker strike in six months had twice the number of strikers than the first. Workers vented their frustration over the city's low minimum wage by chanting, "Hey, hey! Ho, ho! Minimum wage has got to go!"[47] The National Restaurant Association—what some call "the other NRA"—responded by claiming an increase in the minimum wage could jeopardize the thirteen million jobs the industry provides. These jobs, the NRA continued, offer "one of the best paths to achieving the American Dream."[48]

Fast-food workers across the nation did not buy the NRA's argument. Within days following the second NYC job action, McDonald's and Dunkin Donuts workers in Chicago again took to the streets to demonstrate against the Illinois $8.25 minimum wage. An organizing group in St. Louis kicked off a "St. Louis Can't Survive on $7.35" drive for a $15-an-hour minimum wage. On May 10 in Detroit, hundreds of fast-food workers followed suit by walking off their jobs, the first such job action in a right-to-work state. Seattle workers did the same at the end of May. By August, when fast-food strikes had hit almost fifty cities, the Fight for $15 movement had clearly gained unstoppable momentum.[49]

In September, demonstrators for a $15 minimum wage turned to the civil rights movement's practice of civil disobedience as a tactic to embarrass fast-food chains and gain public support. In Kansas City, dozens of members of Stand Up KC rallied, while police arrested about fifty more who had engaged in a sit-in that blocked a road near a McDonald's. One participant carried a sign stating, "I work at McDonald's and I'm going to jail for my five kids."[50] In New York City, police arrested protesters, including an eighty-one-year-old janitor who worked at McDonald's, for blocking traffic. Spreading civil disobedience that September led to the arrests of protesting workers in Chicago, Detroit, Las Vegas, and Little Rock. The growing movement's aim of publicly embarrassing the fast-food giants received another boost in October when activists released a recording of a McResources hotline staffer responding to a worker's request for financial help by giving her telephone numbers to inquire about Medicaid and food stamps.[51]

Political leaders obviously paid close attention to the plight of the fast-food and restaurant workers. In February 2013, President Obama suggested a national minimum of $9 an hour, tied to the cost of living. Democrats in the House and Senate responded by proposing a federal minimum wage of $10.10 an hour in their Fair Minimum Wage Act of 2013 and making the sub-minimum wage 70 percent of the minimum. Responding to the lobbying efforts of the National Restaurant Association, the Republican majority in the House voted unanimously to kill the bill.[52] Despite its failure, the Democratic minimum-wage bill galvanized even more workers to join the struggle, reaching a crescendo in July when sub-minimum wage restaurant employees joined fast-food workers and other low-paid workers in fifteen states and twenty-two cities for a National Day of Action to raise the minimum wage. The National Day of Action also marked the opening of a new ROC struggle to abolish the sub-minimum wage. Backed by the Restaurant Opportunities Center, a worker center supported by organized labor's Unite Here, New York City restaurant workers picketed a Manhattan bar, the Capital Grille, which is owned by Darden Restaurants. Demonstrators held signs saying "Can't Survive on Five," in protest of New York's $5 an hour minimum wage for tipped workers. They chose to rally in front of the Darden property because the corporation had used its vast resources to buy state legislators who would block proposed changes in the minimum wage law. The state's minimum wage was scheduled to reach $8 an hour, but tipped workers were not covered by the increase. "We think [Darden is] a key part of why the tipped minimum wage wasn't increased," an ROC organizer told a *Working in These Times* reporter.[53] The highlight of the new campaign's opening day occurred when several Capital Grille customers began chanting, "We can't stomach the injustice occurring in this restaurant."[54]

The Other NRA

The Fight for $15 and the struggle of full-service restaurant workers received active support from SEIU and UNITE HERE through the Restaurant Opportunities Center. But restaurant chains have a powerful political organization of their own that they rely on to crush the workers' struggle. With a revenue stream of $71 million in 2013, the National Restaurant Association (NRA), the trade association for the multi-billion-dollar restaurant industry, is what *SourceWatch* dubs a "lobbying powerhouse" and major political player on the national, state, and local levels of government. The NRA represents some 500,000 restaurant businesses and has more than 150 corporate members, including, most notably, McDonald's, YUM BRANDS, and Darden Restaurants, as well as all the other major food companies. According to the Center for Responsive Politics, the organization spent $4.7 million lobbying in 2013 and 2014.

The $4.7 million spent in 2013 and 2014 grossly understates the amount the industry spends lobbying. First, it does not include the 2013 political efforts of individual member firms that spent close to another $4.3 million, including McDonald's ($2.3 million), YUM BRANDS ($690,000), and Darden ($1.3 million).[55] Second, as Lee Fang documents in *The Nation*, on paper it appears that lobbying activities are decreasing in Washington. Thousands of Washington lobbyists are deregistering so that in 2013 the number of registered lobbyists—12,281—dipped to the lowest number since 2002. But experts believe this low number is grossly inaccurate because most of the political activities in Washington do not fall under the umbrella of the lobbying registration system. Professor James Thurber, an American University expert on congressional lobbying, estimates that the combination of legal loopholes, poor enforcement, and sophisticated strategies to avoid the law have driven the real number of lobbyists closer to 100,000. Thurber also thinks 2013 spending on lobbying was almost three times the official amount of $3.2 billion. Other experts generally concur with Thurber, suggesting the amount is at least twice the official number.[56]

The NRA's abundant financial resources allow it to employ thirty-seven in-house lobbyists, many of whom previously held top-level positions in government. The organization's financial resources also give it the ability to hire outside political assistance as needed. These outsiders sometimes come from the inner circles of the federal government, which further increases the NRA's ability to gain the ear of public policy makers. In 2013, following the first fast-food walkouts, the NRA brought in a number of outside lobbying and public relations firms to help fine-tune and deliver the industry's message to their former colleagues in government. The NRA and its members use their resources to achieve the industry's objectives in a number of ways. Obviously, they make generous donations to elected officials. In 2014, for instance, the organization gave $1,314,500 to candidates for Congress, with 74 percent going to Republicans. Given the NRA's "generosity" to elected officials, it should surprise no one that Republican House members staunchly oppose increasing the minimum wage. In fact, the NRA's political muscle played a primary role in keeping the federal sub-minimum wage at $2.13 an hour. The NRA donates to state politicians, too, contributing over $3 million between 1998 and 2014. In the early phases of the Fight for $15 movement, the association's political muscle at the state level blocked higher wage laws in a dozen states.[57] It also secured passage of preemption legislation—laws that prohibit municipalities from passing sick-day legislation—in eight of the fourteen states where the laws were introduced.[58] Just as important, the NRA monitors the agendas of state and local governments and uses its funds to fight specific state or local legislative initiatives, such as increases in the minimum wage, paid sick leave, the right to form a union, or just about anything else that might alleviate the poverty wages and poor working conditions endured by fast-food and restaurant workers.

The NRA and its individual member companies rely on their considerable financial and economic assets to keep the sub-minimum wage for restaurant workers at $2.13 hour and to successfully resist the Fight for $15. The NRA and its corporate members have a great deal of economic power, but that doesn't mean the fast-food and restaurant workers who lack economic power are powerless. Power, after all, is a relationship and, as the many foot soldiers involved in the Fight for $15 have demonstrated, the ability to organize large numbers of fed-up workers is a source of power too. Indeed, the power of significant numbers of organized employees can neutralize and even overcome the economic clout of the employers and their political arm. And that's what the Fight for $15 is gradually doing. Over the several years following the civil disobedience of 2013, the struggle continued to gain momentum. A turning point occurred in March of 2015 when the Fight for $15 leaders joined hundreds of others involved in low-wage struggles at the Reverend King's Ebenezer Baptist Church to convert the fast-food battle into a "national movement of all low-wage workers." In addition to a broad spectrum of low-wage workers and Fight for $15 leaders, the meeting included activists from Black Lives Matter and veterans from the civil rights struggle. This meeting, as labor law scholar Kate Andrias observes, demonstrated that the Fight for $15 campaign promotes the interests of all workers.[59] A month later, tens of thousands of workers, students, and activists took to the streets in 200 cities.[60]

The April action marked the movement's increased reliance on social media to garner public support. With limited resources to launch a nationwide media campaign, activists used the internet to reach "every phone and tablet and computer in the nation." The movement claimed to take over Twitter with tweets and trended in cities across the United States. Fight for $15 activists kept the pressure on between strikes with "email campaigns, creative digital video, targeted advertising and powerful social content."[61] The social media operation brought more supporters into the fight and built additional public support.

Now backed by an effective social media campaign, the demonstrations and protests increased as other worker organizations and unions—CWA, AFSCME, and Our Walmart—joined the Fight for $15 movement.[62] Continuing to emulate the nonviolent civil disobedience of the civil rights movement, fast-food workers conducted annual demonstrations and civil disobedience every April 4, the anniversary of Martin Luther King's assassination. The Fight for $15 has revived Dr. King's Poor People's Movement. As more people than ever before participated in an increasing number of demonstrations and protests often marked by the arrest of poorly paid fast-food workers, public opinion changed. According to a survey conducted by the Pew Research Center, by 2019 two-thirds of all Americans favored a $15-an-hour minimum wage.[63]

The goal of taking direct action and going to the streets, according to one SEIU organizer, was to create the perception of the Fight for $15 as "a large and growing movement creating a crisis," but the SEIU supplemented that perception by filing numerous charges of unfair labor practices with the NLRB. In July 2014, the Board, according to the *New York Times*, found merit in forty-three of 181 claims that McDonald's had penalized workers for their union activities.[64] Consequently, the NLRB's General Counsel, Richard E. Griffin Jr., ruled that the fast-food company was liable for labor and wage violations by its franchise operators. In short, McDonald's corporation was now a joint employer with the franchise operator. This meant that SEIU could organize workers on an industry-wide basis rather than store by store. McDonald's promised to appeal. The NRA claimed the decision "would have dire consequences to franchisees, franchise employers, and the economy as a whole."[65] The NRA's fear of a successful union organizing drive was short-lived. In 2019, Trump's NLRB reversed Griffin's ruling and McDonald's was once again not responsible for labor issues at the independent franchises.

Early on, the struggle for a decent wage became regional, with strikes and demonstrations held simultaneously in dozens of cities and towns in various geographical areas of the United States. Over time, the movement evolved, growing beyond the borders of the United States into 300 cities on six continents. Despite the movement's growth and influence, some opponents of the Fight for $15 view activists as more of a nuisance than a problem. One anti-worker lobbyist, Richard Berman, nicknamed Dr. Evil by his critics, is a public relations operative representing restaurant chains. Founder of the pro-corporate Employment Policy Institute, Berman attacks increases in the minimum wage in a number of ways, including full-page ads in the *New York Times* and the *Wall Street Journal* showing a large photo of Nancy Pelosi that reads, "Teens Who Can't Find a Job Should Blame Her."[66] According to the *New York Times*, the Institute employs a full-time economist who writes opinion pieces and letters to newspaper editors arguing against an increase in the minimum wage. Writing for the *Nation's Restaurant News*, an arm of the NRA, Berman declared that worker activism in the industry is just a fad that's not going to change public opinion.[67] But he is wrong.

Making Progress

The Fight for $15 is having an impact despite opposition from the National Restaurant Association and other pro-business lobbying groups. It has influenced public opinion, shaped the public discourse on the issue of "fair pay," and pressured elected officials to take action. Seven states—California, Connecticut, Illinois, Maryland, Massachusetts, New Jersey, and New York—along with Washington, DC, committed to a state minimum wage of $15 before 2015. Washington, DC, and twenty-four states, plus forty-eight cities, raised their minimum wage in 2020.[68] In November 2020, Florida voters approved a ballot initiative to set a $15 minimum wage. According to the Fight for $15 website, the number of cities and counties with a minimum wage of at least $15 doubled in 2020, jumping from sixteen to thirty-two. But that's not all. The struggle for sick pay is also finding some success. Ten states now have mandatory sick leave provisions and eighteen more are considering similar legislation.[69] On the national level, since gaining control of the House in 2018, Democrats annually passed a bill that phases out the sub-minimum wage and raises the federal minimum to $15 by 2025, but the Republican Senate majority leader made sure it never came up for a vote. House Democrats then attempted to raise the minimum wage through the American Rescue Plan Act of 2021, but this effort died again in the Senate when the Senate parliamentarian ruled that actions on minimum wage could not be included in budget legislation.

In capturing the public's attention and support, the Fight for $15—with the help of a healthy and almost full-employment economy—has already achieved much. While the $15 minimum wage continued to encounter roadblocks at the federal level, state and municipal governments have responded to the Fight for $15 by passing minimum-wage legislation that has put $68 billion into the pockets of low-wage American workers.[70] Like their fast-food colleagues, those sub-minimum-wage workers who depend on tips have yet to realize all their goals. The ROC joined the Fight for $15 to kill the sub-minimum wage, but its campaign hasn't received the degree of publicity and public support as that of fast-food employees. Nevertheless, thanks to the ROC and the collective efforts of thousands of fast-food and full-service restaurant workers, tipped workers are making steady progress toward achieving their goals.

The September 11 terrorist attack on the World Trade Center destroyed the Windows of the World restaurant on the 107th floor, killing seventy-three restaurant workers. The attack left another 300 without jobs and destroyed other eateries in the surrounding neighborhood. Many of the businesses that escaped the destruction soon closed their doors for lack of business, putting about 13,000 more restaurant workers on the unemployment lines. The Hotel Employees and Restaurant Employees (HERE) union stepped in and established a temporary relief center that provided emotional and financial assistance to displaced workers, along with a host of desperately needed services. As the need for assistance grew, HERE anted up the initial funds to finance the undertaking and appointed a staffer, Saru Jayaraman, and a former Windows of the World worker, Fekkak Mamdouth, to head the new organization. This is how the ROC—a powerful community-based workers center—was born.[71]

Funded primarily by grants from foundations, most notably the Ford Foundation, and unions, the ROC's initial mission was to organize restaurant workers and improve their working conditions. In the words of Saru Jayaraman, the organization's "first priority . . . was to advocate for displaced workers from Windows of the World."[72] But ROC's goal of helping displaced restaurant workers slowly evolved. In 2006, the organization opened its own cooperative restaurant, Colors, which served as a training center for restaurant workers. The organization's success in helping workers find new jobs eventually led restaurant workers from other cities to convince it to open chapters outside New York City. Two years after opening Colors, it launched the Restaurant Opportunities Center United, a worker center charged with protecting workers' rights and gaining a livable wage nationally. It now has more than 25,000 members in thirty states. ROC and its members fully participated in the Fight for $15, but focused primarily on workers in full-service restaurants. The worker center's influence continued to grow, reaching a high point on May Day, 2017, when it played an instrumental role in a nationwide rally against Trump's immigration policy and for "One Fair Wage." According to media reports, more than 300,000 demonstrators were expected to take to the streets in this mass action.[73] ROC has successfully taken on the NRA on a number of important issues, winning over thirteen workplace justice battles and recovering over $10 million in wage theft and discrimination cases. The organization scored a huge victory against Darden in 2012. After Darden attempted to circumvent the requirements of the Affordable Care Act by reducing workers' hours, ROC's Dignity at Darden campaign caused Darden's profits to drop by more than one-third. Within weeks the company backed off.[74] This successful campaign was mainly a public educational effort supported by a plethora of demonstrations and protests.

Dependence on tips for a living has its roots in the post–Civil War period when freed slaves took positions as servants, waiters, and railroad porters. Rather than paying formerly enslaved people a wage, employers urged patrons to tip the workers for their services. In 1966, Congress set a minimum base salary that combined with tips would bring workers up to the minimum wage. By 1991 the sub-minimum equaled 50 percent of the minimum at $2.13, but, as previously noted, it has remained at that amount since.[75] Thanks to the activism of ROC's members in cooperation with a wide spectrum of progressive community groups, restaurant workers are gradually realizing the goals of their One Fair Wage campaign. Working in conjunction with racial and gender justice groups, the many members of the Food Chain Workers Alliance, the New York Immigration Coalition, and former participants from the Occupy Wall Street movement, ROC has become a formidable opponent to the NRA. It even led the successful fight to block the appointment of Trump's nominee for Secretary of Labor, Andrew Pozder, the CEO of CKE Restaurants, the parent company of Hardees and Carl's Jr., and a vocal opponent of raising the minimum wage.

ROC has also met with some success in realizing the goals of One Fair Wage. Thanks in part to the organization's political efforts, over the past six years, half the states have taken some form of action to increase the minimum wage. The sub-minimum wage has also received much attention. Today, eighteen states still rely on the $2.13 federal standard, but seven have eliminated the sub-minimum wage, and twenty-six others—Washington, DC, included—have a two-tiered minimum above the $7.25 federal standard. But the struggle for One Fair Wage isn't over, and the battle lines appear muddled at times.[76] In Maine, for instance, the legislature removed the sub-minimum only to be greeted by protesting restaurant workers who believed the higher menu prices would drastically reduce their tips. New York's Department of Labor held hearings across the state on the removal of the sub-minimum. After hearing the testimony of hundreds of individuals, including food service workers who felt that a higher minimum wage would cut into their tips, the governor's executive action gave an exemption to employees in the hospitality industry. [77]

ROC's success in advocating for full-service restaurant workers makes the organization a prime target of pro-corporate forces. Its reliance on secondary boycotts, secondary picketing, and its state and federal lobbying activities, including its annual Counter Lobby Day in Washington, DC, led conservative critics to call for the removal of ROC's 501(C)(3) status and reclassify it as a labor union, a familiar charge made by the corporate sector against worker centers. The House Committee on Education and the Workforce subsequently investigated ROC to determine its status as a union, but the organization's status as a worker center remains unchanged. The House Oversight Committee probed the ROC's receipt of $275,000 from OSHA, but found no violations.[78] Republican members of Congress and the conservative media attacked ROC over working conditions at its Colors restaurants. When the restaurants failed to make a profit and closed, corporate spokespersons and the media pointed to the failure as proof that higher wages for restaurant workers wouldn't work.[79] Yet, the ultimate recognition of ROC's political clout might be best expressed by the fact that shutting down ROC is always one of the NRA's top five priorities.

Are the Gains Sustainable?

SEIU backed the Fight for $15 to the tune of at least $70 million. On one level, the union's commitment has brought success beyond the expectations of most of the struggle's original participants. McDonald's recently announced it will no longer resist the $15 minimum, and the U.S. Chamber of Commerce signaled it too could accept a minimum wage hike. Target, Disney, and Amazon have already increased their minimum to $15. In the meantime, states and localities across the nation are raising the minimum wage, passing sick leave legislation, and addressing the pressing economic issues of tipped workers. Perhaps the most obvious success of the movement is how it joined the struggles of Occupy Wall Street and Bernie Sanders' presidential campaign to change the public discourse about the U.S. economy. Thanks in large part to this loosely knit coalition of activists, public discussion of the economy now focuses on economic inequality, and public opinion now backs a $15-per-hour minimum wage. But the victories raise a series of important questions. First, how sustainable are they? Will a $15 minimum wage lead to loss of jobs and hours worked, as NRA spokespeople claim? Or does the evidence suggest that the restaurant industry can absorb a higher minimum wage without a massive displacement of its labor force? Will a decent minimum wage hurt tipped workers because customers tip less as the minimum wage increases? Since SEIU sought to unionize fast-food and restaurant workers when it launched the Fight for a Fair Economy, what are the union's chances for success? Is unionization essential, as some observers claim, to sustain the momentum of the struggle and secure the gains already achieved?

If a $15 minimum wage and the elimination of the sub-minimum are harmful to both businesses and employees, as the NRA contends, the $15 minimum wage would not be sustainable. But the data contradict the NRA's claims. Paul Wolfson and Dale Bellman, for instance, analyzed thirty-seven studies on the economic impact of the minimum wage on employment and found that job loss was "very small."[80] Research by the Economic Policy Institute finds that studies focusing on job loss due to an increase in the minimum wage are misleading because they ignore the larger picture: higher earnings pump more money into the economy, which in turn generates more jobs.[81] According to studies by the ROC and EPI, tipped workers need not fear that an increase in the minimum will reduce their income. Historical experience indicates that not only do restaurants prosper, but tipped workers also earn more when the minimum wage is raised.[82] The bottom line: the Fight for a $15 minimum wage is not going to destroy the fast-food or restaurant business. The struggle for a $15 minimum wage is, in fact, reasonable and economically sustainable.

Workers involved in the struggle had two goals. In addition to a $15 minimum wage they also wanted a union. The Fight for $15 would have died quickly without the backing of SEIU. In addition to spending upward of $70 million on the campaign, the SEIU provided professional organizers, lobbyists, and public relations experts to assist in the campaign to organize an entire industry. In fact, SEIU did so much to promote the Fight for $15 that critics complained the union's approach was not member driven. Instead, they claim, staff played the dominant role and the entire campaign was too top-down.[83] In any case, SEIU's Fight for $15 campaign hasn't brought much success in union building. SEIU originally created fast-food workers committees to unionize the industry on a local basis, but subsequently replaced these local committees with a new organization, the SEIU National Fast Food Workers Union (NFFWU). In its 2018 filing to the DOL, the NFFWU reported having zero members.

CUNY sociologist Frances Fox Piven applauds SEIU for its role in the Fight for $15 battle. But she cautions, "It's not a unionizing campaign . . . Low-wage workers in the United States are searching for a source of worker's power—power against their immediate opponent, the boss."[84] After all, it's the boss, not some legislative body, who decides your work schedule, when and if you get a coffee or bathroom break, and all the other important details that workers face on the job every day. That's one reason workers want a union. Union organizer and author Jane McAlevey, a former student of Piven's, goes further. McAlevey argues that worker power is dependent on well-organized unions capable of waging long-term strikes. The fundamental power of workers, she reminds us, is their collective ability to withhold their labor power. Consequently, the activities of the Fight for $15 Movement are little more than public relations stunts that rely on "protests borrowing the name 'strike.'"[85] There's also the precarious nature of legislative wins. As labor activist and scholar Bill Fletcher observes, "If the political winds shift, minimum wage laws could get repealed or reversed."[86] That's the crucial difference between legislative power and the workers' power that comes with unionization. Is it possible to channel the vitality of the Fight for $15 into a struggle for worker power on the job site in a resurgent union movement?

Organizing fast-food and restaurant workers, always a difficult task, became tougher when the Trump NLRB ruled that McDonald's is not a joint employer. This ruling means that organizing must take place at a store-by-store rather than industry-wide basis. Organizers also must confront the issue of a 150 percent turnover rate in fast-food jobs. This turnover rate makes unionizing almost impossible. Sociologist Ruth Milkman observes that "by the time you get around to organizing folks, they're not on the job anymore."[87] Yet, the $15 minimum wage could reduce the turnover rate and provide a modicum of employment stability favorable to organizing.

An alternative to traditional organizing is voluntary recognition. The Fight for $15 struggle has damaged the public image of fast-food chains and continues to do so. It has also secured a decent minimum wage and other benefits in some regions of the country. This could provide a foundation for unions, SEIU in particular, to seek regionally based industry-wide bargaining similar to the European model of sectoral bargaining. But the question remains: can the movement keep the pressure on fast-food chains until their business drops off and they're ready to recognize some form of collective bargaining? SEIU amped up its own pressure campaign in a number of ways. It played an important role in getting the European Union to investigate McDonald's alleged avoidance of $1 billion in tax payments by funneling money into a Luxembourg subsidiary. The union also worked with Brazil's labor federation to sue McDonald's largest Latin American franchise for wage theft and unsanitary conditions. Still, restaurant profits remain stable and McDonald's and other fast-food giants remain opposed to union representation.[88] Pressuring McDonald's is no easy task since the company makes mega profits through its extensive real estate holdings. According to labor historian Annelise Orleck, the fast-food giant took advantage of the Great Recession by buying up real estate at bargain prices, making it "one of the largest real estate companies on earth." Some observers even claim that McDonald's is a real estate giant "financed by burgers and fries."[89]

It's unlikely that SEIU or any other union will organize fast-food and restaurant workers in the near future. Such is the changing nature of labor struggles in the twenty-first century. The financial and organizational power of SEIU and other unions helped launch a campaign that took to the streets, changed the public dialogue, and made significant gains for some of the most exploited laborers in the workforce. But these fast-food workers don't have a traditional contract with their employer detailing the terms and conditions of employment. They aren't conducting their battles behind closed doors at a negotiations table. Instead, they are waging their battle in the streets as they appeal to justice and fairness. Critics on both the left and right of the political spectrum view the struggle as little more than a public relations campaign with mixed substantive results.[90] But they appear to misunderstand the changes taking place in the American labor movement. While union density numbers continue their decline, support for the Fight for $15 continues to grow, suggesting it is an evolving class-based movement that may someday soon reshape the American political arena as it takes its fight to state and local legislatures instead of the bargaining table.

Economic and workplace conditions were already rough for food service workers when the Covid-19 pandemic hit the restaurant industry like a tsunami. "If Restaurants Disappear, What Happens to Cities?"—that November 2020 headline in the business section of the *New York Times* captures the impact of Covid-19 on restaurant and fast-food workers.[91] For a time, restaurants in many states were mandated to close entirely, then reopened with limited seating, and fast-food sales plummeted as customers stayed home. By May 2020 almost six million workers in the restaurant industry lost their jobs.[92] Millions of these laid-off workers were already living on the fringe of the economy, barely earning enough to put food on the table, and most lack health insurance. Despite the massive drop in business, the industry faced a worker shortage as many chose to leave their jobs rather than risk exposure to the virus. Even when McDonald's and later the Darden chain addressed the worker shortage by offering up to fourteen days sick leave for hourly employees under quarantine, they still couldn't attract enough workers.[93] As more restaurant workers slipped into poverty, they continued their political struggle. Fifty sub-minimum-wage Darden workers who depended on tips walked off their jobs in New York City in September 2020 over management practices that discriminated against women and people of color by assigning them low-occupancy tables that generated fewer tips. Saru Jayaraman, president of One Fair Wage, buoyed by success in getting Darden to provide sick days, emphasized the organization's commitment to keep upping the pressure on Darden to force the company to eliminate the sub-minimum wage.[94] Restaurant and fast-food workers in the Fight for $15 campaign were vital participants in get-out-the-vote drives to elect 2020 candidates who supported a higher minimum wage and expansion of health coverage. As the pandemic slowly abated in 2021, restaurants began reopening, more and more people were fully vaccinated, and work-ers returned to their jobs. While Democrats are still committed to raising the minimum wage, they lack the votes to overcome a filibuster in the Senate, so the Fight for $15 has returned to the streets.

Chapter 7

All Roads Lead to . . .
Sectoral Bargaining?

What is the future of the American labor movement? That is the basic question this book has been examining. Traditional trade unionism and decades-old labor laws are woefully inadequate to meet new labor realities in the twenty-first century. Many workers in the new economy don't even have the right to collective bargaining. With a new militancy, exploited workers have taken to the streets to seek political remedies instead. In other words, the political arena is replacing the bargaining table.

This concluding chapter proposes a roadmap for what workers must do to revitalize the American labor movement. It's a roadmap paved with countless small victories over time that give workers hope by engaging them in winnable collective struggles before arriving at the final destination: sectoral bargaining. What, then, is sectoral bargaining? In their article "What Is Sectoral Bargaining?" David Madland and Malkie Wall give a concise definition: "Sectoral bargaining—also known as multiemployer, industrywide, or broad-based bargaining—is a form of collective bargaining that provides contract coverage and sets compensation floors for most workers in a particular occupation, industry, or region."[1]

But why sectoral bargaining? First, there's a reason most of the groups studied in this book have taken direct action to the streets. They work in industries that are almost impossible to unionize on a shop-by-shop basis. Contacting workers, often part-timers, who move from job to job is difficult. How do you get workers to sign authorization cards when you can't find them or you're blocked from talking to them in the workplace? On their part, many workers fear losing their jobs or other retaliation by their employer. A case in point: SEIU has tried to organize McDonald's for years, despite such obstacles. Then it encountered a fundamental legal challenge whose resolution affects not only McDonald's workers but all workers: who is their employer? In 2012, McDonald's franchises across the country fired numerous employees who participated in Fight for $15 demonstrations. In 2014, the Obama NLRB issued complaints against McDonald's and its franchises and took the case to court in 2015. At issue was the question of whether the McDonald's parent company was a joint employer with its franchises. The case lingered on until late 2019, when the now-Trump NLRB ruled that McDonald's isn't liable for the employment practices of its franchises.[2] This saga illustrates that even when workers have the right to organize under federal laws, enforcement of their fundamental rights is subject to the political vicissitudes of the NLRB. Should the PRO Act become law, it will allow workers to unionize whether they are classified as employees or not, including the subjects of this book, and remove a lot of the legal obstacles to organizing. But the difficulties of organizing one workplace at a time still remain.

Establishing sectoral bargaining as the new norm for labor relations requires big structural changes to our political institutions and to organized labor. One foundational change is to secure a comprehensive national economic and social safety net like those of industrial democracies of western Europe. The workers chronicled in this book have used their developing political clout to achieve some economic security, but it is fragmented, localized, and often minimal. And as the Covid-19 pandemic shows, the safety-net strategy of tying benefits to employment creates a system that is all holes, not netting, when people lose their jobs. Second, the growing coalition of non-union activists, organized labor, and community groups must reform federal labor law to remove obstructions to organizing, lessen the restrictions of Taft-Hartley, and remove road blocks to sectoral bargaining, which the PRO Act aims to do. Third, changes to our political institutions are not enough. Unions must face the fact that competing for members is not the answer to the long-term survival of the union movement. Organized labor needs to unify around common ground. This can be achieved through informal agreements or through restructuring, mergers, and streamlining, but the internecine wars must stop.

A New Movement Brings Old Answers

The political struggle waged by members of direct action movements has achieved some local and statewide success, but it is still in its early stages.

Initial victories highlight what non-union workers and organized labor can achieve by working toward a common goal. The past several decades make clear that organized labor has not been able to right its internal failings or exert sufficient power to effect the political changes it needs to survive and prosper. Similarly, tens of millions of low-wage workers are unlikely to realize their goals without access to the resources of unions. As Larry Cohen, the former president of CWA, notes, "[T]he challenge is how to focus more effectively on the 90 million workers left out of collective bargaining, realizing that more than ever . . . unions cannot realize major gains on their own."[3]

The strategies that worked so well for organized labor in the immediate post–World War II period do not work in our modern economy. There is no better contrast between then and now than the failed union drive by Amazon warehouse workers in Bessemer, Alabama. In March 2021, workers voted two to one against unionization. Amazon's scorched earth campaign against the Retail, Wholesale and Department Store Union (RWDSU) succeeded, in part, because of the strong corporate bias of existing labor law and the weak enforcement of what few protections organizers have. Amazon's high employee turnover rate no doubt contributed to the union's loss, mirroring the difficulties of unionizing workers in the fast-food industry. But in America's increasingly inegalitarian economy, workers are so beaten down that instead of getting angry, they're happy to accept crumbs, such as the many Amazon workers who were willing to trade a $15-an-hour wage and health benefits for sixty-hour weeks and urinating in bottles on the warehouse floor. Alec MacGillis, author of *Fulfillment: Winning and Losing in One-Click America*, summed up his interviews with Amazon workers opposed to unionizing: "What comes through is their incredibly low expectations, like, "It's just a job that will pay $15 an hour, that's basically enough for this kind of entry-level work, better than fast food, I'm probably not going to be here long anyway."[4] David Rolf in his excellent book *The Fight for $15* reminds readers that over the past fifty years legislative attempts to restore organized labor's bargaining power have failed.[5] Even if the combined political clout of unions and direct action groups somehow secures the enactment of the PRO Act, it is not the panacea for growth unions think it is because organized labor is still geared to enterprise organizing. As previously noted, negotiating shop by shop does not represent the reality of the new workforce. But the industry-wide legislative victories of California's gig drivers and activists engaged in the Fight for $15 movement provide clues to a fruitful path to sectoral bargaining.

Sectoral bargaining is not a new idea. It exists throughout most democratic European countries and is, in the words of SEIU president Mary Kay Henry, "unions for all." Rather than traditional enterprise organizing on a workplace-by-workplace basis, sectoral bargaining involves multiple employers and covers all workers in a given labor market or even in entire industries.[6] American labor law currently restricts sectoral bargaining by prohibiting unions from combining bargaining units without the consent of employers. Sectoral bargaining sets uniform wages and benefits industry-wide, ensuring conformity in labor costs in both union and non-union workplaces. It has a number of advantages over enterprise bargaining. Industry wide conformity of labor costs encourages firms to compete by increasing productivity, rather than cutting wages and benefits in a race to the bottom. This broad-based bargaining approach brings more workers under the umbrella of collective bargaining and ends gender, racial, and regional pay differentials.

According to the Center for American Progress, sectoral bargaining might even ease employer resistance to union organizing. With a floor on labor costs set by sectoral bargaining, unions or other worker organizations—worker centers—would still negotiate "shop floor" issues, including work rules, due process, and steps for promotion.[7] The United States is no stranger to the practice of informal structural or broad-based bargaining. In the post–World War II period, as Larry Cohen observes, unions in some manufacturing industries, such as auto, rubber, and steel, engaged in pattern bargaining on wages and benefits for the entire industry, a practice that mirrored sectoral bargaining. But industry-wide bargaining lacked legal sanctions, and the rise of new anti-union companies, attacks on organized labor, and economic globalization have virtually eliminated the practice in most industries.[8]

Still, the growing political clout of the direct action movements opens the possibility of attaining sectoral bargaining in the United States. The 2018 teacher walkouts in Arizona, Kentucky, Oklahoma, and West Virginia culminated in negotiations with state legislatures as opposed to separate school districts. Teachers rallied not only for higher wages and better terms and conditions of employment, but for adequate funding for their public schools.[9] And the Fight for $15 won a vitiated form of sectoral bargaining in 2015 when Governor Cuomo instructed New York's labor commissioner to create a Fast-Food Wage Board. Consisting of a representative from SEIU, a member of the business community, and Buffalo's mayor as a public representative, the board recommended a $15 minimum wage over a six-year period.[10]

The Roots of the Direct Action Movements

In order to understand why sectoral bargaining is the logical next development in direct action movements, we need to understand the relationship between the rise of direct action movements and the decline of organized labor. Thanks to a corporate war on unions and the restructuring of the U.S. economy, when it comes to union membership in the United States there's a growing schism between what American workers want and what they get. Today about half of all non-unionized workers say they would join a union if they had the opportunity to do so.[11] Unfortunately, most don't get that opportunity. Union density in the private sector has collapsed to 6.2 percent, which means that only about one of every sixteen workers belong to a union. In the public sector, union density remains high, at 33.6 percent, but the Supreme Court's *Janus* decision and Republican lawmakers' hostility to unions are likely to reduce that in the coming years.[12]

Why non-union workers support unions is understandable. Compared to union workers, non-union workers earn less and are more likely to live in poverty; benefits such as health care and paid sick and vacation time exist only in their imaginations, and a lot of bad things can happen if the boss is in a bad mood. In non-union shops the boss has almost complete control of the labor process, including the power to deny bathroom or rest breaks, or to punish a worker with an undesirable work assignment or inconvenient schedule. If that's not bad enough, bosses have the right to fire any employee at will. In contrast, union jobs pay more, provide better benefits, and generally come with a modicum of job security. Union workers, with due process, do not have to worry about arbitrarily getting fired because the boss is having a bad day or has a son-in-law looking for a job. Unions also give workers a collective voice in the political process, allowing them to countervail the power of the corporate sector, especially by getting out the vote on election day.

Unions are on the bubble because of an increasing disparity in power between them and the corporate sector. Two simple principles provide a key to understanding this growing power gap. The first is basic to private enterprise: Capital seeks its most profitable outlet. Investors invest with the purpose of maximizing profit. They may, for example, move production overseas or cut production costs by introducing labor-saving technology. There is almost no end to their cost-savings options. The second principle is what often allows capital to seek its most profitable outlet: capital is mobile, but labor is stationary. American companies that move their productive facilities overseas to cut labor costs leave American workers unemployed back home looking for almost any kind of work. In the 1950s, Eisenhower was on the mark when he warned against the rising military-industrial complex, but in the twenty-first century, finance capital now drives our economy.

By the 1970s, after years of benefiting from oligopolistic market structures and all the economic practices that go with controlled markets, U.S. companies faced stiff competition from foreign producers. One response of the American corporate sector was what Bluestone and Harrison call deindustrialization. Unable to compete with more efficient, low-cost foreign producers, U.S. companies closed domestic plants and fled to foreign sites that offered cheap labor and tax havens. Deindustrialization killed tens of thousands of good union jobs. That was just the start of organized labor's decline. Outsourcing union jobs to union-free companies both at home and abroad became a standard corporate practice, displacing thousands more union workers. But corporate offshoring and outsourcing wasn't enough. American corporations declared war on organized labor. According to Heidi Shierholz of the Economic Policy Institute, research suggests that the corporate sector's widespread reliance on aggressive anti-union drives is a crucial cause of the decline of unions.[13] Ronald Reagan's firing of PATCO workers symbolizes the attack on organized labor, but a hostile NLRB, failure to enforce labor rights, legal barriers against organizing, the threat of plant closings, growing dependence on robotics, and the corporate focus on short-term gains all crippled unions and broke the back of America's middle class. And let's not forget the failure of Democrats to pass the Employee Free Choice Act when they controlled both houses in Congress and the presidency in 2008–2010. Thanks in large part to the decline of unions, the middle class is not only losing ground, it barely exists.[14] In short, the United States is no longer a middle-class nation.

Corporate flight and the disappearance of high-paying union jobs helped reshape the U.S. economy. In 1970, manufacturing industries employed more than a quarter of the U.S. workforce. Today less than 10 percent work in manufacturing.[15] The United States remains an important global manufacturing force, but the contemporary American economy is driven by the service sector. Most Americans—about 80 percent—now work in the service economy. The great majority of these jobs are non-union, pay very little, do not provide basic benefits, and offer little or no job security. The decline of unions and the transformation of the economy have resulted in levels of economic inequality not seen since before the Great Depression and have created an underclass that functions on the edge of poverty. To understand this gap better, consider this: in 2018, while almost 30 percent of American households earned below $35,000, the average annual income of the top 1 percent was $1,320,000.[16]

The Bumpy Road to Sectoral Bargaining

Most observers agree that the struggles waged by the groups examined in this book have brought positive results, but there is no consensus on the significance of these battles. On the one hand, most concur that the direct action movements have engendered a tremendous amount of public support that galvanized major legislative victories. Consider, for example, the public's attitude regarding a $15-an-hour minimum wage. Ten years ago, a $15 minimum wage was unthinkable; now it's a reality for millions of low-wage workers. And now its embrace of worker centers as partners rather than competitors has pushed the AFL-CIO a little further to the left on the political spectrum.[17] Now the AFL-CIO executive board includes a worker center member.

Today, almost all labor supporters applaud the protesting workers for their innovative efforts in organizing and their success in bringing the plight of exploited workers to the public. But that's where the consensus ends. Disagreements emerge concerning the significance of these movements and whether they are revitalizing the labor movement. SEIU president Mary Kay Henry, for instance, believes that the legislative victories of non-union workers is opening the way for sectoral bargaining. Sectoral bargaining, the model many European democracies use, allows unions to bargain for all workers in a single industry regardless of union membership. This explains why SEIU has spent millions on the Fight for $15 campaign without recruiting new members. Others claim the wage and job protections won by the protesters are too precarious without the security and protections offered by collective bargaining and backed by organized labor. Still others distinguish between legislative power and worker power on the job and claim that workers must unionize to gain real control of the workplace.[18] No one states this position more clearly than Jane McAlevey, who writes, "It's only . . . when workers decide to harness their only real power—coming together in unity, as a union—that their lives will improve."[19] Before evaluating these assertions, it's important to critically review the achievements of the direct action movements in light of their stated goals.

Florida's tomato pickers and New York's farmworkers have both done well. Neither group has realized all its objectives, but the Immokalee workers have come closest to fulfilling their agenda. These workers—the subject of the documentary *Harvest of Shame*—were grossly underpaid, victimized by wage theft and sexual assault, exposed to hazardous chemicals, occasionally beaten by the field boss, and often required to live in substandard housing. Some were even forced into slavery. Today, thanks to their collective efforts through the CIW, the workers have gained what amounts to nearly a 75 percent wage increase. Of equal importance, they also made remarkable improvements in their working and living conditions. They brought the issue of modern-day slavery into the public's consciousness. And they did all this without any governmental intervention. Instead of trying to get conservative Florida state legislators to address the issues of this mainly migrant workforce, the CIW successfully used a variety of tactics, including secondary boycotts and picketing, to pressure big buyers and growers to address their needs. But how secure are these victories?

Since the gains won by the CIW are not sanctioned by the legislature or backed by a union contract, they are sustainable only as long as the workers can maintain their pressure on the big buyers. In what might signal the fragility of CIW's future, tomato buyers from Wendy's continue to refuse to participate in the agreement. Instead of buying tomatoes from U.S. growers, Wendy's purchases its tomatoes from Mexican growers. After all, their thinking goes, do Americans really care about working conditions in Mexico? If Wendy's approach continues to work and other buyers decide to follow suit, the agreements could collapse and CIW could very easily lose its gains.

New York's farmworkers are doing better now too, but their struggle is only beginning. With much union support and the active backing of the faith community and other progressive groups, the state legislature finally enacted legislation recognizing farmworkers as employees under the New York State Employment Relations Act (NYSERA), which gives them the right to collective bargaining. The new law also provides for overtime pay after sixty hours with a pathway to forty hours, a day of rest every week, eligibility for workers' compensation and disability benefits, and unemployment insurance coverage. The legislation protects farmworkers who file injury claims from reprisals and requires employers to post notices regarding workers compensation obligations in both Spanish and English.[20]

In view of the terrible working conditions New York's farmworkers experienced for decades, these are significant gains. As of this writing, just months after the workers won the right to unionize, potential problems are already surfacing. The challenges inherent in organizing a migrant workforce under the best of circumstances make the chances of a successful organizing campaign difficult enough. But the possibility of different unions engaging in jurisdictional battles threatens to complicate the effort before it even begins. According to Rural & Migrant Ministry board member Alan Lubin, the Retail Clerks International Union (RCIU) and the United Food and Commercial Workers—two unions that have supported the farmworkers' struggle—have agreed to jointly organize the farmworkers in cooperation with the RMM.[21] Since unions are hard pressed to increase membership numbers, others are getting involved too. The United Farm Workers, for instance, also wants the opportunity to organize these workers. And SEIU's powerful 1199 local, a non–AFL-CIO affiliate, has expressed interest. The time wasted in competing for membership weakens the momentum that came with the law's passage and could undercut workers' support for collective bargaining. Some farmworkers in this largely migrant population already look at unions with suspicion, fearing that the overtime pay provision threatens to reduce their working hours and, consequently, their paychecks. Organizing under these conditions is a long-term project with no guarantee of success.

The farmworkers may or may not achieve their goal of unionizing. Nevertheless, thanks to the unions and other groups, they now enjoy important legal protections. Since the New York State Assembly is expected to remain under Democratic control for the foreseeable future, the legislature isn't likely to weaken or repeal the Farm Laborers Fair Labor Practices Act. That gives New York's farmworkers security the Immokalee workers lack. Yet one caveat is in order. Legislative repeal of the law may be unlikely, but the courts will still have an important say about the law's future. Two days before the law took effect, the New York State Vegetable Growers Association and the Northeast Dairy Producers Association, who claim to accept its basic tenets, challenged sections of the law in federal court.[22] However, in July 2020, the U.S. District Court Western District of New York denied their challenge.[23]

In the gig economy much tension exists between those who want flexibility and others who demand employee status with all its legal rights and professional obligations. This tension illustrates the complexity of the gig economy and the difficulty in finding politically workable legislative solutions. After lengthy battles on the streets and in the courts, California's rideshare drivers won what appeared to be a major victory with the passage and eventual enactment of California's AB5 law, a law that classified them and other gig workers as employees. Prior to that, rideshare companies like Uber and Lyft had misclassified them as independent contractors, making drivers responsible for the costs of doing business without any of the benefits granted to traditional employees. In an arrangement most beneficial to the companies, drivers lacked basic governmental protections such as a minimum wage, unemployment insurance, and workers compensation, but they had to pay for all the expenses of doing business. Drivers paid for the car, insurance, gasoline, repairs, and anything else needed to take customers to their destination, even though the rideshare companies basically controlled and dictated the way they perform these services. The reclassification law took effect on January 1, 2020, but its spotty implementation and the desire of many drivers to work as "real" independent contractors undermine any claims to victory. Not surprisingly, the rideshare companies refused to follow the law's requirements. In fact, they successfully used their vast resources to gain passage of Prop 22, which exempted them from AB5. In the meantime, as discussed in chapter 5, California's AB5 provides no relief for rideshare drivers, who still shoulder the obligations of independent contractors.

Opposition to the law is widespread and not limited to the rideshare companies. In addition to the legal challenges filed by Lyft and Uber, at least six other pending legal cases now question the legality of the law. Opposition to the law has galvanized much legislative activity, leading to the introduction of almost three dozen bills in the state legislature directed at modifying the new law. The majority of the bills seek exemptions for different occupations, including truck drivers, freelance writers, photographers, and pharmacists, but some would suspend or repeal AB5 altogether. One Democratic legislator introduced a bill that creates a third category of workers in addition to employee or independent contractor.[24] Despite a judge's rejection of Uber's and Postmates' application to temporarily prevent AB5 from taking effect, the ride companies continued to flaunt the law while they awaited the public's election day decision on the fate of their Proposition 22. In its quest for an exemption from the law, Uber made changes that it claims would give drivers sufficient control over their jobs so they meet the criteria of independent contractors. These changes allow drivers to know their destinations in advance, give them more leeway in rejecting rides, and provide drivers with some control in setting fares.[25] Edward Escobar, the leader of the Alliance for Independent Workers, dismisses these changes as "show business" because they are inconsequential and much too limited to have any real impact.[26]

A sizeable number of drivers already believe that collective bargaining will lead to better wages and working conditions, so the passage of Prop 22 creates an opportunity for unions to build even more support among drivers.[27] Since AB5 was not self-enforcing, workers or their representatives had to file claims charging the companies with labor law violations for the Labor Commissioner to adjudicate. With an eye on organizing drivers, the Transport Workers Union intervened to help workers file the claims.[28] Other unions interested in organizing, most notably the Teamsters and SEIU, also offered assistance. Unfortunately for union organizers, under Prop 22, drivers are not classified as employees and are therefore not covered by the NLRB. The Biden-backed PRO Act, which as of this writing is pending in the U.S. Senate, would not reclassify drivers as employees, but would give them the right to form a union.

New York City's Independent Drivers Guild offers a model for limited collective bargaining, but California's gig drivers have previously rejected that option. Besides, given the secret negotiations between some unions and the companies during the AB5 struggle, many drivers still mistrust organized labor.[29] Escobar claims that some drivers mistrust the motives of unions and want to be classified as legitimate independent contractors. In fact, he adds, "There are two things the drivers want least, unions and employee status."[30] In addition to many drivers not trusting unions and others wanting to be seen as legitimate independent contractors, the majority of drivers work part-time making it extraordinarily difficult for organizers to identify and contact them. Finally, unions lack consensus on how best to organize the drivers. Some unions want industry-wide sectoral bargaining; others aim for smaller bargaining units.

Despite its demise in California, AB5 started a national movement, a movement limited so far to states dominated by the Democratic Party. Thanks to the efforts of California's gig drivers, drivers in Illinois, New Jersey, and New York managed to get similar legislation on their state's political agenda. The proposed laws have already triggered resistance from gig workers in a variety of occupations who want exemptions, particularly truck drivers and freelancers in the creative economy. As of this writing, legislators in these states have not given up on the idea of reclassifying some gig workers as employees. They just need to decide what occupations to exempt. Meanwhile, the rideshare companies are prepared to launch Prop 22-style attacks when any state allowing ballot initiatives passes an AB5-type law.

Among the groups this book examines, the Freelancers Union is the outlier. Jurisdictional battles, strikes, and civil disobedience are not part of this organization's story. Nevertheless, Freelancers Union founder Sara Horowitz believes her organization embodies the future of the labor movement, even though it never bargains directly with employers. She bases her assertion on the rising number of freelance workers in the labor force and on the Union's delivery of services through what she calls the new mutualism, cooperative-like entrepreneurial solutions to address free-lancers' interests. There is no doubt that the Freelancers Union provides its members with a wide range of services and effective political advocacy. It is a valuable and useful organization. But is it in itself a viable model for a new labor movement? The short answer is no.

The answer is no for several reasons. First, as discussed in chapter 5, the number of gig workers in the labor force is overstated. Horowitz and others claim that about fifty million workers toil in the gig econ-omy. But this number includes part-timers and counts those who con-tract with more than one company each time they get a new assignment in the course of a year. An EPI study suggests that the real number is around eleven million, and the Bureau of Labor Statistics concludes that the number of gig workers is actually shrinking.[31] More important than the numbers is the organization's underlying model. The practice of new mutualism is based on the concept of mutual aid rooted deeply in the American experience. Horowitz rightly points to the work of Sidney Hillman as her avatar. Much like the organizations created by Hillman, the Freelancers Union does much good for its constituents. Yet over the years similar voluntary organizations have made major contributions to American workers and their families without significantly changing the labor movement. The Union's long-range goal of providing an adequate social safety net to freelancers hasn't yet materialized, mainly because social safety nets are the responsibility of government. During the Great Depression, Sidney Hillman rejected voluntarism for a political solution by turning to the political arena and becoming an architect of Roosevelt's New Deal. The Freelancers Union attained some of its most important victories in the political arena, too. But these legislative victories were largely confined to New York City, where the bulk of the organization's members live.

When it comes to building coalitions and creating public support for exploited workers that result in legislative action, the Fight for $15 and the One Fair Wage campaign are models for others to emulate. These closely coordinated struggles successfully address the important issues of wage theft, violence and safety on the job, sexual harassment, paid sick leave, and a decent minimum wage. As of 2019, the Fight for $15 had put $68 billion into the pockets of low-wage workers. Fast-food workers and tipped restaurant workers are winning legislative victories through a nationwide campaign that directs their bargaining at an entire industry in the public arena, rather than at the bargaining table. The Restaurant Opportunities Center (ROC), working closely with the Fight for $15 campaign, speaks for full-service restaurant workers. These two organizations are part of a larger coalition involved in the Fight for $15. Our Walmart, Black Lives Matter, AFSCME, and CWA also seek worker justice under the banner of the Fight for $15. ROC's membership in the Food Chain Workers Alliance connects the movement to a numerically powerful coalition consisting of several unions and worker centers. The United Food and Commercial Workers, the Teamsters, and UNITE HERE are all involved in the struggle, as are the Coalition of Immokalee Workers, Organization United for Respect at Walmart, the International Labor-Rights Forum, Fair World Project, and the Brand Workers International.

The broad-based coalition that brought important legislative wins for restaurant workers has also gained important concessions from the fast-food companies and their business allies. McDonald's announcement that it would not resist a $15-per-hour minimum wage is a major breakthrough, as was the company's willingness to provide employee sick leave when faced with Covid-19–induced workforce shortages.[32] Another possible breakthrough is the U.S. Chamber of Commerce's signal that it too might accept a hike in the minimum wage. Clearly, the direct action protests taken by workers across the country have shifted debate about the economy from the virtues of supply-side economics to the growing problems of income inequality. Public opinion now supports a higher minimum wage, and the Fight for $15 struggle has become part of a new political crusade tied to the former Occupy Wall Street movement and the progressive politics associated with Bernie Sanders, Elizabeth Warren, Alexandria Ocasio-Cortez, and others. Unions provide worker power at the point of production, but these new political movements are now giving workers significant legislative power. How these two roads merge is now the question.

A Viable New Partnership?

The victories won by the direct action groups studied here are impressive but incomplete. They tend to be regional, or, with the exception of the Immokalee Workers, restricted to blue states. These groups are responding to a variety of different issues, too, as they emerge from many different occupations. The only thing they have in common is that they are all exploited. What, if anything, ties these groups together then? The Fight for $15, full-service restaurant staff, and California's gig workers resist the structural changes in the economy by fighting for a decent wage and the right to unionize. The Freelancers Union takes a very different approach. Rather than contest the economic changes leading to a rise in gig work, the Union accepts the inevitability of change and works to cushion its impact. Unlike California's gig workers who fought for the reclassification of contract workers as employees, the Freelancers Union provides the benefits and services that traditional employees enjoy. The Immokalee Workers and New York's farmworkers are attempting to right the wrongs of the racist policies that excluded them from the New Deal's labor protections.

All these organizations come together through worker centers, a new operational arm of the non-union sector of the labor movement. Now worker centers are even an essential part of the AFL-CIO's New Strategic Initiative. Worker centers circumvent legal prohibitions barring unions from using secondary boycotts, mass and secondary picketing, and a host of other tactics unionized workers are legally barred from using. It is no surprise that anti-labor conservatives see worker centers as front organizations for unions and continually try to place them under the same restrictive laws and regulations that govern unions. Worker centers are not unions, but they depend on organized labor for financial and professional support. With the exception of the Freelancers Union, which generates income by using grant money to start new entrepreneurial services and then selling the services back to its members, all the other protest organizations depend on unions for support. Organized labor's support of worker centers runs the gamut from providing organizers and financing their campaigns to financing their entire operation. SEIU, for instance, foots the bill for the Fight for $15 campaign. Dependence on unions for fiscal support threatens the independence of worker centers, but without the patronage of unions the direct action organizations could not sustain their activities.

The groups studied act independently of each other, but sometimes work together as part of a larger movement. The gig workers in California, for instance, joined protests in support of fast-food workers. The National Day of Protest conducted by the Fight for $15 had the active support and backing of most of the groups as well as many unions. Other direct action organizations and unions—Our Walmart, AFSCME, and CWA—participate in the Fight for $15 struggle. The ROC's membership in the Food Chain Workers Alliance brings a spate of other unions and worker centers into the struggle. These coalitions tend to unite for a specific event and then dissolve, only to form again for another action.

Finally, all these struggles gained political leverage through social bargaining rather than traditional collective bargaining. By bringing their issues to the public, the Immokalee Workers literally shamed big buyers into major concessions. The Fight for $15 and California's gig drivers used public pressure to push legislative bodies to redress basic working conditions and improve wages. Even the Freelancers Union, an organization that sidesteps politics whenever possible, garnered public support to achieve important local political victories.

Despite diverse occupations, distinctively different struggles, and the infrequent and somewhat unsystematic way in which the groups join forces, they are part of a developing movement of exploited workers united in their quest to raise the public's consciousness of the human and economic costs of worker exploitation. The implications of this nascent movement for American politics and organized labor are far-reaching.

On the political level, this workers' movement seeks a strong, comprehensive social safety net that a revitalized labor movement can build upon. In short, it is pursuing the progressive economic agenda articulated in what Bernie Sanders calls "Our Revolution," an agenda that appeals to nonvoters and those many white working-class voters who support the GOP. Pursuit of this agenda by direct action movements and Sanders' supporters has driven the Democratic Party further to the left and is turning it into a vehicle for far-reaching structural change. Unions will still play an instrumental role in waging the battle to achieve the goals of a progressive economic program. Direct action groups represent millions of workers, but unions have the fiscal resources and the committed professional staff needed to mobilize and sustain activists for a long-term fight.[33] Direct action movements have already won significant legislative victories in the coastal states and in big cities throughout the United States, gains that reflect the movement's influence on public opinion. Public opinion polls show a majority of Americans now favor a $15 minimum wage, a universal health care plan, and paid sick and family leave.[34] By bringing its struggles to the streets, the worker's grassroots movement has even improved the public image of unions. According to a 2019 Gallup Poll, public approval of unions reached a twenty-year high when nearly two-thirds of Americans said they favored unions.[35] Yet in 2016, Donald Trump won significant support from working-class voters, including union members. Such support should not be that surprising, considering that the United States electorate leans center-right. Is it reasonable, then, to expect the continuing rise of the left leaning movements this book has chronicled? The answer is yes.

Public attitudes toward progressive issues and changing demographics suggest the movements studied in this book are not only likely to continue, but will probably move further leftward and become a much larger force in American politics. As already noted, a significant majority of the voting population supports a $15 minimum wage and the right to join a union. Some 60 percent of the populace believes it is government's responsibility to provide universal health care, with about half of this group favoring a single-payer system.[36] According to a Pew Research Center study, 85 percent of U.S. adults surveyed support paid medical leave; more than 80 percent believe that mothers should receive a paid leave following birth or adoption of a child, and almost 70 percent think fathers should receive the same leave benefit.[37]

Social change comes through political struggle in the broadest sense, and previous chapters have documented the current labor movement's struggle to change the dynamics of power. Going forward, changing demographics predict an emergent generation of progressive voters. Millennials now consist of about 27 percent of the population, soon outnumbering the Boomers.[38] They tend to hold progressive views, support unions, overwhelmingly back the Democratic Party, and expect government to play an activist role in providing health care and paid family and medical leave. In fact, a 2020 *Economist*/YouGov poll found that 60 percent of Democrats under the age of thirty voted for either Bernie Sanders or Elizabeth Warren, the two most progressive candidates in the 2020 Democratic presidential primary.[39] Millennials are not alone with their leftward leanings. Pew researchers found that the even younger Gen Z generation members expect more from government than do the millennials.[40]

Age is just one demographic shift pushing U.S. politics to the left. Ethnicity is another. According to the U.S. Census Bureau, by 2042 non-Hispanic whites will become a minority. Residents identified as Hispanic, Black, Asian, American Indian, Native Hawaiian, and Pacific Islander will make up a majority of the population. Polls show that these groups generally support an activist government. Over 70 percent of Hispanic voters, numerically the largest ethnic bloc of the new majority, want government to do more to solve social and economic problems.[41] All these demographic predictions can prove wrong because they are abstractions that do not take into consideration countervailing forces such as voter suppression, gerrymandering, election hijacking by foreign agents, and plain old right-wing agitprop. Those who hold power now will not give it up easily.

Nevertheless, if predictions hold, demographic shifts clearly do not augur well for the Republican Party. It is important to note here that when we talk about American political parties, the labels "Democrat" and "Republican" have remained constant, but their values have changed over time. The Republican Party of Lincoln and Eisenhower is now the racist, extreme anti-government party of Donald Trump. The Democratic Party of Bill Clinton, who claimed "the era of big government is over," was not the party of FDR. But now Democrats are looking at the New Deal as a model for the future. President Biden's first hundred days in office emulated the premise of the New Deal that big government is the solution, not the problem.

The political attitudes of the groups studied in this book reflect larger national views on progressive issues. Clearly, the Sanders' agenda appeals to movement leaders and activists, but much evidence indicates that rank-and-file members hold similar views and vote accordingly. Since the majority of farmworkers are migrants who do not vote, their influence is mostly restricted to the effect their moral appeal has on the public's political consciousness, an appeal supported and conveyed by progressive activist community groups and the faith community. As discussed in chapter 5, the Freelancers Union assigns a secondary role to politics, but its members are highly politically motivated and favor an intervention-ist government that provides affordable health care and other benefits, including rent control and the ability to contribute to a retirement fund. They tend to be young: 84 percent are below age forty, hold "Bohemian" views, and vote at a much higher rate than their nonfreelancing peers.

California's gig drivers may not all agree on AB5, but all want fair treatment on the job, and demographics suggest they lean left politically. A spate of recent demographical studies indicates that on-demand platform workers, such as Uber and Lyft drivers, are more highly educated than salary and wage earners, with about 50 percent holding college degrees. Compared to wage and salary workers, they earn less, and are dispropor-tionately young males. Studies differ concerning race and ethnicity. For instance, a 2016 survey by Intuit and Emergent Researcher found that over 60 percent of platform workers are white, but a study by the Pew Foundation claims that Blacks and Latinos participate in the platform economy at higher rates than whites. Most other research concurs with Intuit and Emergent Researcher.[42] What do these demographics tell us about the voting tendencies of these working-class drivers? Are they part of the working class that voted for and supported Donald Trump, or are they more likely to side with a progressive Democratic Party that's in step with the demands of the movements representing their occupations? It is important to note that the Democratic Party moved left even in 2016 when it included a $15 minimum wage in its national platform. Since then, the Democratic-led House passed a $15-minimum-wage bill, and all 2020 Democratic presidential primary candidates called for some form of universal health care and paid family leave. More recently, driven by the economic chaos and hardship wrought by the Covid-19 pandemic, the Democratic Party is moving further leftward. Senator Mark Warner, a moderate who views the pandemic as more transformative than the fall of the Berlin Wall, claims that his party's moderates have started thinking "about a legislative vision for overhauling the economy." The pandemic also prompted then presidential candidate Joe Biden to work with Bernie Sanders' advisors and others to "not just . . . rebuild the economy, but to transform it."[43] From time to time, progressive third-party candidates emerge, but, let's face it, in our winner-take-all electoral system, they always end up playing the role of spoiler. Many progressives still harbor doubts about the Democratic Party and its Wall Street connections, but at this moment in history the Democratic Party is the only vehicle capable of bringing significant progressive change.

Studies indicate that highly educated low-wage earners are becoming the heart of the new Democratic Party. This cohort that now makes up about 50 percent of California's platform workers was almost nonexistent seventy-five years ago. Today it constitutes 16 percent of the total electorate. Low-wage earners of color are concerned with redistributionist economic policies as well as issues of racial equality. Their voting participation rates are low for many reasons, including concentrated voter suppression, but in the 2018 midterm elections, 90 percent of people of color voted Democratic.[44] In the low-wage / low-education category of working-class whites, a large portion of whom voted for Trump in 2016, many support redistributionist economic policies and sometimes vote Democratic. In 2016, Trump's now broken promise of protecting Social Security and Medicare "put him on the side of core adherents of the welfare state."[45] Many in this group of economically motivated voters—some of whom are likely participants in the gig drivers' demonstrations—could easily join the political fight for progressive change. A small group of on-demand platform workers—high-earning whites without college degrees—are opposed to change. Studies indicate that non-college-educated whites earning between $77,552 and $130,000 oppose progressive economic policies and are now solidly committed to Trump's Republican Party. They are basically shopkeepers and small business owners in the trades, retail, and construction industries. High-earners in manufacturing are not as solidly committed to the Republican Party, but enough blue-collar union workers supported Trump in 2016 to give him narrow victories in the important swing states of the Midwest. As political scientist Herbert Kitschelt puts it:

> . . . the "white working class"—concentrated in the low-education / low-income sector of the white population—is not the category that has most ardently realigned toward Republicans. It's higher income ($77, 552–$130,000) / low education whites who are still doing well, but fear that in the knowledge society their life chances are shrinking as higher education becomes increasingly the ticket to economic and social success.[46]

This cohort now makes up more than a quarter of the Republican Party, but its numbers among gig drivers is small and shrinking.[47] Also, almost

60 percent of these on-demand platform workers are between the ages of eighteen and forty-four, an age cohort that voted Democratic by more than 60 percent in the 2018 midterm elections.[48]

Voluminous literature documents how working-class voters often vote against their own interests. Racism and sexism frequently trump the economic interests of working-class voters when they cast their ballot.[49] But there are several reasons to believe that workers involved in the Fight for $15 overwhelmingly support a progressive economic and political agenda. In the fast-food industry, more than half receive some form of public assistance. A somewhat outdated Maxwell Poll conducted in 2004–2007 found that 60% to 80% of those who receive some form of welfare identify as Democrats.[50] Other studies suggest that similar trends still hold. A 2015 study by the National Employment Project found that women make up less than half the U.S. workforce but account for almost 55 percent of all workers earning less than $15. This "feminization of poverty" moves women to vote Democratic. As widely reported, Trump's narrow margin of support from college-educated white women put him over the top in 2016, but in 2018 enough of this group abandoned the Republican Party to deliver record victories to Democrats in the House races. Then in the 2020 presidential election, 57 percent of women voted for Biden.[51] Another exploited bloc of workers likely to vote Democratic is African American and Latino. About 60 percent of Latinos earn less than $15, and more than half of all African American workers earn less than $15.[52] Still another study found that the lower the income among Democratic voters, the greater the support for Bernie Sanders and his political revolution. Unfortunately, for many reasons, voter turnout among the poor is very low.[53]

In a word, those involved in the movements studied here tend to vote for the progressive issues their movements represent. Getting the poor out to vote is the challenge. In their influential book, *Why Americans Don't Vote*, Piven and Cloward, who engineered the passage of the Motor Voter Act of 1993, discuss the many barriers to voting faced by the poor and why neither political party wants the poor to vote.[54] Incumbents try to keep the poor from voting so they can maintain the status quo they view as essential to their reelection. E.E. Schattschneider's seminal work *The Semi-Sovereign People* documents how issues relevant to the poor are not the same as those that motivate the middle-class electorate.[55] But the Fight for $15 and other movements shifted the public dialogue to include issues relevant to the now organized poor, which has pressured the Democratic Party to respond to their needs. Even before the Covid-19 outbreak, then Democratic presidential nominee Joe Biden, who said he planned to restructure the economy, supported a $15 minimum wage and lower age for Medicare eligibility. He also said he had a plan for college loan forgiveness, supported extending federal labor protections to all farmworkers and domestics, and wanted tougher penalties on companies that violate labor laws. Upon observing Biden's move left, *New York Times* columnist Michelle Goldberg declared that "Biden's leftward drift offers the chance for a generational change."[56] As president, Biden continues to move left, at least on domestic policies.

As the tragic and deadly coronavirus pandemic devastated the U.S. economy, even congressional Republicans had to take a big-government response, at least initially. Challenging the Reagan Republican view that government is the problem, a bi-partisan Congress passed the Coronavirus Aid, Relief, and Economic Security Act (CARES Act), a $2.2 trillion relief package to cushion the economic collapse. As the death toll skyrocketed and the main-street economy worsened, a bi-partisan Congress passed another $900 billion relief bill in January 2021. Bi-partisanship abruptly ended when the Democrats took power and passed President Biden's $1.9 trillion American Rescue Plan without the vote of a single Republican in the House or Senate. Under Joe Biden, big government is back.

The pandemic has unmasked the many holes in America's social safety net and exposed the human consequences of social and economic inequality. Thanks to the deepening economic crunch, as of this writing, Democrats in the White House and Congress are exploring additional legislation, including universal income, New Deal–style infrastructure jobs programs, and expansion of health coverage. These social democratic proposals reflect the demands of the vast majority of voters and might even signal the rise of a democratically responsive administrative state. Even some major restaurant chains and box stores responded to the rumblings of their exploited workers by providing them with limited paid sick leave during the pandemic.[57] As Jamelle Bouie of the *New York Times* observed, "at this moment in American life, it feels as if one movement, a reactionary one, is beginning to unravel and another, very different in its outlook, is beginning to take shape."[58]

When the public discourse becomes more relevant to poor and working people, they are more likely to flock to the polls in large numbers. But if progressive legislation is their road for change, they should expect roadblocks. Enter voter suppression, a tool of election manipulation with a long history in the United States.[59] In 2011 and 2012, for instance, several states enacted restrictions to make registering to vote more difficult, if not impossible. If you can't register to vote, you can't vote. Rulings by the Roberts Supreme Court gutted the 1965 Voting Rights Act, spurring states both north and south to take actions restricting the right to vote. The methods used to suppress voting run the gamut of shameful tactics such as removing eligible voters from the registration rolls without telling them; requiring difficult-to-obtain voter identification; and an unsuccessful attempt to impose a modern-day poll tax, a scheme used in Florida to prevent felons who have served their time from voting after the state's voters amended Florida's constitution to give these felons the right to vote.[60] An extraordinary instance of the U.S. Supreme Court's role in voter suppression is its ruling that Wisconsin could not extend the mail balloting deadline for its April 2020 state election despite the governor's "stay home" order to protect citizens during the pandemic. The goal of Wisconsin's Republican-controlled legislature that brought the case to the U.S. Supreme Court was, of course, to restrict the number of voters in order to protect an unpopular Republican candidate for the state's Supreme Court. Thanks to Wisconsin's Republican Party and the U.S. Supreme Court, citizens had to risk their lives in order to exercise their constitutional right to vote. Within two weeks, over two dozen voters and poll workers had been diagnosed with Covid-19.

On the chance that the poor and people of color somehow manage to cast a ballot, elected guardians of the status quo rely on gerrymandering to reduce the value of that vote. Gerrymandering is the practice of carving up state voting districts to give the dominant political party an overwhelming advantage in the election. While gerrymandering is a tool used by both political parties, Republican-controlled legislatures typically use it to dilute the Democratic vote of people of color and urban voters. In Greensboro, North Carolina, for instance, the Republican Party in 2016 split the thousands of African American voters at North Carolina Agricultural and Technical State University into two districts. By dividing a predominantly black Democratic district in half and attaching each half to mostly white Republican congressional districts, an African American female Democrat was replaced by two white Republican males. The 2018 state assembly elections in Wisconsin provide another flagrant example of gerrymandering. In that election, Democrats cast 190,000 more votes than Republicans, yet Republicans won sixty-three of the state's ninety-nine assembly seats.[61] In keeping with its clear commitment to restrict voting, the U.S. Supreme Court ruled that gerrymandering was a political question for legislatures, not the courts, to decide.[62]

The Fight for $15 movement is actively resisting these restrictions on voting by promoting voter turnout. On the fiftieth anniversary of the Memphis sanitation workers' 1968 march for economic justice, the occasion of Martin Luther King Jr.'s assassination, the Reverend William Barber announced that his new Poor People's Campaign would join fast-food workers in the struggle for voting rights and racial justice by waging fast-food strikes across the South. "We're bringing two movements together," he proclaimed, "people fighting for a living wage, a lot of young people, along with poor people, moral leaders, people of faith."[63] Later that year, the Fight for $15 movement, led by SEIU, launched a massive canvassing campaign to promote workers' rights in eleven states. Focusing on ousting anti-labor Republican governors in Rust Belt states, the efforts of hundreds of workers knocking on thousands of doors paid off. The election of Democratic governors who favor the right to unionize and a $15 minimum wage in Wisconsin and Michigan in 2018 illustrates the growing political power of the developing workers movement.[64] Since then, the movement has upped its emphasis on getting out the vote. With the November 2020 election still months away, the Fight for $15 joined a massive campaign to turn out voters of color in Wisconsin and Michigan, where gerrymandered legislatures remained in Republican control. Members of Fight for $15 successfully challenged a Michigan law that made it illegal to hire someone to drive voters to polling locations. Many poor who cannot afford a car often pool their limited resources to hire someone to drive them to their polling places. Fight for $15 members publicly challenged the law by hiring a bus to take people to vote. Their aim was to bring public attention to this anti-democratic law and the legislators who voted for it.[65]

For a full-fledged working-class movement to emerge, the struggles must continue to grow and play an increasingly larger role in shaping public opinion. The fights examined in this book are not winding down—they're just beginning. In this era of social networking and fast traveling 24/7 news cycles, the victories won by one group lead others in similar circumstances to ask, why not us too? The success of gig workers in California, however tentative, triggered demands for similar legislation in other states. New York City already has a minimum wage for gig drivers; others are pushing for that, too. Farmworkers can join unions in California, Oregon, Washington, and, most recently, New York. New

Jersey farmworkers may soon gain this right as well. New York City's gig workers in the creative economy led the way in winning very effective protections against wage theft for all workers. Workers in other localities now want the same protections. To understand how the movement's victories have become models, recall the early stages of the Fight for $15. When the Fight for $15 began, not many people gave fast-food workers much of a chance to win. *Forbes* labeled the idea as nearly insane, and *The Nation* said it was unwinnable—but today millions are enjoying a $15 minimum wage, and millions more want the same.[66] Thanks to media coverage and the workers' astute and ceaseless use of social networking and the media, the Fight for $15 has become a struggle for *all* low-wage workers. Domestics, home care aides, warehouse and hospitality workers, clerks, cashiers, and workers from virtually every other low-wage industry have now joined the movement, while millions of others now support the workers in their struggle.

What Is to be Done?

Regardless of where the labor movement is going in the twenty-first century, establishing a comprehensive economic safety net is the foundational step. So how do we get there? Direct action as chronicled in this book can go only so far without a fundamental change in federal laws. First, since the Sanders political revolution has moved the Democratic Party to the left, the grassroots struggle must focus on pushing the party further left and electing Democrats who back the progressive movement. However, this realignment cannot be achieved until voter rights are protected and expanded.

Democratic Party supporters of the Sanders revolution received a boost from the federal government's social-welfare-like response to the coronavirus pandemic. The trillions of dollars in emergency aid is a temporary rejection of the Republican Party's anti-statism. The health crisis has exposed the precarious nature of benefits tied to employment. Now, social safety net concepts such as guaranteed annual income and universal health care are major topics of public discourse. The nation's changing political dynamics and demographics favor progressive Democrats. In contrast, the Republican Party's racism, sexism, homophobia, xenophobia, anti-semitism, rejection of science, and rejection of the rule of law and basic democratic principles are now far out of mainstream public opinion. Former President Trump's comment in a Fox News interview that "you'd never have another Republican elected in this country again" if states made voting easy says it all.[67]

Voting is the hammer over the head of politicians. Consequently, Republicans are trying to stop voters from swinging the hammer by launching a nationwide assault on voter rights. They justify this attack by embracing the Trump narrative that Joe Biden and the Democrats stole the 2020 election with the help of massive voter fraud, a narrative commonly called the "Big Lie." Trump and right-wing media incessantly propagated the Big Lie, which in turn fueled Trump's "Stop the Steal" campaign and culminated with his supporters sacking the U.S. Capitol on January 6, 2021. The Brennan Center for Justice reports that at the end of March 2021 Republican legislators in forty-seven states introduced 361 bills restricting voting rights, "a 43 percent increase in little more than a month."[68] In contrast, House Democrats passed two sweeping voter reform bills that are pending in the Senate, as of this writing. The John Lewis Voting Rights Act would restore the provisions of the 1965 Voting Rights Act struck down by the Roberts Supreme Court in *Shelby County v. Holder*. An even broader bill, the For the People Act, not only expands voter rights and access to the ballot significantly, but reforms campaign financing laws and restricts partisan gerrymandering, among a longer list of provisions to strengthen democracy.

To mobilize voters, the struggles that take workers off the job and onto the streets must continue. The mobilization by Fight for $15 and other groups is essential to educating American voters and winning their support to pressure politicians. For workers, these struggles are lessons in empowerment that raise their expectations and show them that change is possible. Unions alone cannot deliver a resurgent labor movement. Unions have been playing defense for decades, with organizing drives bringing in fewer and fewer new members and with strikers fighting mostly losing battles as previous gains slip away. In contrast, direct action initiatives have led to the most recent labor victories. But activists could not have succeeded without union help. Clearly, unions and worker centers must continue working together. Neither institution has the resources to go it alone. Unions have the "guns"—money, political, and technical skills; worker centers have the numbers.

Beyond its work with unions, the success of the new labor movement has depended on its ability to build broad coalitions. But these various coalitions are somewhat fragmented, each working toward its own goals. An umbrella board of workers, union leaders, and community organizations, such as Reverend Barber's Poor People's Campaign, could play a pivotal role by bringing together all these coalitions to plan and coordinate activities in pursuit of broader national change. These struggles also unite different identity groups under the larger category of class. Differences like race, ethnicity, gender, and religion are crucial to shaping individual experiences, but all direct action workers are united in their struggle to fight exploitation. Organizers must build on this common ground.

Pursuit of securing a strong social safety net must go hand in hand with reforming American labor laws to open the door to union membership for the millions who want it. As discussed in chapter 2, Taft-Hartley put a brake on union power and gave management the tools to turn back the power of organized labor. It prohibited secondary boycotts, placed limitations on the ability to strike, gave states the right to pass right-to-work laws, and made organizing more difficult by giving management a host of new powers that weakened the Wagner Act, organized labor's Magna Carta. The Supreme Court's ruling in the 1938 case of *NLRB v. Mackay* that employers could fire striking workers had no impact as long as unions were strong and politically powerful. Ronald Reagan's firing of striking PATCO workers in 1981 illuminated the law's hostility toward unions and exposed organized labors' loss of power. Workers obviously need to mobilize to change the law, and they also need to force government to vigorously enforce existing union protections, something the federal government often refuses to do. This is a formidable task given the current reality of a politically weakened union movement that could not garner the passage of EFCA even during Obama's first term, despite Democrats controlling both houses of the legislature.

In addition to all the reforms that EFCA and a chiseling away of Taft-Hartley would have secured, labor law reform must include provisions for sectoral bargaining. Under current labor law, companies have to consent to sectoral bargaining, which most will not. Clearly, attempts to attain the legal right for sectoral bargaining will meet with much resistance from the corporate sector and its ideological allies and simply will not happen until the electorate votes in politicians willing to change the laws.

In her 2020 presidential primary campaign, Senator Elizabeth Warren argued that the country needs "big structural change, not tinkering around the edges." And sectoral bargaining is a big structural change. But until progressives gain more political power, the road to sectoral bargaining will be built mile by mile on smaller victories such as the reclassification of gig drivers as employees, securing for all the right to unionize, a $15 minimum wage, and paid family and sick leave. For instance, if at first sectoral bargaining is not gained, aim for the smaller win of establishing wage boards as a step toward the larger goal.[69] Given that New York State created a fast-food wage board that raised the minimum wage, activists should continue to focus on New York and other more worker-friendly states and localities to secure more rights. Another winnable local or statewide battle, according to labor journalist David Madland, is the extension of prevailing wage laws. Prevailing wage laws require governmental projects to pay wages and benefits equal to the rate paid for similar work in the region or industry. Once activists convince their local or state officials that all government spending must conform to prevailing wage requirements, they need to make sure the calculation of that wage is tied to union wages. These victories provide a platform for activists to seek an even bigger one by pressuring private employers in the same industry to meet the prevailing wage standard.[70] The Gay Rights movement is a good example of this approach. Same-sex marriage victories prevailed first in localities, then in a handful of states, and now is protected by the U.S. Constitution. In other words, local victories can pave the way to national standards.

Labor law reform without changes in the behavior of unions is not enough. Labor needs visionary leaders who will put the interests of workers before the interests of their own organizations. This includes expanding rank-and-file participation in union governance and activities. For sectoral bargaining to work, unions must work together. The loss of membership over the decades has turned union organizing into battlefields in which survival of the organization overshadows serving workers. These jurisdictional wars weaken organized labor in the long run by wasting scarce financial resources, alienating the unorganized targets of the campaign, and sometimes resulting in outcomes where the victor has little expertise or experience in the industry the organization now must represent. Think UAW representing college faculty. Better yet, imagine a teachers union representing steel workers. If organized labor does not consolidate into sectoral/industry-wide organizations, unions must at least find informal ways to stop the competition and work as a more unified movement, as *Labor Notes* writers have suggested.[71]

We do not need to imagine what the benefits of sectoral bargaining are. We need only look to the industrialized nations of Europe. In his

New York Times op-ed piece "McDonald's Workers in Denmark Pity Us" describing Denmark's response to the coronavirus pandemic, Nicholas Kristof considers the plight of American workers versus the relative comfort of their Danish counterparts during this crisis. He compares America's fast-food workers' who are fighting for a $15 minimum wage to the $22 per hour starting pay for a Danish McDonald's worker. The Danish social safety net provides all Danish workers, including hamburger-flippers, six weeks' paid vacation, universal medical coverage, paid sick leave, pensions, life insurance, up to a year of paid maternity leave, free child care, and free public education through college. These basic economic benefits are the foundation on which sectoral bargaining is based. Danes employed by McDonald's enjoy a livable starting wage, receive their work schedules a month in advance, and cannot be assigned to work back-to-back shifts, but so do Burger King workers and all employees covered by the fast-food industry's sectoral bargaining compact. By treating its workers decently, Danish society reaps benefits such as higher productivity rates and a more egalitarian society with less poverty and all the negative social and economic consequences that go with it.[72]

In the United States, the gap between rich and poor increases by the minute, and the Supreme Court's ruling in Citizens United ensures that the country's political institutions mirror its economic inequality. Nevertheless, there is hope for progressive change: the corporate sector and its allies have abundant cash and infinite other resources to pour into elections in support of their candidates. But the potential voting power of tens of millions of politically motivated workers reminds corporations and their political protectors that wealth is not always enough. As that old worker's slogan goes, "the rich have their money, and the poor have their politics."[73] That's why voter suppression and opposition to expanding the vote have become scripture to the Republican Party

The constant attack on voting rights is a tell-tale sign of how much the corporate sector and its right-wing allies fear the power of a united workers movement. Government's response to the coronavirus epidemic suggests that New Deal–type policies may become part of a new political reality. The ink had barely dried on the CARES Act and other pandemic relief packages when the political right in Congress began trotting out their old deficit hawk song and dance about runaway inflation, impending economic ruin, and so on. But voters are no longer buying this story. Public opinion polls show that the overwhelming majority of voters, including a majority of Republicans, support Biden's big government spending programs and they want corporations and the richest Americans to foot the bill.[74] Fear, as the adage goes, is the basis of tyranny. As the GOP base shrinks, it relies more and more on stoking fear. Trump's one talent was his uncanny ability to play on voter fears as he brought our democratic institutions to the brink of authoritarian rule. The fight of American workers for a revitalized labor movement through political action, then, is ultimately a struggle for democracy.[75]

Notes

Introduction

1. WRGB Albany, Staff, "Paid Sick Days," October 17, 2018. https://cbs6-albany.com/news/local/albany-county-workers-rally-for-paid-sick-days

2. Kata Guillaume, "Workers Demand Action on Paid Sick Leave," WTEN Albany County. www.news10.com/news/local-news/protest-held-to-call-for-paid-sick-days/1366516264

3. Ravi Mangla, "Westchester County Passes Paid Sick Days, Albany County Expected to Follow," October 2, 2018. https://citizenactionny.org/2018/10/westchester-county-passes-paid-sick-days-albany-county-expected-to-follow/29781

4. Rachel L. Swarns, "New York's Paid Sick Leave Law Quietly Takes Effect," *New York Times*, April 6, 2014. www.nytimes.com/2014/04/07/nyregion/new-yorks-paid-sick-leave-law-quietly-takes-effect.html

5. For a discussion, see William E. Scheuerman, *Civil Disobedience* (Cambridge, UK: Polity Press, 2018), 81–100.

6. Regarding the idea of direct action used in the civil rights movement, see Martin Luther King Jr., "Letter from a Birmingham Jail." African Studies Center-University of Pennsylvania. www.africa.upenn.edu/Articles_Gen/Letters_Birmingham.html

7. Elizabeth Warren, speech announcing her presidential candidacy, Lawrence, Massachusetts, February, 9, 2019.

8. The literature is voluminous. Good examples include Stanley Aronowitz, "On the Future of American Labor," *Working USA* (Spring 2005): 271–291; Amy B. Dean and David B. Reynolds, *A New New Deal: How Regional Activism Will Reshape the American Labor Movement* (Ithaca & London: Cornell University Press, 2009); Phillip Dine, *State of the Unions: How Labor Can Strengthen the Middle Class, Improve Our Economy and Regain Political Influence* (New York: McGraw Hill, 2008); Bill Fletcher Jr. and Fernando Gaspin, *Solidarity Divided: The Crisis in Organized Labor and a New Path toward Social Justice* (Berkeley, Los Angeles, & London: University of California Press, 2008); Richard Hurd, "Contesting the

Dinosaur Image: The Labor Movement's Search for a Future," *European Review of Labour and Research* 7 (Autumn 2001): 451–465; Kim Moody, *U.S. Labor in Trouble and Transition: The Failure of Reform from Above, the Promise of Revival from Below* (London & New York: Verso, 2007; Jane F. McAlevey, *No Shortcuts: Organizing for Power in the New Gilded Age* (New York: Oxford University Press, 2016); Patricia Cayo Sexton, *The War on Labor and the Left: Understanding America's Unique Conservatism* (Boulder, CO: Westview Press, 1991).

9. Andre Gorz, *Paths to Paradise: On the Liberation from Work*, translated by Malcolm Imrie (Boston: South End Press, 1985); see also Stanley Aronowitz and William Difazio, *The Jobless Future: Sci-tech and the Dogma of Work* (Minneapolis & London: University of Minneapolis Press, 1994).

10. Friedrich Hayek, *The Road to Serfdom* (Chicago & London: University of Chicago Press, 1944); Nancy Maclean, *Democracy in Chains: The Deep History of the Radical Right's Stealth Plan For America* (New York: Viking Press, 2017), xxii.

11. According to a news account, within weeks after the *Janus* decision, the powerful New York State United Teachers union experienced a 6 percent drop in its membership. Very few members resigned from the union, but new hires were not joining as in the past. See Rick Karlin, "Impact of Ruling on Union Debated," *Albany Times Union*, December 4, 2018, A-3.

12. Cal Winslow, *Labor's Civil War in California* (Oakland, CA: PM Press, 2010).

13. Annelise Orleck, *We Are All Fast-Food Workers Now* (Boston: Beacon Press, 2018).

14. David Rolf, *The Fight for $15: The Right Wage for a Working America* (New York & London: The Free Press, 2016).

15. Eric Blanc, *Red State Revolt: The Teachers' Strike Wave and Working Class Politics* (London & New York: Verso, 2019).

16. Ziad Resian, "Freelancers Rights Come of Age as Gig Economy Booms," TechCrunch, 2018. htpp://techcrunch.com/22018/freelancers-rights-come-of-age-as-gig-economy-boom

Chapter 1

1. Elizabeth Warren's speech in Lawrence, Massachusetts, February 9, 2019.

2. Ibid.

3. Robert B. Reich, *After-Shock: The Next Economy and America's Future* (New York: Knopf, 2010), 42–50.

4. Robert B. Reich, *Saving Capitalism: For the Many, Not the Few* (New York: Knopf, 2015), 128–129.

5. Henry S. Faber, Daniel Herbst, Ilyana Kuziemko, and Suresh Naidu, "Unions and Inequality over the Twentieth Century; New Evidence from Survey Data," Working Paper #24587, The National Bureau of Economic Research website,

September 20, 2018. See also Bruce Western and Jake Rosenfeld, "Unions, Norms, and the Rise of Wage Inequality," *American Sociological Review* 76, no. 4: 513–537.

6. Matthew Walters and Lawrence Mishel, "How Unions Help All Workers," Economic Policy Institute, briefing paper #143, August 26, 2003.

7. For a good summary on the importance of unions, see Michael D. Yates, *Why Unions Matter* (New York: Monthly Review Press, 2009).

8. Jake Rosenfeld, Patrick Denice, and Jennifer Laird, "Union Decline Lowers Wages of Nonunion Workers, Economic Policy Institute, August 30, 2016.

9. Christain Weller, David Madland, and Alex Rowell, "Building Middle-Class Wealth Through Unions," Center for American Progress Action Fund, Dec. 1, 2016. www.americanprogressactionfund.org/issues/economy/reports/2016/12/01/164578/building-middle-class-wealth-through-unions; Christain Weller, "Unions Help Middle-Class families Save for the Future," www.forbes.com/sites/christainweller/2018/08/30 unions-help-middle-class-families save-for-the-future

10. John Kenneth Galbraith, *American Capitalism: The Concept of Countervailing Power* (New Brunswick, NJ & London: Transition Press, 1993), esp. 135–153.

11. Timothy J. Minchin, *Labor under Fire: A History of the AFL-CIO Since 1979* (Chapel Hill: University of North Carolina Press, 2017), 53.

12. Sean McElwee, "How Unions Boost Democratic Participation," *The American Prospect*, September 16, 2015. www.prospect.org/article/how-unions-boost-democraic-participation

13. Benjamin Radcliff and Patricia Davis, "Labor Organization and Electoral Participation in Industrial Democracies," *American Journal of Political Science* 44, no. 1: 132–141.

14. David Madland and Nick Bunker, "Unions Make Democracy Work for the Middle-Class," Center for American Democracy, website, January 25, 2012. Report # 10895.

15. For a good summary of unions and Donald Trump, see Steven Greenhouse, "The Unions That Like Trump," *New York Times*, April 8, 2017. www.nytimes.com/2017/04/08/opinion/sunday/the-union-that-likes-trump

16. Drew Silver, "American Unions Membership Declines as Public Support Fluctuates," PEW Research Center, Fact Team, February 20, 2014. www.pewresearch.org/fact-tank/2014/02/20/for-american-unions-membership-trails-far-behind-public-support

17. Bureau of Labor Statistics, News Release, Friday, January 19, 2018. www.blsgov/news.release/pdf/union2.pdf

18. Alana Semuels, "How to Kill the Middle Class," *The Atlantic*, December 7, 2016. www.theatlantic.com/business/archive/2016/12/unions-wisconsin/509798

19. Ibid.

20. Estelle Sommeiller and Mark Price, "The New Gilded Age: Income Inequality in the U.S. by State, Metropolitan Area and County," Economic Policy Institute, July 19, 2018. www.epi.org/publication/the-new-gilded-age-income-inequality-in-the-us-by-state-metropolitan-area-and-county

21. David Morris, "When Unions Are Strong, Americans Enjoy the Fruits of Their Labor," Institute for Local Self-Reliance, March 31, 2011. https://ilsr.org/when-unions-are-strong-americans-enjoy-the-fruits-of-their-labor

22. Robert B. Reich, *After-Shock*, 20.

23. Carter C. Price and Kathryn A. Edwards, "Trends in Income from 1975 to 2018," RAND Corporation, 2020. www.rand.org/pubs/working-papers/WRA 516-1.htm; Nick Hanauer and David M. Rolf, "The Top 1% of Americans Have Taken $50 Trillion from the Bottom 90%—and That's Made the U.S. Less Secure," *Time*, October 21, 2020. https://time.com/5888024/50-trillion-income-inequality-america

24. Jennifer Erickson, ed., "The Middle Class Squeeze: A Picture of Stagnate Incomes, Rising Costs and What We Can Do To Strengthen America's Middle Class," Center For American Progress 2014, 5.

25. Elise Gould, "Decades of Rising Economic Inequality in the United States," testimony before the U.S. House of Ways and Means Committee, for a hearing on "The 2017 Tax law and Who it Left Behind," March 27, 2017.

26. Robert B. Reich, *Saving Capitalism*, 127.

27. Josh Bivens, Elise Gould, Lawrence Mishel, and Heidi Sheirholz, "Raising America's Pay: Why It's Our Central Policy Challenge," Economic Policy Institute, Briefing Paper No. 378, June 2014; "Corporate Profits in the United States," www.statista.com/statistics/222130/annual-corporate-profits-in-the-us

28. Estelle Sommeiller and Mark Price, *The New Gilded Age*.

29. AFL-CIO.org/paywatch/highest-paid-ceos

30. Gillian B. White, "A Conversation With Joseph Stiglitz," *The Atlantic*, April 28, 2016. www.theatlantic.com/business/archive/2016/04/stiglitz-inequality/479952; Joseph Stiglitz, *The Great Divide: Unequal Societies and What We Can Do about Them*, (New York & London: W.W. Norton & Company, 2015).

31. Philo Hutcheson, "Shared Goals, Different Politics, and Differing Outcomes: The Truman Commission and the Dewey Commission" in, *SUNY at Sixty: The Promise of the State University of New York* John W. Clark, W. Bruce Leslie and Kenneth O'Brien, eds. (Albany, NY: SUNY Press, 2010), 3–15.

32. Robert Reich, op. cit., 49.

33. Elizabeth McNichol, Douglas Hall, David Cooper, and Vincent Palacios, "Pulling Apart: A State-by-State Analysis of Income Trends," Center on Budget and Policy Priorities, November 15, 2012.

34. Thomas Piketty suggests that economic inequality in the United States today is so entrenched that it is perpetuated more on inherited wealth than earnings. In that sense, the United States is returning to the "patrimonial" capitalism of the nineteenth century. Thomas Piketty, *Capital in the Twenty-First Century* (Cambridge & London: Belknap Press of Harvard University Press, 2014).

35. Joseph E. Stiglitz, *The Price of Inequality: How Today's Divided Society Endangers Our Future* (New York & London: W.W. Norton and Company, 2012), 73.

36. James O'Connor, *The Fiscal Crisis of the State* (New Brunswick, NJ: Transaction Publishers, 2002).

37. Barry Lynn, "America's Monopolies Are Holding Back the Economy," *The Atlantic*, February 22, 2017. www.theAtlantic.com/business/archives/2017/02/antimonopoly-big-busines/514358

38. Jason Furman, "Prepared Testimony to the Hearing on Market Competition," before the Directorate for Financial and Enterprise Affairs Competition Committee, Organization for Economic Co-operation and Development, June 7, 2018.

39. Hillary Clinton, "Hillary Clinton: Being Pro-Business Doesn't Mean Hanging Consumers Out to Dry," *Quartz*, October 20, 2015. https://concentrationcrisis.openmarketinstitute.org/industry/domestic-airlines

40. In 1981 the Reagan Administration's Federal Trade Commission stopped collecting data on economic concentration in American industries. The private sector Open Market Institute is now garnering much of these data.

41. Richard Felon, "Nobel Prize Winning Economist Joseph Stiglitz Says the U.S. Has a Major Monopoly Problem," *Business Insider*, September 6, 2018. www.businessinsider.com/joseph-stiglitz-says-that-the-us-has a-major monopoly-problem-2018

42. AFL-CIO Executive Paywatch news release, May 22, 2018.

43. Kathleen Elkins, "Median CEO Pay Reaches $12.1 Million—Here's How Much the 5 Highest Leaders Earn," *Closing the Gap*, www.cnbc.com/2018/05/09/how-much-the-5-highest-paid-ceos-earn-html

44. Bryce Covert, "Does Monopoly Power Explain Workers' Stagnate Wages," *The Nation*, February 15, 2018. www.thenation.com/article/does-monopoly-power-explain-workers'-stagnate-wages; Jose Azar, Ioana Marinescu, and Marshall I. Steinbaum, "Labor Market Concentration," National Bureau of Economic Research, NBER Working paper 24147, December 2017.

45. Fatih Guvenen, David J. Price, Jae Song, and Till M. von Wachter, "Inequality Inside United States Mega Firms." Paper presented at the annual meeting of the American Economics Association, January 6, 2017.

46. "What Market Concentration, Monopsony, and Monopoly Can and Can't Explain About Wage Trends," News from EPI, Press Release, April 25, 2018.

47. Ibid.

48. Robert Reich, *Saving Capitalism: For the Many, Not the Few*, 173.

49. Jane Mayer, *Dark Money: The Hidden History of the Billionaires behind the Rise of the Radical Right* (New York: Doubleday, 2016). Nancy MacLean argues that the Koch brothers, who view democracy as an impediment to economic liberty, that is, property rights, are financing a stealth attack on the nation's democratic institutions. See Nancy MacLean, *Democracy in Chains: The Deep History of the Radical Right's Stealth Plan For America* (New York: Viking Press, 2017).

50. For a concise summary of the importance of the *Speech Now* and *Citizens United* Decision, see John Dunbar, "The Citizens United Decision and Why it Matters," The Center for Public Integrity, October 18, 2012. www.publicintegrity.org/2012/10/18/11527/citizens-united-decision-and-why-it-matters

51. Ibid.

52. Matea Gold, "Koch-Backed Political Network, Built to Shield Donors, Raised $400 million in 2012 Elections," *Washington Post*, January 5, 2014.

53. A. Bonica, N. McCarty, K. Poole, and H. Rosenthal, "Why Hasn't Democracy Slowed Rising Inequality?" *Journal of Economic Perspectives* 27, no. 3, 113.

54. Ibid., 107.

55. "Voter Turnout Rates, 1916–2016," Fair Vote, www.fairvote.org/voter-turnout#voter-turnout-101

56. Timothy J. Minchin, *Labor under Fire: A History of the AFL-CIO Since 1979*, 8.

57. A. Bonica, N. McCarty, K. Poole, and H. Rosenthal, op. cit., 577.

Chapter 2

1. The literature is voluminous. Good examples include Stanley Aronowitz, "On the Future of American Labor," *Working USA* (Spring 2005): 271–291; Stanley Aronowitz, *The Death and Life of American Labor: Toward a New Workers' Movement* (London & New York: Verso, 2014); Phillip Dine, *State of the Unions: How Labor Can Strengthen the Middleclass, Improve our Economy and Regain Political Influence* (New York: McGraw Hill, 2008); Bill Fletcher Jr. and Fernando Gaspin, *Solidarity Divided* (Berkeley, Los Angeles, & London: University of California Press, 2008); Richard Hurd, "Contesting the Dinosaur Image: The Labor Movement's Search for a Future," *European Review of Labour and Research* 7 (Autumn 2001): 451–465; Kim Moody, *US Labor in Trouble and Transition: The Failure of Reform from Above, the Promise of Revival from Below* (London & New York: Verso, 2007).

2. Doris Goodwin, "The Way We Won America's Economic Breakthrough during World War II," *The American Prospect*, Fall 1992. prospect.org/article/way-we-won-americas-economic-breakthrough-during world-war-ii

3. Nelson Lichtenstein, *The Most Dangerous Man in Detroit: Walter Reuther and the Fate of American Labor* (New York: Basic Books, 1995), 220–240.

4. The then emerging Austrian school of economics provided one of many ideological justifications to attack unions. This group feared that democratic institution of any kind that interfered in the marketplace threatened an individual's economic liberty. In other words, popular democracy, of which unions are an expression, must be limited if it is not to threaten capital. See Friedrich Hayek, *The Road To Serfdom* (Chicago & London: University of Chicago Press, 1944).

5. Lichtenstein, 225.

6. Lichtenstein, 226

7. Lichtenstein, 224.

8. Lichtenstein, 228.

9. Victor G. Reuther, *The Brothers Reuther and the Story of the UAW* (Boston: Houghton Mifflin Company, 1976), 246–256; Kevin Boyle, *The UAW and the Heyday of American Liberalism: 1945–1968* (Ithaca, NY & London: Cornell University Press, 1995), 30.

10. Robert H. Zieger, Timothy J. Minchin, and Gilbert J. Gall, *American Workers, American Unions: The 20th & Early 21st Centuries* (Baltimore: Johns Hopkins Press, 2014), 144–181.

11. Victor Reuther, 254–255.

12. Lichtenstein, xxx.

13. For a good analysis of the Southern response to "Operation Dixie," see Ira Katznelson, *When Affirmative Action Was White: An Untold History of Racial Equality in Twentieth Century America* (New York & London: W.W. Norton, 2005).

14. Louis Hyman, *Temp: How American Work, American Business, and the American Dream Became Temporary* (New York: Viking, 2018), 47.

15. James O'Connor, *The Fiscal Crisis of the State* (New Brunswick & London: Transaction, 2002), 19–21.

16. Chris Isidore, "When American Steel Was King," @CNNMoney, March 9, 2018.

17. *Federal Trade Commission, The United States Steel Industry and its International Rivals: Trends and Factors Determining International Competitiveness* (Washington, DC: Government Printing Office, 1977), 41–93.

18. Barry Bluestone, Bennett Harrison, and Lawrence Baker, *Corporate Flight: The Causes and Consequences of Economic Dislocation* (Washington, DC: Progressive Alliance Book, 1981), 39.

19. Council on Economic Advisors, *Report to the President on Steel Prices* (Washington, DC: U.S. Government Printing Office, 1965), 8–9; William Scheuerman, *The Steel Crisis: The Economics and Politics of a Declining Industry* (New York: Praeger, 1986), 45–63.

20. Stan Luger, *Corporate Power, American Democracy, and the Automobile Industry* (New York: Cambridge University Press, 2000), 40–41; Bradford Snell, "Annual Style Changes in the Automobile Industry as an Unfair Method of Competition," *Yale Law Journal* 80, no. 3 (January 1971): 567–613.

21. *Business Week* (November 16, 1963): 144–146; see also Walter Adams and Joel Dirlam, "Big Steel, Invention and Innovation," *Quarterly Journal of Economics* 80, no. 2 (May 1966): 167–189.

22. Paul A. Baron and Paul M. Sweezy, *Monopoly Capital: An Essay on the American Economic and Social Order* (New York & London: Monthly Review Press, 1968).

23. William Scheuerman, *The Steel Crisis: The Economics and Politics of a Declining Industry* (New York: Praeger, 1986), 64–97.

24. Ibid.

25. Barry Bluestone and Bennett Harrison, *The Deindustrialization of America: Plant Closings, Community Abandonment, and the Dismantling of Basic Industry* (New York: Basic Books, 1982), 7.

26. Bennett Harrison and Barry Bluestone, *The Great U-Turn: Corporate Restructuring and the Polarizing of America* (New York: Basic Books, 1990), 25.

27. "Where America's Jobs Went," *The Week Staff*, March 18, 2011. theweek. com/articles/486362/where-americas-jobs-went. See also David Leonhardt, "When C.E.O.s Cared about America," *New York Times*, December 3, 2018, p. A27.

28. Bluestone, Harrison, and Baker, *Corporate Flight*, 45.

29. *Corporate Flight*, 13.

30. "The Changing Situation of Workers and Their Unions," A Report by the AFL-CIO Committee on the Evolution of Work, February 1985.

31. Jeff Faux, "NAFTA's Impact on U.S. Workers," Economic Policy Institute, Working Economics Blog, December 9, 2013.

32. Eric Schaal, "The Companies Offshoring Jobs at a Record Pace Under Trump," Cheat Sheet, April 21, 2018, www.cheatsheet.com/money-career/the-companies-offshoring-at-a-record-pace-under-trump.html

33. Timothy J. Minchin, *Labor Under Fire: A History of the AFL-CIO since 1979* (Chapel Hill: University of North Carolina Press, 2017), 271; Eric Schaal, "The Companies Offshoring Jobs at a Record Pace Under Trump," Cheat Sheet, April 21, 2018, www.cheatsheet.com/money-career/the-companies-offshoring-at-a-record-pace-under-trump.html; David Madland, Olugbenga Ajilore, Michael Madowitz, and Daniella Zessoules, "Under President Trump, Workers Continue to Struggle," Center for American Progress, September 11, 2018.

34. International Federation of Robotics, *2015 World Robotics Statistics*; Robotics on Line Marketing Team, "The History of Robotics in the Automotive Industry," Robotics on Line, January 17, 2017.

35. William E. Scheuerman, "Joint Ventures in the U.S. Steel Industry," *The American Journal of Economic and Social Policy* 18, no. 2 (Winter 1989–1990).

36. Mark J. Perry, "The Main Reason for the Loss of U.S. Steel Jobs Is a Huge Increase in Worker Productivity, Not Imports, and the Jobs Are Not Coming Back," *Carpe Diem*, March 7, 2018; *Trending Economics*, U.S. Steel Production, trendingeconomics.com/united-states/steel-production

37. Mark Mauro, Robert Maxim, and Jacob Whiton, "Automation and Artificial Intelligence: How Machines Are Affecting People and Places," Report, Brookings Institute, January 24, 2018. www.brookings.edu/research/automation-and-artificial-intelligence-how-machines-affect-people-and-places. For an analysis of the impact of technology on the labor process, see Harry Braverman, *Labor and Monopoly Capital: The Degradation of Work in the Twentieth Century* (New York & London: Monthly Review Press, 1974); see also Richard Edwards, *Contested Terrain: The Transformation of Work in the Twentieth Century* (New York: Basic Books, 1979).

38. Stanley Aronowitz, *From the Ashes of the Old: America's Labor and America's Future* (Boston & New York: Houghton Mifflin, 1998), 139.

39. AFL-CIO report, "The Changing Situation of Workers and Their Unions," 8.

40. Barry Bluestone and Bennett Harrison, "The Great American Job Machine: The Proliferation of Low Wage Employment in the U.S. Economy," United States Congress, Joint Economic Committee, December 1986.

41. U.S. Department of Labor, Bureau of Labor Statistics, "Employment by Major Industry Sector," www.bls.gov/emp/tables/employment-by-major-industry-sector.htm

42. Hyman, 8.

43. Ibid., 8–9.

44. Sarah Kessler, *Gigged: The Gig Economy, the End of the Job and the Future of Work* (London: Random House, 2018).

45. Philip M. Dine, *State of the Unions: How Labor Can Strengthen the Middle Class, Improve Our Economy, and Regain Political Influence* (New York: McGraw Hill, 2008), xxviii.

46. Pattern bargaining takes wages and benefits out of competition through industry-wide standardization achieved at the bargaining table. Pattern bargaining provides a floor to build on in future negotiations. Also, by negotiating contracts that removed wages and benefits from competition among firms in the same industry, unions essentially prevented a "race to the bottom." For a brief but clear description of pattern bargaining and the implication of the end of this practice, see Kim Moody, "A Pattern of Retreat: The Decline of Pattern Bargaining," *Labor Notes*, February 16, 2010, https://labornotes.org/2010/02/pattern-retreat-decline-pattern-bargaining

47. Moody, *An Injury to All: The Decline of Industrial Unionism*; see also Garth L. Mangum and R. Scott McNabb, *The Rise, Fall and Replacement of Industrial Bargaining in the Basic Steel Industry* (New York: M.E. Sharpe, 1997); Scott A. Kruse, "Regressive or Concession Bargaining and Corporate Restructuring," unpublished paper, www.americanbar.org/content/dam/aba/administrative/labor-law/meetings/2009/ac2009/028.pdf; Anne Scheetz, "Behind the UAW 'Health Care Co-Op' Scam," Illinois Single Payer Coalition, October 16, 2015. www.singlepayer.org/article/behind-uaw-health-care-co-op-scam

48. A recent example is Jane McAlevey, *A Collective Bargain: Unions, Organizing, and the Fight for Democracy* (New York: Harper Collins, 2020).

49. David Yaffe-Bellany, "Key Points about the U.A.W. Strike against General Motors," *New York Times*, September 16, 2019. www.nytimes.com/2019/09/16/business/gm-strike-uaw.html?auth=login-email&login=email

50. Alexia Fernandez Campbell, "The GM Strike Has Officially Ended. Here's What Workers Won and Lost," *Vox*, October 25, 2019. www.nytimes.com/2019/09/16/business/gm-strike-uaw.html?auth=login-email&login=email

51. Harold L. Sirkin, Michael Zinser, and Douglas Hohner, "Made in America Again: Why Manufacturing Will Return to the U.S.," The Boston Consulting Group, August 2011.

52. Harold Meyerson, "How the American South Drives the Low Wage Economy," *American Prospect*, Summer 2015, www.prospect.org/article/how-american-south-drive-low-wage-economy

53. Ibid.

54. Brian Snavely, "GOP Legislators Accuse Volkswagen of Backing the UAW as Election Nears," *Detroit Free Press*, February 11, 2014.

55. Bernie Woodall, "Loss at Volkswagen Plant Upends Union's Plan for U.S. South," Reuters, February 14, 2014. www.reuters.com/article/us-auto-vw-election/loss-at-volkswagen-plant-upends-unions-plan-for-u-s-south-idUSBREH1D1DP20140251

56. Erik Schelzig, "UAW Reports 55% Membership at VW Plant in Tennessee," *Detroit Free Press*, April 29, 2015.

57. David Morris, "When Unions Are Strong, Americans Enjoy the Fruit of Their Labor,." Institute for Local Self-Reliance, March 31,2011. Ilsr.org/when-unions-are-strong-americans-enjoy-the-fruit-of-their-labor

58. For a detailed analysis of the impact of Taft-Hartley on unions, see Steven E. Abraham, "How the Taft-Hartley Act Hindered Unions," *Hofstra Labor and Employment Journal* 12, no. 1, article 1.

59. Paul D'Amato, "Labor and the Cold War," *Socialist Worker.Org* July 29, 2011.

60. D'Amato, "Labor and the Cold War"; Stanley Aronowitz, *The Death and Life of American Labor: Toward a New Workers' Movement* (London & New York: Verso, 2014); Nelson Lichtenstein, *Labor's War at Home: The CIO in World War II* (Cambridge: Cambridge University Press, 1982); Patricia Cayo Sexton, *The War on Labor and the Left: Understanding America's Unique Conservatism* (San Francisco: Westview Press, 1991).

61. AFL-CIO report, "The Changing Situation of Workers and Their Unions," 10.

62. Bluestone and Harrison, *The Great U-Turn*, 25.

63. For a good summary of the role played by union-breaking consulting firms, see John Logan, "Consultants, Lawyers, and the 'Union Free' Movement in the USA since the 1970s," *Industrial Relations Journal* 33, no. 2: 197–214.

64. Freeman and Medoff, *What Do Unions Do?* (New York: Basic Books, 1984).

65. Kate Bronfenbrenner, "No Holds Barred: The Intensification of Employer Opposition to Organizing," Economic Policy Institute Briefing Paper #235, May 20, 2009.

66. John Logan, Erin Johannson, and Ryan Lamare, "New Data; NLRB Process Fails to Ensure a Fair Vote," University of California, Berkeley, Labor Center, June 29, 2011.

67. Steven E Abraham, "How the Taft-Hartley Act Hindered Unions." *Hofstra Labor and Employment Journal*, Vol. 12, Iss. 1, January 1994.

68. R.W. Hurd, "Assault on Workers' Rights" (Electronic Version). Washington, DC: AFL-CIO. Retrieved from Cornell University, ILR School site: http://digital commons.ilr.cornell.edu/laborunions/34

69. Dorian T. Warren, "Union Organizing in National Labor Relations Board Elections," Roosevelt Institute, October 7, 2015.

70. R.W. Hurd, Union Free Bargaining Strategies and First Contract Failures (Electronics Version), Proceedings of the Forty-Eighth Annual Meeting of the Industrial Relations Research Association (1996), 145–152; William M. Cook, "Union Organizing and Public Policy: Failure to Secure Contracts," Kalamazoo, MI: WEUP Dots Institute for Employment Research. doi.org/10.12848/9780880996136; Minchin, 141.

71. AFL-CIO report, "The Changing Situation of Workers and Their Unions," 10–11; Paul Weiler, "Promises to Keep: Securing Workers' Right to Self-Organization Under the NLRA," *Harvard Law Review* 96, no. 8 (June 1983): 1769–1780. Charles Morris, Researchers, V. Case Studies of Violations of Workers Freedom of Association, Human Rights Watch (2000). www.hrw.org/reports/2000/uslabor/USLBR008-07.htm

72. Hurd, "Assault on Workers' Rights," 34.

73. Kate Bronfenbrenner, "No Holds Barred."

74. Economic News Release, "Work Stoppages Involving 1,000 or More Workers, 1947–2017." United States Department of Labor, Bureau of Labor Statistics.www.bls.gov/news-release/wkstp.toi.htm

75. U.S. Bureau of Labor Statistics, Work Stoppages, February 11, 2020. www.bls.gov/wsp

76. David Leonhardt, "Where Have You Gone, Resistance?" *New York Times*, January 21, 2019, p. A19; see also James Gray Pope, Ed Bruno, and Peter Kellman, "The Right to Strike," *Boston Review*, May 22, 2017. http://bostonreview.net/forum/james-gray-pope-ed-bruno-peter-kellman-right-strike

77. Dick Meister, "It Has Become a National Anti-Labor Relations Board," *Chicago Tribune*, April 6, 1988; see also David P. Gregory, "The NLRB and the Politics of Labor Law," 27 *B.C.L. Rev.* 39 (1985), http://lawdigitalcommons.bc.edu/bclr/vol27/iss1/2

78. "Anti-Worker Lawyer Appointed to Chair NLRB as GOP Regains Control of Board," IBEW Media Center, April 16, 2018. www.ibew.org/media-center/articles/18Daily/1804/180416-anti-worker

79. Letter Concerning Nomination of Peter Robb as NLRB General Counsel, October 2, 2017. https://aflcio.org/about/advocacy/legislative-alerts/letter-concerning nomination-peter-robb-nlrb-counsel

80. See "Unions Fear Rollback of Rights under Republicans," Steven Greenhouse, *New York Times,* November 2, 2010, p. A19.

81. "Unions Are Losers in Court Decision," WSJ.com, March 18, 2010.

82. Moody, *An Injury to All*, xx.

83. Stanley Aronowitz, "On the Future of American Labor;" Kim Moody, *US Labor in Trouble*.

84. Robert H. Zieger, Timothy J. Minchin, and Gilbert J. Gall, *American Workers, American Unions*.

85. Jeffery H. Keefe, "Are Wisconsin Public Employees Over Compensated?" Economic Policy Institute briefing paper, February 10, 2011; Andrea Orr, "Scapegoating Public Sector Workers," Economic Policy Institute, March 8, 2011.

86. "Out of Balance? Comparing Public and Private Sector Compensation over 20 Years," A report commissioned by the Center for State and Local Government Excellence and the National Institute on Retirement Security (NIRS), April 2010.

87. Sid Plotkin and Bill Scheuerman, "Tea Party Creams Labor," MRZine, May 5, 2011. http://mrzine.monthlyreview.org/2011/ps050511.html; John Nichols, *Uprising: How Wisconsin Renewed the Politics of Protest, from Madison to Wall Street* (New York: Nation Books, 2012).

88. Here again the literature on the bureaucratization of unions is voluminous, to say the least. Three representative examples are Kim Moody, *An Injury to All: The Decline of American Unions* (New York & London: Verso, 1988); James Wallihan (Washington, DC: Bureau of National Affairs, 1985); and Michael Goldfield, *The Decline of Organized labor in the United States* (Chicago: University of Chicago Press, 1987).

89. Gallop, Labor Unions, "Do you approve or disapprove of labor unions?" https://news.gallop.com/poll/12751/labor-unions.aspx

90. Jack Goldsmith, the stepson of a close associate of Jimmy Hoffa, claims that the McClellan hearings played a primary role in labor's decline. Jack Goldsmith, *In Hoffa's Shadow* (New York: Farrar, Straus and Giroux, 2019), 98–108; see also Robert Fitch, *Solidarity for Sale: How Corruption Destroyed the Labor Movement and Undermined America's Promise* (New York: Public Affairs, 2006).

91. Minchin, *Labor under Fire*, 276–278; see also Steven Greenhouse, "AFL-CIO Lays Off 105, but Discord Grows Louder," *New York Times*, May 8, 2005.

92. Robert Combs, "Labor Stats and Facts: Has Change to Win Out-Organized AFL-CIO?" *Bloomberg BNA*, June 13, 2012. www.bna.com/labor-stats-facts--b12884910076

93. Ibid.

94. Bill J. Fletcher, Jr. and Nelson Lichtenstein, "SEIU's Civil War," *In These Times*, December 16, 2009. www.inthesetimes.com/aricle/5309

95. Ibid.

96. Ibid.

97. Cal Winslow, *Labor's Civil War in California* (Oakland, CA: PM Press, 2010); Steve Early, *The Civil Wars in U.S. Labor: Birth of a New Workers Movement or the Death Throes of the Old*? (Chicago: Hay Market Books, 2011).

98. Labor Notes Staff, "SEIU International Attempts Disruption at 2008 Labor Notes Conference," *Labor Notes*, March 13, 2008. www.labornotes.org/2008/03/seiu-international-attempts-disruption-2008-labor-notes-conference

99. Alec MacGillis, "Union Leader Leaving with a Mixed Legacy," *Washington Post*, May 15, 2010, p. A2.

100. Steve Greenhouse, "Two Unions in Marriage Now Face Divorce Talks," *New York Times*, February 7, 2009.

101. Peter Dreier, "Divorce-Union Style: Can the Labor Movement Overcome UNITE HERE's Messy Breakup?" *The Nation*, August 12, 2009. www.thenation.com/article/divorce-union-style

102. Steve Early, "Change to Win's Lack of Change," Socialist Worker. org/2011/10/18change-to-wins-lack-of-change

103. Stephen Lerner, "An Immodest Proposal: A New Architecture for the House of Labor," *New Labor Forum* 1, no. 2 (2003): 7–30.

104. Kate Gibson, "Americans Still Support Unions—Even if They Don't Belong to One," CBS News Money Watch. www.cbsnews.com/news/majority-of-americans-support-labor-unions-fewer-belong-to-one; Lydia Saad," Labor Union Approval Study at 15-Year High," Gallup, Economy, August 30, 2018. https://news.gallup.com/poll/241679/labor-unions-approval-steady-year-high.aspx

105. David Rolf, *The Fight for $15: The Right Wage for a Working America* (New York: The New Press, 2016).

Chapter 3

1. NPR News, "In Confronting Poverty, 'Harvest of Shame' Reaped Praise and Criticism," May 31, 2014, www.npr.org/2014/05/31/317364146/in-confronting-poverty-harvest-of-shame-reaped-praise-and-criticism. The entire documentary can be viewed on YouTube at www.youtube.com/watch?v=1Am9oaWsIEE

2. Susan L. Marquis, *I Am Not a Tractor: How Florida Farmworkers Took On the Fast Food Giants and Won* (Ithaca, NY & London: Cornell University Press, 2017).

3. Colin Austin, "The Struggle for Health in Times of Plenty," in Charles D. Thompson and Melinda F. Wiggins, eds., *The Human Cost of Food* (Austin: University of Texas Press, 2002), 198–217.

4. Nano Riley, *Florida's Farmworkers in the Twenty-First Century* (Gainesville: University Press of Florida, 2002); Christopher Holden, "Bitter Harvest: Housing Conditions of Migrant and Seasonal Farmworkers," in Thompson and Wiggins, *The Human Cost of Food*, 169–193; Margaret Gray with Emma Kreyche, "The Hudson Valley Farmworker Report: Understanding the Needs and Aspirations of a Voiceless Population," Bard College Migrant Labor Project, n.d.

5. Seth Holmes, "Farmers Are Dying, COVID-19 Cases Are Spiking and The Food System Is In Peril," *Salon*, May, 31, 2020, www.salon.com/2020/05/31/farmworkers-are-dying-covid-19-cases-are-spiking-and-the-food-system-is-in-peril

6. Pete Daniel, *The Shadow of Slavery: Peonage in the South, 1901–1969* (Urbana: University of Illinois Press, 1972), 174.

7. Risa L. Goluboff, *The Lost Promise of Civil Rights* (Cambridge MA.: Harvard University Press, 2010).

8. C. Vann Woodward (Boston: Little, Brown, 1966).

9. Juan F. Perea, "The Echoes of Slavery: Recognizing the Racist Origins of the Agricultural and Domestic Worker Exclusion from the National Labor Relations Act," *Ohio State Law Journal* 72, no. 1 (2011): 101. Marc Linder, *Migrant Workers and Minimum Wages: Regulating the Exploitation of Agricultural Labor in the United States* (Boulder, CO: Westview Press, 1992), especially ch. 4; Greg Schell, "Farmworker Exceptionalism Under the Law: How the Legal System Contributes to Farmworker Poverty and Powerlessness," in Thompson and Wiggins, *The Human Cost of Food.*

10. Linder, *Migrant Workers and Minimum* Wages, 129.

11. Linder, *Migrant Workers and Minimum* Wages, 130. See also David Conrad, *The Forgotten Farmers: The Story of Sharecroppers in the New Deal* (Urbana: University of Illinois Press, 1965); Ira Katznelson, *When Affirmative Action Was White: An Untold History of Racial Inequality in Twentieth Century America* (New York: W.W. Norton, 2005).

12. Perea, "The Echoes of Slavery," 100.

13. Greg Hall, *The Harvest Wobblies: The International Workers of the World and Agricultural Laborers in the American West, 1905–1930* (Corvallis: Oregon State University Press, 2001); Phillip S. Foner, *History of the Labor Movement in the United States. Vol IV, The Industrial Workers of the World, 1905–1917* (New York: International Publishers, 1965).

14. Linder, *Migrant Workers and Minimum* Wages, 135–136.

15. *Schecter Poultry v. United States*, 295 U.S. 495 (1935).

16. Greg Schell, "Farmworker Exceptionalism under the Law," 141.

17. Laura Jordan, "States Granting Bargaining Rights to Agricultural Workers," OLR Research Report, September 13, 2000, www.cga.ct.gov/2000/rpt/2000-R-0894.htm. In June 2019, New York State lawmakers gave farmworkers the right to unionize.

18. EC55-801 Revised 1956 Farm Families and Social Security, Historical Materials from University of Nebraska-Lincoln Extension, 11–56, http://digitalcommons.unl.edu/cgi/viewcontent.cgi?article=4288&context=extensionhist

19. Cindy Hahamovitch, "Standing Idly By: 'Organized' Farmworkers in South Florida During the Depression and WWII," in Thompson and Wiggins, *The Human Cost of Food*, 55–86.

20. Roger Bruns, *Cesar Chavez and the United Farm Workers Movement* (Westport, CT: Greenwood Press, 2011); Ronald B. Taylor, *Chavez and the Farm Workers* (Boston: Beacon Press, 1975); Mario T. Garcia, ed., *A Dolores Huerta Reader* (Albuquerque: University of New Mexico Press, 2008).

21. W.K. Barger and Ernesto M. Reza, *The Farm Labor Movement in the Midwest: Social Change and Adaptation among Migrant Farmworkers* (Austin:

University of Texas Press, 1994); Rene Perez Rosenbaum, "Unionization of Tomato Field Workers in Northwest Ohio, 1967–1969," *Labor History* 35, no. 3 (Summer 1994): 329–344.

22. Marquis, *I Am Not a Tractor!*, 4–5.

23. Linder, *Migrant Workers and Minimum* Wages, 140; Hahamovitch, "Standing Idly By."

24. *New York Times*, February 7, 1972.

25. Bret McCabe, "Farmworkers to Table," *John Hopkins Magazine*, Fall 2018, https://hub.jhu.edu/magazine/2018/fall/greg-asbed-coalition-immokalee-workers

26. Marquis, *I Am Not a Tractor!*, 11–13.

27. Marquis, ibid.; Richard W. Coughlin and Peter S. Stedman, "The Moral Economy of Farm Labor: Notes on the Coalition of Immokalee Workers," paper presented at the 2000 Latin American Studies Association Conference, Miami, Florida, http://itech.fgcu.edu/faculty/rcoughlin/ciw.htm; Shaun Harkin interview of Marc Rodrigues, April 6, 2007; "Immokalee Workers Target Fast-Food Giant," *Socialist Worker*, www.socialistworker.org/2007-1/626/626_15_ciw_php

28. McCabe, "Farmworkers to Table."

29. Elly Leary, "Immokalee Workers Take Down Taco Bell," *Monthly Review*, October 1, 2005, https://monthlyreview.org/2005/10/01/immokalee-workers-take-down-taco-bell

30. Ibid.; Coughlin and Stedman, "The Moral Economy of Farm Labor."

31. Ibid.

32. Marquis, *I Am Not a Tractor!*, 34.

33. Ibid., 26; "Immokalee Workers Target Fast-Food Giant"; McCabe, "Farmworkers to Table."

34. Aaron Dorfman, "How Philanthropy Contributed to Improved Conditions for Tomato Pickers," *Washington Post*, July 02, 2014, www.huffpost.com/entry/how-philanthropy-contributed-tomato-pickers_b_5256316

35. Marquis, *I Am Not a Tractor!*, 45.

36. Ibid.

37. Ibid., 46.

38. Elly Leary, "Coalition of Immokalee Workers Campaign against Taco Bell (Boycott the Bell), 2001–2005," Global Non-Violent Action Database, Swarthmore College. https://nvdatabase.swarthmore.edu/content/coalition-immokalee-workers-campaign-against-taco-bell-boycott-bell-2001-2005

39. Marquis, *I Am Not a Tractor!*, 54.

40. Leary, "Immokalee Workers Take Down Taco Bell."

41. Ibid.; "Endorsements of the CIW Taco Bell Boycott," Coalition of Immokalee Workers, Blog, February 28, 2003, https://ciw-online.org/blog/2003/02/endorsementspg; Elly Leary, "Victory for Florida Farmworkers: Taco Bell Settles Boycott," *Labor Notes*, April 1, 2005, www.labornotes.org/2005/04/victory-florida-farmworkers-taco-bell-settles-boycott

42. Student/farmworker website, http://www.sfalliance.org

43. Ibid.

44. Marquis, *I Am Not a Tractor!*, 60.

45. "Coalition of Immokalee Workers Campaign against Taco Bell (Boycott the Bell), 2001–2005," Global Non-Violent Action Database, Swarthmore College, https://nvdatabase.swarthmore.edu/content/coalition-immokalee-workers-campaign-against-taco-bell-boycott-bell-2001-2005

46. McCabe, "Farmworkers to Table."

47. Marquis, *I Am Not a Tractor*, 59; Leary, "Immokalee Workers Take Down Taco Bell."

48. Marquis, *I Am Not a Tractor!*, 65.

49. "Taco Bell Agreement Analysis," Coalition of Immokalee Workers, Blog, March 10, 2005, https://ciw-online.org/blog/2005/03/agreement-analysis

50. Ibid.

51. Ibid.

52. U.S. Senate, Committee on Health, Education, Labor and Pensions, *Hearing of the Committee on Health, Education, Labor and Pensions: Examining Ending Abuses and Improving Working Conditions for Tomato Workers*, April 15, 2008.

53. Marquis, *I am Not a Tractor!*, 114–138.

54. "Fair Food Program: The Leading Edge of Human Rights in Agriculture," Coalition of Immokalee Workers, http://ciw-online.org/fair-food-program

55. WSR: Worker-Driven Social Responsibility Network, Fair Food Program. https://wsr-network.org/success-stories/fair-food-program

56. "Fair Food Program Takes United Nation's Annual Forum on Business and Human Rights in Geneva by Storm," Coalition of Immokalee Workers, Blog, November 30, 2015, http://ciw-online.org/blog/2015/11/ffp-united-nations; Marquis, *I Am Not a Tractor!*

57. Marquis, *I Am Not a Tractor!*, 3–4.

58. "U.S. Chamber Report Profiles Five Leading Worker Centers at the Forefront of New Union Organizing Push," U.S. Chamber of Commerce, February 26, 2014, www.uschamber.com/press-release/us-chamber-report-profiles-five-leading-worker-centers-the-forefront-new-union

59. Letter, Richard Berman, Executive Director, Center for Union Facts to Internal Revenue Service, TE/GE Division, November 6, 2017, www.unionfacts.com/article/wp-content/uploads/2017/11/CIW-Complaint.pdf

60. "IRS Should Crack Down on Coalition of Immokalee Workers," *Labor-Pains*, November 13, 2017, https://laborpains.org/2017/11/13/irs-should-crack-down-on-coalition-of-immokalee-workers

61. Chris Berardi, "Worker Centers: How Unions Circumvent Federal Rules," Congressman Francis Rooney website, March 2, 2018, https://francisrooney.house.gov/news/documentsingle.aspx?DocumentID=319

62. Leary, "Immokalee Workers Take Down Taco Bell."

63. Ibid.

64. "When Labor Laws Left Farm Workers Behind—and Vulnerable to Abuse," PBS News Hour (weekend), September 18, 2016, www.pbs.org/newshour/nation/labor-laws-left-farm-workers-behind-vulnerable-abuse

65. Justice for Farmworkers Campaign, http://ruralmigrantministry.org/en/justice-farmworkers-campaign

66. U.S. Department of Labor, Bureau of Labor Statistics, "Newsletter," January 18, 2019. https://www.bls.gov/news.release/pdf/union2.pdf

67. Ai-jen Poo and Tammy Kim, "Organizing to Transform Ourselves and Our Laws: The New Yok Domestic Workers Bill of Rights Campaign," *Clearing House Review: Journal of Poverty Law and Policy* 44, no. 12 (March–April 2011): 577–580.

68. "Small Farm Statistics," Cornell Small Farms Program, Cornell University. https://smallfarms.cornell.edu/contact/statistics-and-information-resources

69. Author's interview with Brian O'Shaugnessey, April 25, 2019.

70. "Forge a Better Food Chain," *Albany Times Union*, March 7, 2019, p. A12.

71. Cornell Small Farms Program, Small farm Statistics. https://smallfarms.cornell.edu/contact/statistics-and-information-resources; New York Farm Bureau, "New Ag. Census Shows Drop in New York Farms," www.nyfb.org/news/news-articles/new-ag-census-shows-drop-ny-farms

72. Author's interview with Brian O'Shaugnessey, April 25, 2019.

73. Carly Fox, Rebecca Fuentes, Fabiola Ortiz Valdez, Gretchen Purser, and Kathleen Sexsmith, "Milked: Immigrant Dairy Farmworkers in New York State." A 2017 report by the Workers' Center of Central New York and the Worker Justice Center of New York, pp. 19–20.

74. Emily Hamilton and Mary Jo Dudley, "The 'Yogurt Boom': Job Creation and the Role of Dairy Farmworkers in the Finger Lakes Region," PathStone Corporation, Cornell Farmworker Program, and Cornell Cooperative Extension. November 2013, https://cardi.cals.cornell.edu/sites/cardi.cals.cornell.edu/files/shared/documents/CFP/The-Yogurt-Boom.pdf; see also Mary Jo Dudley, "The Importance of Farm Labor in the New York State Yogurt Boom," Research and Policy Brief 62, October 2014, Cornell College of Agricultural and Life Sciences. https://cardi.cals.cornell.edu/sites/cardi.cals.cornell.edu/files/shared/documents/CFP/The-Yogurt-Boom.pdf

75. "Farmworkers' Overtime Pay Is Affordable and Long Overdue," Fiscal Policy Institute, May 2019, http://ruralmigrantministry.org/sites/default/files/docs/Support-the-Farm-Worker-Fair-Labor-Practices-Act.pdf

76. New York Economy, Agriculture, www.netstate.com/economy/ny_economy.htm; *New York Agriculture*, New York Farm Bureau, www.nyfb.org/about/about-ny-ag; Thomas P.P. Dinapoli, "Agriculture by the Numbers: New York

Farming is Big Business," New York State Comptroller, report 7-2013, August 2012.

77. Governor Andrew M. Cuomo's Task Force to Combat Worker Exploitation, 2016 Report, www.governor.ny.gov/sites/governor.ny.gov/files/atoms/files/EWTFReport_27.pdf

78. Fox et al., "Milked: Immigrant Dairy Farmworkers in New York State."

79. Margaret Gray with Emma Kreyche, "The Hudson Valley Farmworker Report: Understanding the Needs and Aspirations of a Voiceless Population." Bard College Migrant Labor Project.

80. "Attention Farm Workers," New York State Department of Labor, www.labor.ny.gov/formsdocs/wp/LS110.pdf

81. Fox et al., "Milked: Immigrant Dairy Farmworkers in New York State," 11.

82. Lisa Foderaro, "Study Finds Farmworkers Unaware of Job Protections," *New York Times*, October 24, 2007, www.nytimes.com/2007/10/24/nyregion/24report.html

83. Brian O'Shaugnessey, the retired director of the Labor Religion Coalition and consultant to the RMM, explains that the farmer's relationship to the sheriff is of crucial importance in determining whether nondocumented workers can work. This relationship puts "troublesome workers" in peril. Interview with author, March 8, 2019.

84. Rosa Goldensohn, "Ice Arrests New York Farm Workers, Alarming Industry and Advocates," Crain's New York Business, March 23, 2017, www.crainsnewyork.com/article/20170323/BLOGS04/170329954/ice-arrests-new-york-farm-workers-alarming-industry-and-advocates. Trump's aggressive approach squeezed farmers by exacerbating the tight labor market. In fact, according to the financial services firm of Farm Credit East, strict enforcement of the order had the potential to put about 1,000 of New York's farms out of business.

85. Margaret Gray, *Labor and the Locavore: The Making of a Comprehensive Food Ethic* (Berkeley, Los Angeles, & London: University of California Press, 2014)

86. "The Hudson Valley Farmworker Report: Understanding the Needs and Aspirations of a Voiceless Population." See also U.S. Department of Labor, Occupational Safety and Health Administration, "Agricultural Operations," www.osha.gov/dsg/topics/agriculturaloperations/index.html

87. "Small Farm Statistics," Cornell Small Farms Program, Cornell University, Ithaca, New York, https://smallfarms.cornell.edu/contact/statistics-and-information-resources

88. Robert Downen, "Eighty Years after Jim Crow, NY Farmers Still Fighting for Rights," *Albany Times Union*, May 27, 2017.

89. "Advocates Rally in Albany for Farmworker Rights," Press Release, New York Civil Liberties Union, May 15, 2018, www.nyclu.org/en/press-releases/advocates-rally-albany-farmworker-rights

90. Fox et al., "Milked: Immigrant Dairy Farmworkers in New York State," 31.

91. Jocelyn Sherman, "Stopping Sexual Harassment in the Fields," United Farmworkers blog, October 24, 2018, https://ufw.org/metoo

92. "Labor Problems Are the Bitter Fruit of Farmers Markets," Takepart, https://ufw.org/metoo

93. Lauren Kaori Gurley, "A Sexual Harassment Nightmare in Rural New York," National Public Radio, Latino, USA, February 14, 2018, www.latinousa. org/2018/02/14/sexual-harassment-nightmare-rural-new-york

94. Ibid.

95. Gwendolyn Craig, "Owasco Farm under Investigation for Worker Living Conditions," auburnpub.com, May 17, 2017, https://auburnpub.com/news/local/ owasco-farm-under-investigation-for-worker-living-conditions/article_a3321f03- ddad-5411-847b-85aca95d07d8.html

96. Two days prior to the session's conclusion, the legislature also passed the Green Light New York bill, a law that restores the right of undocumented immigrants to obtain a driver's license, a right taken away by Governor Pataki through executive order in 2001. Farmworkers again have the possibility of driving legally to shop, commute, go to the doctor's, and other such activities that are now dependent on the farmer's assistance. Governor Cuomo signed the bill into law almost immediately. Tara Smith, "Update: New York State Approves Licenses for Undocumented Immigrants," *The Suffolk Times*, June 17, 2019, https://suffolktimes.timesreview.com/2019/06/ update-new-york-state-approves-licenses-for-undocumented-immigrants

97. Amy Roth, David Robinson, and Sarah Teddeo, "Living to Work: Massive New York Greenhouse Coronavirus Outbreak Exposes Migrant Workers Vulnerability," *Utica-Observer Dispatch*, June 17, 2020, www.uticaod.com/story/ news/2020/06/17/living-to-work-massive-ny-greenhouse-coronavirus-outbreak- exposes-migrant-workersrsquo-vulnerability/113463258

98. History of RMM. http://ruralmigrantministry.org/en/history-rmm

99. Gray, *Labor and the Locavore*, 133.

100. Author's interview with Brian O'Shaugnessey, March 8, 2019.

101. Farmworker Albany Day. http://ruralmigrantministry.org/en/farmworker- albany-day

102. Gray, *Labor and the Locavore*, 133.

103. Actually the first State Assembly and Senate bills granting collective bargaining rights and overtime pay for farmworkers were introduced in 1994 and 1995. In 2000, these two bills were merged with other provisions into what is called the Farmworker Fair Labor Practices Act. See Stanley W. Telega and Thomas R. Maloney, "Legislative Actions on Overtime Pay and Collective Bargaining and Their Implications for Farm Employers in New York State, 2009–2010," College of Agriculture and Life Science, Cornell University, CE 2010-19, http://publications. dyson.cornell.edu/outreach/extensionpdf/2010/Cornell-Dyson-eb1019.pdf

104. Farmworker Albany Day. http://ruralmigrantministry.org/en/farmworker- albany-day

105. Gray, *Labor and the Locavore*, xxx.

106. For a clear and thoughtful analysis of worker conditions on the state's small farms, see Margaret Gray, "The Dark Side of Local," *Jacobin*, August 21, 2016, https://www.jacobinmag.com/2016/08/farmworkers-local-locavore-agriculture-exploitation

107. Workers Center, https://workerscny.org/en/about-2

108. Kerry Kennedy, "This Must be New York's Final Harvest of Shame: Let Us Finally Protect Exploited Farmworkers," *New York Daily News*, November 25, 2009, www.nydailynews.com/opinion/new-york-final-harvest-shame-finally-protect-exploited-farmworkers-article-1.420101

109. Stanley W. Telega and Thomas R. Maloney, "Legislative Actions on Overtime Pay and Collective Bargaining and Their Implications for Farm Employers in New York State, 2009–2010," 10–11.

110. Jude Seymour, "Farmworker Bill Fails in Senate," *Watertown Daily Times*, August 3, 2010. www.watertowndailytimes.com/article/20100803/BLOGS09/100809957/&

111. Telega and Maloney, "Legislative Actions," 11.

112. New York Civil Liberties Union. Legislative Memo: Regarding the Farmworkers Fair Labor Practices Act. May 18, 2015. www.nyclu.org/en/node/1661

113. "March for Farmworker Justice: New York Farmworkers Deserve Equal Rights," Event Calendar, Episcopal Church, www.episcopalchurch.org/events/march-farmworker-justice-new-york-farmworkers-deserve-equal-rights

114. Sarah Maslin Nir, "New York Farmworkers to Argue in State Supreme Court for Right to Organize," *New York Times*, July 19, 2017, www.nytimes.com/2017/07/19/nyregion/new-york-farmworkers-to-argue-in-state-supreme-court-for-right-to-organize.html?login=email&auth=login-email; *Harvard Civil Rights-Civil Liberties Law Review*, "Labor Law Left Farm Workers Behind. This State Constitutional Case May Change That," November, 30, 2018, https://harvardcrcl.org/labor-law-left-farm-workers-behind-this-state-constitutional-case-may-change-that

115. H. Claire Brown, "A New York Farmworker Was Fired for Organizing. State Supreme Court Says That's Legal," *The New Food Economy*, January 18, 2018, https://newfoodeconomy.org/new-york-state-supreme-court-dismisses-farmworker-unionization-suit

116. Mallory Moench and Diego-Mendoza-Moyers, "Court: Farm Staff Can Unionize," *Albany Times Union*, May 24, 2019.

117. New York Senate Standing Committees on Agriculture and Labor, Public Hearing on the Farmworkers Fair Labor Practices Act, April 25, 2019.

118. Email from Richard Witt to colleagues and supporters, June 17, 2019.

119. Miriam Pawel, "The Sad Lesson from California," *New York Times*, July 16, 2019, www.nytimes.com/2019/07/16/opinion/labor-laws-california-new-york-lesson.html?login=email&auth=login-email

120. Dennis Slattery, "Justice Sprouts for Farmworkers," *New York Daily News*, http://enewspaper.nydailynews.com/infinity/article_share.aspx?guid=1d0af969-110d-43ba-89e3-0d2c983fbe5d

Chapter 4

1. This summary of Jesse's experience is taken from Steven Blum, "Frustrated L.A. Rideshare Drivers Protest Uber's Latest Painful Pay Cut," *Los Angeles Magazine*, March 26, 2019, www.lamag.com/citythinkblog/uber-protest-los-angeles

2. Janice Fine, "How Innovative Worker Centers Help America's Most Vulnerable Wage Earners," Scholars Strategy Network, August 1, 2013, www.nytimes.com/2014/01/17/business/as-worker-advocacy-groups-gain-momentum-businesses-fight-back.html; Janice Fine, "Worker Centers: Organizing Communities at the Edge of the Dream," Fiscal Policy Institute, Briefing Paper #159, December 13, 2005.

3. The definitive study of worker centers, mainly immigrant centers, was conducted by Janice Fine in conjunction with the AFL-CIO's Fiscal Policy Institute. See Fine, *Worker Centers: Organizing Communities at the Edge of the Dream* (Ithaca, NY: Cornell University Press, 2006).

4. The Immigrant Act of 1924 (Johnson-Reed Act) limited immigration by reducing national origin quotas from 3 percent to 2 percent and pushing the calculation of the quotas from 1910 to 1890. Asians were totally excluded from entry into the United States. For a concise summary, see "The Immigration Act of 1924 (The Johnson-Reed Act)," Office of the Historian, Milestones, 1921–1936, https://history.state.gov/milestones/1921-1936/immigration-act

5. It's important to note that three-fifths of the working poor held full-time jobs. See "A Profile of the Working Poor," U.S. Department of Labor, Bureau of Labor Statistics. March 2002, Report 957. www.census.gov/library/publications/2001/demo/p60-214.html

6. Kati L. Griffith, "Worker Centers and Labor Law Protections: Why Aren't They Having Their Cake?," *Berkley Journal of Employment and Labor Law* 36, no. 331 (2015): 334, https://papers.ssrn.com/sol3/papers.cfm?abstract_id=2671391

7. Quoted in Benjamin Sachs, "Worker Centers and the 'Labor Organization' Question," *On Labor*, September 1, 2013, https://onlabor.org/worker-centers-and-the-labor-organization-question

8. Janice Fine, "How Innovative Worker Centers Help America's Most Vulnerable Wage Earners"; Fiscal Policy Institute briefing paper #159.

9. Fine, "Worker Centers: Organizing Communities at the Edge of the Dream."

10. For a detailed discussion of centers' outreach programs, see Fine, "Worker Centers: Organizing Communities at the Edge of the Dream," 42–71.

11. Ibid; see also Fine's analysis of nine major worker centers, "Worker Centers: Organizing Communities at the Edge of the Dream," *New York Law School Law Review* 50 (2005–2006): 417–463, www.nylslawreview.com/wp-content/uploads/sites/16/2013/11/50-2.Fine_.pdf

12. Fine, *Worker Centers: Organizing Communities at the Edge of the Dream*, 51.

13. C. Wright Mills, *The Sociological Imagination* (New York: Oxford University Press, 1959), esp. chapter 1, "The Promise," 3–24.

14. Jarol B. Manheim, "The Emerging Role of Worker Centers in Union Organizing: An Update and Supplement," U.S. Chamber of Commerce, Workforce Freedom Initiative, 13, www.uschamber.com/sites/default/files/uscc_wfi_worker centerreport_2017.pdf

15. Ibid., 55.

16. Josh Eidelson, "Who Should Fund Alt-Labor?" *The Nation*, July 17, 2013, www.thenation.com/article/who-should-fund-alt-labor

17. Ibid.

18. See the National Day Laborer Organizing network website at https://ndlon.org/about-us

19. Laura Flanders, "Bhairavi Desai of Taxi Workers Alliance Elected to AFL-CIO Executive Council," *The Nation*, September 16, 2013.

20. David Moberg, "The New AFL-CIO," *In These Times*, October 8, 2013. http://inthesetimes.com/article/15704/the_new_afl_cio

21. For a concise summary of the achievements of the Taxi Workers Alliance, see Josh Eidelson, "Alt-Labor," *The American Prospect*, January 29, 2013, https://prospect.org/article/alt-labor

22. Steve Early, "House of Labor Needs Repairs, Not Just New roommates," *Labor Notes*, September 16, 2013, https://www.labornotes.org/2013/09/house-labor-needs-repairs-not-just-new-roommates

23. Josh Eidelson, "A Reboot for the AFL-CIO?" *The Nation*, September 25, 2013, www.thenation.com/article/reboot-afl-cio

24. Steve Early, Report on AFL-CIO Convention: Labor's Days in La La Land," *Socialist Worker*.org, September 18, 2013, https://socialistworker.org/2013/09/18/labors-days-in-la-la-land

25. Ibid.

26. Quoted in Michael J. Lotito, Maury Baskin, and Tessa Gelbman, "A Special Labor Day 2013 Report: Is Labor Poised for Rebirth?" Littler Work Policy Institute, August 2013.

27. Steven Greenhouse, "Advocates for Workers Raise the Ire of Business," *New York Times*, January 16, 2014, www.nytimes.com/2014/01/17/business/as-worker-advocacy-groups-gain-momentum-businesses-fight-back.html

28. Sharon Block. "Backhanded Compliment: Acosta Threatens Workers Centers." Originally published at onLabor.org, November 20, 2017. https://lwp.law.harvard.edu/publications/backhanded-compliment-acosta-threatens-workers-centers

29. Letter, Virginia Fox, Chairwoman of the Committee on Education and the Workforce, and Tim Walberg, Chairman, Subcommittee on Health, Employment, Labor and Pensions, to Secretary Acosta, January 18, 2018, https://republicans-edlabor.house.gov/news/documentsingle.aspx?DocumentID=402413

30. Ben Penn and Jacquie Lee, " 'Worker Center or Union Probe May Be Sign of Things to Come," Bloomberg law, daily labor reports, March 15, 2018,

https://news.bloomberglaw.com/daily-labor-report/worker-center-or-union-probe-may-be-sign-of-things-to-come. For an analysis of worker centers and labor law, see Eli Naduris-Weissman, "The Worker Center Movement and Traditional Labor Law: A Contextual Analysis," 30 *Berkeley J. Emp.* 7 Lab L469 (2006).

31. Nathan Mehrens, Letter Re: Tax Exempt Status of "Worker Centers" to Senator Orin G. Hatch, Chairman of U.S. Senate Committee on Finance, October 23, 2015; Mehrens, "Big Labor's Tax Deductible Organizing Scam," *NetRightDaily*, October 26, 2015, http://netrightdaily.com/2015/10/big-labors-tax-deductible-organizing-scam

32. Penn and Lee, "'Worker Centers or Union Probe May Be Sign of Things to Come."

33. Mehrens, "Big Labor's Tax Deduction Scam," *NetRightDaily*, October 26, 2015, http://netrightdaily.com/2015/10/big-labors-tax-deductible-organizing-scam

34. See Griffith, "Worker Centers and Labor Law Protections"; see also Griffith, "The NLRA Defamation Defense: Doomed Dinosaur or Diamond in the Rough?" *American University Law Review* 59, no. 1 (2009), https://papers.ssrn.com/sol3/papers.cfm?abstract_id=1499771

35. National Labor Relations Act (1935) 29 U.S.C.

36. *NLRB v. Washington Aluminum Co.*, 370 U.S. 9 (1962).

37. *Lynn v. United Plant Guard Workers of America, Local 114*, 383 U.S.53 (86 S. Ct. 657, 15 L. Ed 2d582). A comprehensive discussion of this issue is found in Griffith, "The NLRA Defamation Defense: Doomed Dinosaur or Diamond in the Rough?"

38. Griffith, "The NLRA Defamation Defense," 118–119.

39. Cynthia L. Estlund, "Free Speech and Due Process in the Workplace," *Indiana Law Journal* 71, no. 1 (Winter 1995): 118n68.

40. Griffith, "Worker Centers and Labor Law Protections," 336.

41. Fine, *Worker Centers: Organizing Communities at the Edge of the Dream*, 245–248.

42. "Worker Centers: Union Corporate Campaigns Reinvented," U.S. Chamber of Commerce, March 31, 2017, www.uschamber.com/issue-brief/worker-centers-union-corporate-campaigns-reinvented

43. Sam Jewler, "Corporate Center Points Finger at Worker Centers," *CITIZENVOX*, April 21, 2014, https://citizenvox.org/2014/04/21/corporate-center-points-finger-at-worker-centers

44. Alexia Fernandez Campbell, "McDonald's Workers Are on Strike. 3 Presidential Candidates Join Them," *Vox*, May 23, 2019.

45. Steven Greenhouse, *Beaten Down, Worked Up: The Past, Present and Future of American Labor* (New York: Knopf, 2019), 217.

46. "The Gig Economy: 2020 Freelance Workforce Predicted to Rise to 43%," Nasdaq Latest news, June 14,2017, www.nasdaq.com/articles/gig-economy-2020-freelance-workforce-predicted-rise-43-2017-06-14

47. Diana Farrell and Fiona Greig, "The Online Platform Economy: Has Growth Peaked?" JP Morgan Chase Institute, November 2016.

48. Lawrence Mishel, "Uber and the Labor Market: Uber Drivers' Compensation, Wages, and the Scale of Uber and the Gig Economy," Economic Policy Institute, Report May 15, 2018, www.epi.org/publication/uber-and-the-labor-market-uber-drivers-compensation-wages-and-the-scale-of-uber-and-the-gig-economy

49. Louis Hyman, *Temp: How American Work, American Business, and the American Dream Became Temporary*, 298.

50. Ibid.

51. Mishel, "Uber and the Labor Market."

52. Lauren Kaori Gurley, "California Looks to Give Gig Workers Their Due," *The New Republic*, Jul 24, 2019, https://newrepublic.com/article/154517/california-ab5-gig-workers-employees; Sarah Kessler, *Gigged*, 6–7.

53. Sarah Leberstein, "Uber's Car leasing Program Turns Its Drivers Into Modern-day Sharecroppers," *Quartz*, June 6, 2016, https://qz.com/700473/ubers-car-leasing-program-turns-its-drivers-into-modern-day-sharecroppers

54. The Los Angeles driver who complained of taking passengers to northern California and even to Las Vegas not only lost flex time but was not remunerated for the long trip back to Los Angeles.

55. Gurley, "California Looks to Give Gig Workers Their Due"; Kessler, *Gigged*, 6–7.

56. Gurley, "California Looks to Give Gig Workers Their Due"; Kessler, *Gigged*, 6–7.

57. Alexia Fernandez Campbell, "California Just Passed a Landmark Law to Regulate Uber and Lyft," *Vox*, September 18, 2019, www.vox.com/2019/9/11/20850878/california-passes-ab5-bill-uber-lyft

58. Steven Blum, "Frustrated L.A. Rideshare Drivers Protest Uber's Latest Painful Pay Cut," *Los Angeles Magazine*, March 26, 2019, www.lamag.com/citythinkblog/uber-protest-los-angeles

59. Scott Cohen, "America's Ten Most Expensive Cities to Live in 2019," CNBC, July 10, 2019, www.cnbc.com/2019/07/10/americas-10-most-expensive-states-to-live-in-2019.html

60. *Douglas O'Connor, Thomas Colopy, Matthew Manahan, and Elie Gurfinkel v. Uber Technologies, Inc., U.S. District Court, Northern California*, case No. CV 13-3826-EMC. August 16, 2013.

61. Carolyn Said, "Uber Drivers Get Big Boost in Lawsuit against Company," *San Francisco Chronicle*, December 9, 2015, www.sfchronicle.com/business/article/Drivers-get-big-boost-in-lawsuit-vs-Uber-6687261.php

62. Ibid.

63. Michael Hiltzik, "California Regulators Blast a Big Hole in Uber's 'Sharing Economy' Dodge," *Los Angeles Times*, June 17, 2015, www.latimes.com/business/hiltzik/la-fi-mh-california-shoots-a-big-hole-in-uber-20150617-column.html

64. Ibid.

65. Carolyn Said, "Uber Bans Drivers from Class-Action Lawsuit Participation," *San Francisco Chronicle*, December 14, 2015, www.govtech.com/applications/Uber-Bans-Drivers-From-Class-Action-Lawsuit-Participation.html

66. After chipping away at worker's rights in numerous decisions, in *Epic Systems v. Lewis* the court ruled that arbitration provisions in employment contracts can be used by companies to prevent workers from collectively taking legal action regarding workplace issues. *O'Connor v. Uber*, No. 14—16078 (9th Cir. 2018); see also Adam Liptak, "Supreme Court Upholds Workplace Arbitration Barring Class Actions," *New York Times*, May 21, 2018, www.nytimes.com/2018/05/21/business/supreme-court-upholds-workplace-arbitration-contracts.html?auth=login-email&login=email

67. Diana Kapp, "Uber's Worst Nightmare," *San Francisco Magazine*, May 18, 2016, www.uberlawsuit.com/Uber's%20Worst%20Nightmare.pdf

68. Ibid.

69. Julie Carrie Wong, "Uber Reaches $100M Settlement in Fight with Drivers, Who Will Stay as Contractors," *The Guardian*, April 21, 2016, www.theguardian.com/technology/2016/apr/21/uber-driver-settlement-labor-dispute-california-massachusetts

70. Laura Waxmann, "Uber Drivers Push Back against Proposed Settlement in Suit," *SFGate*, June 3, 2016, https://blog.sfgate.com/inthemission/2016/06/03/uber-drivers-push-back-against-proposed-settlement-in-suit

71. Kapp, "Uber's Worst Nightmare."

72. Mike Isaac, "Judge Overturns Uber's Settlement With Drivers," *New York Times*, August 18, 2016, www.nytimes.com/2016/08/19/technology/uber-settlement-california-drivers.html

73. Ibid.

74. Author telephone interview with Edward Escobar, November 10, 2019.

75. Heather Somerville, "U.S. Judge Rejects $12.25 Million Settlement in Lyft Driver Lawsuit," Reuters, April 7, 2016, www.reuters.com/article/us-classaction-lyft/federal-judge-rejects-12-25-million-settlement-in-lyft-driver-lawsuit-idUSKCN0X42MN

76. Ibid.

77. Sarah Kessler, "What Does a Union Look Like in The Gig Economy?" *FastCompany*, February 19, 2015, www.fastcompany.com/3042081/what-does-a-union-look-like-in-the-gig-economy

78. Author telephone interview with Edward Escobar, November 10, 2019.

79. Joel Rosenblatt, "Uber Gambled on Driver Arbitration and Might Have Come Up the Loser," *Los Angeles Times*, May 8, 2019, www.latimes.com/business/la-fi-uber-ipo-arbitration-miscalculation-20190508-story.html; Somerville, "U.S. Judge Rejects $12.25."

80. Rosenblatt, "Uber Gambled on Driver Arbitration."

81. "Uber Drivers In Southern California Form Association with Teamsters Local 986," *TEAMSTERS*, August 27, 2014, https://teamster.org/news/2014/08/uber-drivers-southern-california-form-association-teamsters-local-986

82. Rideshare professor interview with Edward Escobar, September 2, 2019. www.youtube.com/watch?v=hbvZcybuzOk

83. Alan Feuer, "Uber Drivers Up Against the App," *New York Times*, February 19, 2016, www.nytimes.com/2016/02/21/nyregion/uber-drivers-up-against-the-app. html?auth=login-email&login=email

84. Rideshare Professor interview with Edward Escobar, September 2, 2019, www.youtube.com/watch?v=hbvZcybuzOk

85. Davey Alba, "Angry Uber Drivers Threaten to Make a Mess of the Super Bowl," *Wired*, February 6, 2016, www.wired.com/2016/02/uber-drivers-protest-san-francisco-super-bowl

86. Cora Lewis and Johanna Bhuiyan, "What Striking Uber Drivers Are Up Against," *BuzzFeed News*, February 9, 2016, www.buzzfeednews.com/article/coralewis/what-uber-strikers-are-up-against

87. Faiz Sidiqui, "Uber Drivers to Join Fight for $15 Demonstrations for Higher Wages," *The Washington Post*, November 29, 2016, www.washington-post.com/news/dr-gridlock/wp/2016/11/29/uber-drivers-to-join-fight-for-15-demonstrations-for-higher-wages

88. Rideshare professor interview with Edward Escobar, September 2, 2019, www.youtube.com/watch?v=hbvZcybuzOk

89. Marie Targonski-O'Brien, "Uber, Lyft Drivers Crowd LAX, Protest Low Pay," *KCET*, August 22, 2017, www.kcet.org/shows/socal-connected/uber-lyft-drivers-crowd-lax-protest-low-pay

90. Noam Scheiber and Kate Conger, "Uber and Lyft Gain Labor Clout, with Help From an App," *New York Times*, September 20, 2019, www.nytimes. com/2019/09/20/business/uber-lyft-drivers.html

91. *Dynamex Operations West, Inc. v. Superior Court of Los Angeles County* 4 cal. 5th 903 (2018) Supreme Court of California. April 30, 2018; Larry Buhl, "New Legislation Aims to Clarify Who Is an Employee," *The American Prospect*, February 22, 2019, https://prospect.org/labor/new-legislation-aims-clarify-employee

92. Veena Dubal, "Op-Ed; The Courts Have Decided Gig Workers Are Covered by Wage and Overtime Protections. Now Their Bosses Are Trying to Evade the Law." *Los Angeles Times*, August 14, 2018, www.latimes.com/opinion/op-ed/la-oe-dubal-gig-companies-undercut-california-wage-law-20180814-story.html

93. Rachel M. Cohen, "A California Bill Could Transform the Lives of Gig Workers. Silicon Valley Wants Labor's help to Stop it," *The Intercept*, July 18, 2019, https://theintercept.com/2019/07/18/uber-lyft-california-gig-economy-labor-unions

94. Barclay's estimated that classification of drivers as employees would cost Uber more than $500 million and Lyft about $290 million annually. See Alison Griswold, "How Much It Would Cost Uber and Lyft If Drivers Were Employ-

ees," *Quartz*, June 14, 2019, https://qz.com/1643263/the-cost-to-uber-and-lyft-if-drivers-were-employees

95. Johanna Bhuiyan, "'I'm Really Struggling': Facing Pay Cuts Some Ride-Hailing Drivers Prepare to Strike," *Los Angeles Times*, March 23, 2019, www.latimes.com/business/technology/la-fi-tn-uber-driver-strike-la-pay-cut-20190323-story.html; Paige Austin, "Uber Drivers Strike in Los Angeles, Sort Of," *Patch*, March 25, 2019, https://patch.com/california/los-angeles/uber-drivers-strike-los-angeles-sort

96. Johanna Bhuiyan, "'I'm Really Struggling.'"

97. Paige Austin, "Uber Drivers Strike in Los Angeles, Sort Of."

98. Dawn Kawamoto, "San Francisco Uber Drivers to Launch Protest, Blackout on Eve of IPO," *San Francisco Business Times*, May 1, 2019, www.bizjournals.com/sanfrancisco/news/2019/05/01/san-francisco-uber-drivers-launch-protest-ipo.html

99. Sara Ashley O'Brien, "Why Uber and Lyft Drivers Are Striking," CNN Business, May 8, 2019, www.cnn.com/2019/05/07/tech/uber-driver-strike-ipo/index.html

100. Associated Press, "Uber & Lyft Drivers Try to Organize Gig Workers," Courthouse News Service, May 10, 2019, www.courthousenews.com/uber-lyft-drivers-try-to-organize-gig-workers

101. Beth Daley, "Uber Drivers Strike: Organizing Labour in the Gig Economy," *The Conversation*, May 6, 2019, http://theconversation.com/uber-drivers-strike-organizing-labour-in-the-gig-economy-115911; Dawn Kawamoto, "San Francisco Uber Drivers to Launch Protest, Blackout on Eve of IPO."

102. Noam Scheiber, "Uber Drivers Are Contractors, Agency Finds," *New York Times*, May 15, 2019, B4, New York edition.

103. National Employment Law Project, News Release, "Report Exposes Gig Companies Campaign to Strip Workers of Employee Rights," March 26, 2019, www.nelp.org/news-releases/nelp-report-exposes-gig-companies-campaign-strip-workers-employee-rights; see also Maya Pinto, Rebecca Smith, and Irene Tung, "Rights at Risk: Gig Companies' Campaign to Upend Employment as We Know It," National Employment Law Project, March 25, 2019, www.nelp.org/publication/rights-at-risk-gig-companies-campaign-to-upend-employment-as-we-know-it

104. Dara Khosrowshahi and John Zimmer, "Open Forum: Uber, Lyft Ready to Do Our Part for Drivers," *San Francisco Chronicle*, June 12, 2019, www.sfchronicle.com/opinion/openforum/article/Open-Forum-Uber-Lyft-ready-to-do-our-part-for-13969843.php; see also Alexia Fernandez Campbell, "The High Stakes Battle Between Uber Executives and Drivers in California Explained," *Vox*, June 18, 2019, www.vox.com/2019/6/18/18682002/uber-lyft-drivers-california-ab5-bill

105. Gurley, "California Looks to Give Gig Workers Their Due."

106. Fernandez, "The High Stakes Battle."

107. Lauren Swiger, "This Rideshare Driver Demands a Voice—And a Living Wage," *San Francisco Chronicle*, June 19, 2019.

108. Joshua Sabatini and Joe Fitzgerald Rodriguez, "Mandelman to Hold Hearing on Working Conditions for Gig Workers to Boost Push For Labor Protections," *San Francisco Examiner*, June 18, 2019, www.sfexaminer.com/the-city/mandelman-to-hold-hearing-on-working-conditions-for-gig-workers-to-boost-push-for-labor-protections

109. Johanna Bhuiyan, "Uber and Lyft Drivers Swarm Sacramento as Lawmakers Advance Gig Workers' Rights Bill," *Los Angeles Times*, July 10, 2019, www.latimes.com/business/technology/la-fi-tn-gig-workers-ab5-lorena-gonzalez-uber-lyft-sacramento-20190710-story.html

110. "Editorial: California Legislators Could Save Gig Workers—Or Ruin the Part-Time Economy," *Los Angeles Times*, July 6, 2019, www.latimes.com/opinion/editorials/la-ed-dynamex-ab5-ride-sharing-20190706-story.html

111. Noam Scheiber, "Debate over Uber and Lyft Drivers' Rights in California Has Split Labor," *New York Times*, June 29, 2019, www.nytimes.com/2019/06/29/business/economy/uber-lyft-drivers-unions.html?auth=login-email&login=email; Alexia Fernandez Campbell, "Secret Meetings between Uber and Labor Unions Are Causing an Uproar," *Vox*, July 1, 2019, www.vox.com/2019/7/1/20677095/uber-lyft-labor-unions-ab5-california

112. Josh Eidelson, "Teamsters Union Splits from Uber and Lyft on California Worker Rights Law," *Bloomberg LP*, July 25, 2019, www.bloomberg.com/news/articles/2019-07-25/union-splits-from-uber-and-lyft-on-california-worker-rights-law

113. Dara Kerr, "Uber, Lyft Pull Out All Stops to Defeat Bill That'd Make Drivers Employees," *C/NET*, August 30, 2019, www.cnet.com/news/uber-lyft-pull-out-the-stops-to-defeat-bill-that-would-make-drivers-employees

114. Josh Eidelson, "California Governor Signs labor Law, Setting Up Bitter Gig Economy Fight," September 19, 2019, www.benefitnews.com/articles/law-could-force-gig-companies-to-reclassify-employees

115. "Calling an Employee and Employee," *New York Times*, A34, September 12, 2019.

116. Graham Rapier, "Uber, Lyft and DoorDash Have Now Spent More than $200 Million on Prop. 22—But There's No Guarantee It'll Pass," *Business Insider*, October 30, 2020, www.businessinsider.com/uber-doordash-lyft-prop-22-spending-200-million-close-polling-2020-10

117. Kerr, "Uber, Lyft Pull Out All Stops"; see also, Joe Kukara, "Uber and Lyft Drivers Plan Protest Caravan to Fight for Employee Rights," *SFiST*, August 23, 2019, https://sfist.com/2019/08/23/uber-and-lyft-driver-plan-protest-caravan-to-fight-for-employee-rights

118. Josh Eidelson, "The Gig Economy is Coming for Millions of American Jobs," Bloomberg Businessweek, February 17, 2021, 8. www.bloomberg.com/news/features/2021-02-17/gig-economy-coming-for-millions-of-u-s-jobs-after-california-s-uber-lyft-vote

119. Michelle Chen, "Uber and Lyft Hate This Bill," *The Nation*, August 2, 2019, www.thenation.com/article/uber-lyft-california-ab5

120. Shirin Ghaffary and Alexia Fernandez Campbell, "A Landmark Law Disrupted the Gig Economy in California. But What Comes Next for Uber Drivers?" *Vox*, October 4, 2019, www.vox.com/recode/2019/10/4/20898940/uber-lyft-drivers-ab5-law-california-minimum-wage-benefits-gig-economy-disrupted

121. Taryn Luna, "After Winning Prop. 22, Lyft President Says He Still Wants a Deal With Unions," *Los Angeles Times*, November 5, 2020, www.latimes.com/california/story/2020-11-05/prop-22-win-lyft-founder-union-deal-california; Josh Eidelson, "The Gig Economy is Coming for Millions of American Jobs," 9.

122. Email from Edward Escobar to author on November 12, 2019.

123. Janelle Orsi and Emily Doskow, *The Sharing Solution: How to save Money, Simplify Your Life and Build Community* (Berkeley: Nolo, 2009), 33–55; Janelle Orsi, *Practicing law in the Sharing Economy: Helping People Build Cooperatives, Social Enterprises and Local Sustainable Economies* (Chicago: American Bar Association Press, 2002).

124. Kessler, "What Does a Union Look Like in the Gig Economy?"

125. Sarah Kessler, "Fed Up With Uber and Lyft, Drivers Plan to Launch Competing App," *Fast Company*, February 23, 2016, www.fastcompany.com/user/sarah-kessler

126. Andrew Wolf, "The City Is Ours, Not Uber's," *Jacobin*, May 8, 2019, https://jacobinmag.com/2019/05/ubers-ipo-strike-lyft-cities-governance; see also, Benjamin Sachs, "The Uber/Lyft 'Workers' Association Debate," *OnLabor*, June 19, 2019, https://onlabor.org/the-uber-lyft-workers-association-debate; Sarah Kessler, "In Quest to Organize Gig Economy Workers, Unions Sometimes Clash," *Fast Company*, May 24, 2016, www.fastcompany.com/3060161/in-quest-to-organize-gig-economy-workers-unions-sometimes-clash

127. Josh Eidelson, "California Governor Signs Labor Law, Setting Up Bitter Gig Economy Fight," *Bloomberg News*, September 19, 2019, www.bloomberg.com/news/articles/2019-09-18/california-governor-signs-labor-law-setting-up-bitter-gig-economy-fight

128. Rideshare professor interview with Edward Escobar, September 2, 2019, www.youtube.com/watch?v=hbvZcybuzOk

129. Jessica Bursztynsky, "Uber Lays Off 17% of Workforce, Furloughs Hundreds More," CNBC, April 29, 2020.

130. Robert Booth, "Uber Driver Dies from Covid-19 after Hiding It Over Fear of Eviction," *The Guardian*, April 17, 2020, www.theguardian.com/world/2020/apr/17/uber-driver-dies-from-covid-9-after-hiding-it-over-fear-of-eviction

Chapter 5

1. This story taken from Natasha Burton and Levo League, "5 True Stories All Freelancers Dread," Fast Company, July 7, 2015, www.fastcompany.com/3048090/5-true-stories-all-freelancers-dread

2. Abdullahi Muhammed, "58% of Freelancers have Experienced Not getting paid for Their Work," Forbes, April 24, 2018, www.forbes.com/sites/ abdullahimuhammed/2018/04/24/shocker-58-of-freelancers-have-experienced-not-getting-paid-study-shows/#28dcce19175e

3. "Promising Protection: An Assessment of New York City's Free Lance Isn't Free," www.kentlaw.iit.edu/sites/ck/files/public/institutes-centers/ilw/Jackson_Louis_Competition/Promising_Protection_An_Assessment_of_New_York_City%27s_Freelance_Isn%27t_Free_Act.pdf

4. Quoted in Richard A. Greenwald, "Contingent, Transient and at Risk: Modern Workers in a Gig Economy," in Daniel Katz and Richard A Greenwald, eds. Labor Rising: The Past and Future of Working people in America (New York: The New Press, 2012), 112.

5. Sara Horowitz, "Freelancers in the U.S. Workforce," Monthly Labor Review, October 2015, www.bls.gov/opub/mlr/2015/article/freelancers-in-the-us-workforce.htm

6. Ibid.

7. Charles Heckscher, Sara Horowitz, and Althea Erickson, "Civil Society and The Provision of Services: The Freelancers Union Experience," in David Feingold, Mary Gatta, Hal Saltzman, and Susan Schurman, eds., Transforming the U.S. Workforce Development System: Lessons from Research and Practice (Ithaca, NY: Cornell University Press, 2010).

8. Ibid.

9. Steven Hill, Raw Deal: How the "Uber Economy" and Runaway Capitalism Are Screwing American Workers (New York: St. Martin's Press, 2015)

10. Amy Wilkinson, "The Entrepreneurial Union: The Freelancers Union is Modernizing the Labor Movement for Independent Workers," Stanford Social Innovation Review, Fall 2009, https://ssir.org/articles/entry/the_entrepreneurial_union

11. "About the Freelancers Union," www.freelancersunion.org/about

12. Testimony of Sara Horowitz, Founder and Executive Director, Freelancers Union Before the House Oversight and Government Reform Committee, Subcommittee on Economic Growth, Job Creation and Regulatory Affairs and Subcommittee on Energy Policy, Health Care, and Entitlements. February 5, 2014, https://republicans-oversight.house.gov/wp-content/uploads/2014/02/Horowitz_Testimony.pdf

13. Martha W. King, "Protecting and Representing Workers in the New Gig Economy," in Ruth Milkman and Ed Ott, eds., New Labor in New York: Precarious Workers and the Future of the Labor Movement (Ithaca, NY & London: Cornell University Press, 2014), 150.

14. Greenwald, "Contingent, Transient and at Risk," 120.

15. Guy Standing, The Precariat: The New Dangerous Class (New York: Bloomsbury Academic, 2011).

16. Michelle V. Rafter, "10 Things You Didn't Know About the Freelancers Union," https://michellerafter.com/2013/04/08/10-things-you-didnt-know-about-freelancers-union

17. Tejal Rao, "Hive Mind," *The Village Voice*, http://digitalissue.villagevoice.com/publication/?i=146601&article_id=1314909&view=articleBrowser &ver=html5#{"issue_id":146601,"view":"articleBrowser","article_id":"1314909"}; see also Anya Kamenetz, "Why Freelancers Are So Depressed, *Fast Company*, February 27, 2013, www.fastcompany.com/3006208/why-freelancers-are-so-depressed

18. William H. Whyte, Jr., *The Organization Man* (New York: Simon and Schuster, 1956); see also, C. Wright Mills, *White Collar* (London, Oxford, & New York: Oxford University Press, 1951).

19. Sara Horowitz with Sciarra Poynter, *The Freelancer's Bible* (New York: Workman Publishing Company, 2012), 7

20. Sara Horowitz, "Freelancers in the U.S. Workforce."

21. Sara Horowitz, "Welcome to Middle-Class Poverty—Does Anybody Know the Way Out?" *The Atlantic*, September 23, 2011, www.theatlantic.com/business/archive/2011/09/welcome-to-middle-class-poverty-does-anybody-know-the-way-out/245447; see also Sara Horowitz, "Future of Work 2.0: Building the Next Safety Net," A Medium Corporation, July 31, 2018, https://medium.com/@sara_horowitz/future-of-work-2-0-building-the-next-safety-net-7fdae89904a1

22. Horowitz, "Freelancers in the U.S. Workforce."

23. "Mutual Support for the Information Age," https://blog.freelancersunion.org/2011/01/24/mutual-support-for-the-information-age

24. Sara Horowitz, "How Do You Build a Union for the 21st Century? (Step 1: Learn from History)," *The Atlantic*, September 3, 2012, www.theatlantic.com/business/archive/2012/09/how-do-you-build-a-union-for-the-21st-century-step-1-learn-from-history/261884

25. Steven Fraser, *Labor Will Rule: Sidney Hillman and the Rise of American Labor* (New York: The Free Press, 1991), 83.

26. A classic on this period is Robert K. Murray, *Red Scare: A Study in National Hysteria, 1919–20* (New York: McGraw Hill, 1964); for government's treatment of unions, see Robert H. Zeiger, *Republicans and Labor: 1919–1920* (Lexington: University of Kentucky Press, 1969).

27. Mike Mariana, "The New Generation of Self-Created Utopias," *New York Times*, January 16, 2020, www.nytimes.com/2020/01/16/t-magazine/intentional-communities.html?auth=login-email&login=email; regarding the cooperative efforts of the Knights of Labor, see Leon Fink, *Workingman's Democracy: The Knights of Labor and American Politics* (Champaign: University of Illinois Press, 1983).

28. Fraser, *Labor Will Rule*, 153.

29. Amalgamated Bank, "Our Story: A Legacy of Access, Affordability and Advocacy," www.amalgamatedbank.com/our-story

30. Ibid.

31. David Thompson, "Housing Case Study 4: U.S. Unions Help Build Housing Co-operatives," *COOP News*, May 22, 2014, www.thenews.coop/85298/ sector/housing-case-study-4-us-unions-help-build-housing-co-operatives

32. Ibid.

33. Horowitz, "How Do You Build a Union?" Much has been written about the Amalgamated Bank and Sidney Hillman's battles against industrial capitalism, but the seminal work on the subject remains Steven Fraser's *Labor Will Rule: Sidney Hillman and the Rise of American Labor.*

34. Horowitz, "How Do You Build a Union?"

35. "Freelancers Union: Branding a Social Innovation," Cultural Strategy Group. Abridged chapter from Douglas Holt and Douglas Cameron, *Cultural Strategy: Using Innovative Ideologies to Build Breakthrough Brands* (New York: Oxford University Press, 2010), https://culturalbranding.org/wp-content/uploads/2010/10/ FLU-case-website.pdf

36. Ibid.

37. Sara Horowitz with Toni Sciarra, *The Freelancer's Bible*, 14.

38. Ibid.

39. See "Freelancer Union Subway Ads," contributed by Nick Sherman, April 20, 2012. Artwork published circa 2012, https://fontsinuse.com/uses/1448/ freelancers-union-subway-ads; Martha W. King's "Protecting and Representing Workers in the New Gig Economy: The Case of the Freelancers Union" has a nice summary of the subway ads (pp. 164–166).

40. "Freelancers Union: Branding a Social Innovation," Cultural Strategy Group.

41. Ibid.

42. About Freelancers Union https://www.freelancersunion.org/about

43. Rana Foroohar, "Strong Unions Will Boost America's Economy," *Financial Times*, July 31, 2017, www.ft.com/content/6965239a-6e30-11e7-bfeb-33fe0c5b7eaa

44. Upwork Press Release, "Sixth Annual 'Freelancing in America' Study Finds That More People Than Ever See Freelancing as a Long-Term Career Path," Upwork, October 3, 2019, www.upwork.com/press/2019/10/03/freelancing-in-america-2019

45. King, "Protecting and Representing Workers," 169–170.

46. Ibid.

47. Adam Warner, "30+ Freelance Stats for 2019," Website Planet, September 8, 2019, www.websiteplanet.com/blog/freelance-stats

48. Anthony Cilluffo and Richard Fry, "Gen Z, Millennials and Gen X Outvoted Older Generations in 2018 Midterms," Pew Research Center, *FactTank*, May 29, 2019, www.pewresearch.org/fact-tank/2019/05/29/gen-z-millennials-and-gen-x-outvoted- older-generations-in-2018-midterms

49. Kim Parker, Nikki Graf, and Ruth Igielnik, "Generation Z Looks a Lot Like Millennials on Key Social and Political Issues," Pew Research Center, January 17, 2019, www.pewsocialtrends.org/2019/01/17/generation-z-looks-a-lot-like-millennials- on-key-social-and-political-issues

50. Ziad Reslan, "Freelancers Rights Come of Age as Gig Economy Booms," Helewix, October 31, 2018, http://helewix.com/howto/freelancers-rights-come-of-age-as-gig-economy-booms

51. "Freelancing in America: 2019," Commissioned by UpWork and Freelancers Union, October 2019, slide 42, www.slideshare.net/upwork/freelancing-in-america-2019

52. Ibid., slide 27.

53. Freelancers Union, "The Costs of Non-Payment: A Study of Non-payment and Late Payment in the Freelance Workforce," December 10, 2015, https://blog.freelancersunion.org/2015/12/10/costs-nonpayment

54. "Freelancing in America: 2019," Commissioned by UpWork and Freelancers Union, October 2019, slides 47–49.

55. Halley Bondy telephone interview with author, March 12, 2020.

56. "Freelancing in America: 2019," slides 13 and 58.

57. Blog Freelancers Union, "Misclassification Laws Must Not Threaten the Livelihoods of Freelancers," December 16, 2019, https://blog.freelancersunion.org/2019/12/16/misclassification-laws-must-not-encroach-upon-the-livelihoods-of-freelancers

58. "Freelancing in America: 2019," slide 38.

59. Sarah Laskow, "Freelancers Insurance Evolves, Again (and Again)," *Politico*, October 1, 2014, www.politico.com/states/new-york/albany/story/2016/05/freelancers-insurance-evolves-again-and-again-049831

60. King, "Protecting and Representing Workers," 155.

61. Laskow, "Freelancers Insurance Evolves."

62. Wilkinson, "The Entrepreneurial Union."

63. Upset Freelancers Union members, "An Open letter to Freelancers Union," November 20, 2008, https://upsetfu.blogspot.com

64. Steven Greenhouse, "Freelancers Balk at a Change in Health Benefits," *New York* Times, December 7, 2008, www.nytimes.com/2008/12/08/nyregion/08freelancers.html

65. Richard Pollack, "Nonprofit Health Insurance Pioneer Closes Its Doors Due to Obama Care Costs," *Washington Examiner*, October 8, 2014, www.washingtonexaminer.com/nonprofit-health-insurance-pioneer-closes-its-doors-due-to-obamacare-costs

66. Clinton Global Initiative, A National Benefits Platform for the New Workforce, www.clintonfoundation.org/clinton-global-initiative/commitments/national-benefits-platform-new-workforce

67. Testimony of Sara Horowitz at Joint Hearing on "Health Insurance CO-OPs: Examining Obamacare's $2 Billion Loan Gamble," before the Subcommittee on Economic Growth, Job Creation, and Regulatory Affairs, and the Subcommittee on Energy Policy, Health Care, and Entitlements of the Committee on Oversight and Government Reform, House of Representatives, 113th Congress, Second Session, February 5, 2014.

68. Julia James, "The CO-OP Health Insurance Company," *Health Affairs*, February 28, 2013, www.healthaffairs.org/do/10.1377/hpb20130228.47227/full

69. U.S. House of Representatives, Committee on Oversight and Government Reform, "Examining the Administration's $2 Billion Obamacare Loan Guarantee Gamble: Two Case Studies of Political Influence Peddling and Millions of Taxpayer Dollars Wasted," Staff Report, 113th Congress, February 4, 2014.

70. Testimony of Sara Horowitz at Joint Hearing on "Health Insurance CO-OPs: Examining Obamacare's $2 Billion Loan Gamble."

71. Ibid.

72. Guadalupe Gonzalez, "This Entrepreneur Is Teaming Up with Silicon Valley Royalty to Bring Short-Term Disability to Gig Workers," *Inc.*, August 1, 2018, www.inc.com/guadalupe-gonzalez/trupo-sara-horowitz-short-term-disability-insurance-freelancers-gig-economy.html

73. "Meet Trupo: A New Kind of Insurance Company to Offer First-of-its Kind Safety Net to Freelancers," Press Release, Trupo, July 31, 2018, www.bloomberg.com/press-releases/2018-07-31/meet-trupo-a-new-kind-of-insurance-company-to-offer-first-of-its-kind-safety-net-to-freelancers

74. Steven Greenhouse, "Tackling Concerns of Independent Workers," *New York Times*, March 23, 2013, www.nytimes.com/2013/03/24/business/freelancers-union-tackles-concerns-of-independent-workers.html

75. Adam Bluestein, "Sara Horowitz: Labor's Renaissance Woman," *Fast Company*, October 14, 2012, www.fastcompany.com/3002367/sara-horowitz-labors-renaissance-woman

76. King, "Protecting and Representing Workers," 158; United States Government Accountability Office, "Employment Arrangements: Improved Outreach Could Help Ensure Proper Worker Classification," Report to the Ranking Minority Member, Committee on Health, Education, Labor, and Pensions, July 2006, www.gao.gov/new.items/d06656.pdf

77. Blog Freelancers Union, "Freelance Politics: The Unincorporated Business Tax Campaign Heats Up," June 1, 2009.

78. Wilkinson, "The Entrepreneurial Union."

79. "New York's Paid Family Leave Law: What Freelancers Need to Know," Blog, Freelancers Union, December 14, 2017, https://blog.freelancersunion.org/2017/12/14/new-yorks-paid-family-leave-law-what-freelancers-need-to-know

80. New York City, Office of the Mayor, Press Release, "Freelancers Aren't Free: Mayor Announces First in Nation Protections for Freelance Workers," May 15, 2017, www1.nyc.gov/office-of-the-mayor/news/307-17/freelancers-aren-t-free-mayor-first-nation-protections-freelance-workers

81. Rafter, "10 Things You Didn't Know about the Freelancers Union."

82. "5 Ways Freelancers Got the Freelance Isn't Free Act Passed," Blog, Freelancers Union, Nov. 1, 2016, https://blog.freelancersunion.org/2016/11/01/5-ways-nyc

83. New York City, Office of the Mayor, Press Release, "Freelancers Aren't Free: Mayor Announces First in Nation Protections for Freelance Workers."

84. New York City Council, District 39, Brad Lander, "NYC Council Member Brad Lander and Freelancers Union Celebrate passage of Legislation to protect Freelance Workers From Discrimination and Harassment," September 12, 2019.

85. "8 Ways Freelancers Union Helps Freelancers," Blog, World of Freelancers, May 28, 2019, www.worldoffreelancers.com/8-ways-freelancers-union-helps-freelancers

86. Gabrielle Wuolo, "New Tool Lets Freelancers Rate Clients and Companies," Freelancers Union Blog, May 31, 2011, https://blog.freelancersunion.org/2011/05/31/new-tool-lets-freelancers-rate-clients-and-companies

87. Freelancers Union, "The Freelance Contract: Make Your Contract Yours," www.freelancersunion.org/resources/contract-creator

88. LaToya Irby, "Book Review: The Freelancers Bible," All Freelance Writing, January 28, 2013, https://allfreelancewriting.com/book-review-the-freelancers-bible

89. Elaine Pofeldt, "A New Safety Net For Freelancers," *Forbes*, June 25, 2014, www.forbes.com/sites/elainepofeldt/2014/06/25/a-new-safety-net-for-freelancers/#54f200113bf9

90. Yuki Noguchi, "This New Program Aims to Train the Growing Freelance Workforce," NPR, January 4, 2019, www.npr.org/2019/01/04/681807327/this-new-program-aims-to-train-the-growing-freelance-workforce

91. "Freelancing in America: 2019," Commissioned by UpWork and Freelancers Union, October 2019.

92. Steven Greenhouse, "Tackling Concerns of Independent Workers."

93. Michelle Miller, "The Union of the Future," The Roosevelt Institute, July 6, 2015, https://rooseveltinstitute.org/union-future

94. Eugene Meyer, "Founder Advocates a 'New Mutualism' between Workers and Communities," in *Selections from CQ Researcher*, 18th edition, https://books.google.com/books?id=aOiVDgAAQBAJ&pg=PT234&lpg=PT234&dq=criticisms+of+freelancers+union&source=bl&ots=Oyoezwq4Rr&sig=ACfU3U2kXJoVtfK1m1TlP--4pflXGDBnMA&hIssues for Debate in American Policy

95. Larry Mishel, "Despite Freelancers Union/Upwork Claim, Freelancing Is Not Becoming American's Main Source of Income," Economic Policy Institute, Briefing Paper #415, December 9, 2015. See also "Freelancing in America: 2019," Commissioned by UpWork and Freelancers Union, October 2019; Colton Cox, "The BLS Just Released Its First Research on the Freelance Economy in 13 Years," *The Freelancer*, June 8, 2018, https://contently.net/2018/06/08/resources/news/bls-research-freelance-economy

96. Mishel, ibid.

97. Jonathan Rothwell, "Earning Income on the Side Is a Large and Growing Slice of American Life," *New York Times*, December 18, 2019, www.nytimes.com/2019/12/18/upshot/multiple-jobs-united-states.html

98. Kim Moody, *On New Terrain: How Capital Is Reshaping the Battleground of Class War* (Chicago: Haymarket Books, 2017), 28.

99. Larry Mishel, "Despite Freelancers Union/Upwork Claim."

100. Freelancers Union, "New Freelancers Union Study Reveals the Scope of Coronavirus Losses," April 2, 2020, https://blog.freelancersunion.org/2020/04/02/new-freelancers-union-study-reveals-the-scope-of-coronavirus-losses

101. Uri Berliner, "Jobs in the Pandemic: More Are Freelance and May Stay That Way Forever, Northeast Public Radio, September 16, 2020, www.npr.org/2020/09/16/912744566/jobs-in-the-pandemic-more-are-freelance-and-may-stay-that-way-forever

102. Upwork Press, News & Media Coverage, "New Upwork Study Finds 36% of U.S. Workforce Freelance Amid the COVID-19 Pandemic," September 15, 2020, www.upwork.com/press/releases/new-upwork-study-finds-36-of-the-us-workforce-freelance-amid-the-covid-19-pandemic

103. A good example is Ari Paul, "A Union of One," *Jacobin*, October 2014, www.jacobinmag.com/2014/10/freelancers-union

104. Author interview with Rafael Espinal, May 11, 2020.

105. Steve Fraser, *The Age of Acquiescence: The Life and Death of American Resistance to Organized Wealth and Power* (New York, Boston, & London: Little, Brown, 2015).

106. C. Wright Mills, *Sociological Imagination*.

107. Some conservatives such as Eli Lehrer argue that worker centers are a good conservative alternative to unions that could be used to split the political commitment of workers to the Democratic Party. See Eli Lehrer, "How the Trump Administration Should Help Nontraditional Labor Organizations," *NR Plus Magazine*, November 25, 2019.

108. Steven Hill, *Raw Deal*.

Chapter 6

1. Steven Greenhouse, "How to Get Low-Wage Workers into the Middle Class," *The Atlantic*, August 19, 2015, www.theatlantic.com/business/archive/2015/08/fifteen-dollars-minimum-wage/401540

2. William Finnegan, "Dignity: Fast Food Workers and a New Form of Labor Activism," *The New Yorker*, September 8, 2014, www.newyorker.com/magazine/2014/09/15/dignity-william-finnegan

3. Ibid.

4. Max Zahn, "First the Fight for $15, Then West Virginia Teachers: Can a New Playbook Rescue the Labor Movement?" *In These Times*, March 27, 2018, http://inthesetimes.com/working/entry/21015/fight-for-15-west-virginia-teachers-unions-labor-movement-Disney; see also, Eric Blanc, *Red State Revolt: The Teachers' Strike Wave and Working-Class Politics* (London: Verso, 2019).

5. According to Popeyes owner and founder, the company does not use an apostrophe because he couldn't afford it when he started the company.

6. Dominic Rushe with video by Tom Silverstone, "Fran Works Six Days a Week in Fast Food, and Yet She's Homeless: 'It's Economic Slavery,'" *The Guardian*, August 21, 2017, www.theguardian.com/us-news/2017/aug/21/missouri-fast-food-workers-better-pay-popeyes-economics

7. Ibid.

8. Laura Flanders, "Workers ROC the Restaurant Industry," *The Nation*, August 14, 2013, www.thenation.com/article/archive/workers-roc-restaurant-industry

9. Amanda Marcotte, "Who's behind the Fast Food Strikes? Working Women," *Slate*, September 2, 2013, https://slate.com/human-interest/2013/09/fast-food-strikes-low-wage-female-workers-are-driving-this-labor-movement.html

10. Saru Jayaraman, Forked: *A New Standard for American Dining* (New York: Oxford University Press, 2016), 94.

11. Finnegan, "Dignity: Fast Food Workers and a New Form of Labor Activism."

12. "Restaurants Flourish with One Fair Wage," Restaurant Opportunities Center United, February 13, 2018, https://chapters.rocunited.org/wp-content/uploads/2018/02/OneFairWage_W.pdf

13. Sylvia A. Allegretto and Kai Filion, "Waiting for Change," Briefing Paper #297, Economic Policy Institute and Center on Wage and Employment Dynamics, February 23, 2011.

14. Aaron Hotfelder, "New York Laws for Tipped Employees," *NOLO*. n.d., www.nolo.com/legal-encyclopedia/new-york-laws-tipped-employees.html

15. Flanders, "Workers ROC."

16. Madeline Aulseer, "Checkmate: U.S. Payroll Card Programs Trump Paper Checks," *Aite* Group, April 8, 2015, https://aitegroup.com/report/checkmate-us-payroll-card-programs-trump-paper-checks

17. "The High Cost of Getting Paid: How Payroll Cards Cost Darden Employees," The Restaurant Opportunities Center United, May 2016, https://chapters.rocunited.org/wp-content/uploads/2016/05/HighCostGettingPaid_Report_Web-2.pdf

18. Caroline Fairchild, "Low-wage Workers Are Robbed More than Banks, Gas Stations and Convenience Stores Combined," *HUFFPOST*, updated December 6, 2017, www.huffpost.com/entry/low-wage-workers-robbed_n_4178706; Brady Meixell and Ross Eisenbrey, "An Epidemic of Wage Theft Is Costing Hundreds of Millions of Dollars a Year," *Economic Policy Institute*, Issue Brief #385 September 11, 2014, www.epi.org/publication/epidemic-wage-theft-costing-workers-hundreds

19. Dana Hatic, "How Restaurants Get Away with Stealing Millions from Workers Every Year," *EATER*, September 25, 2018, www.eater.com/2018/9/25/17886990/how-restaurants-steal-from-workers-wage-theft

20. Corporate Research Project of Good Jobs First, "Violation Tracker Parent Company Summary," 2019 https://violationtracker.goodjobsfirst.org/industry/restaurants%20and%20foodservice

21. "Our Tips Belong to Us," Restaurant Opportunities Center United, October 2017, https://rocunited.org/wp-content/uploads/2017/10/OurTips_2017_W.pdf

22. Lewis Jackson, "Department of Labor to Rescind 2011 Tip Pooling Regulation," *The National Law Review*, July 20, 2017, www.natlawreview.com/article/department-labor-to-rescind-2011-tip-pooling-regulation

23. Kate Tornone, "DOL Takes a Second Swing at Tip Credit, Pooling Regs," *HRDIVE*, October 7, 2019, www.hrdive.com/news/dol-takes-a-second-swing-at-tip-credit-pooling-regs/564498; Andrea Strong, "Trump Is About to Make Tip Pooling Legal Again. Here's What It Means for Restaurant Workers," *EATER*, December 5, 2017, www.eater.com/2017/12/5/16708374/tipping-laws-trump-department-of-labor-changes

24. Y. Douglas Yang, "Share the Tip Jar: Department of Labor Finalizes Rule Opening Tip Pooling to Back-of-the-House Workers," Sheppard Mullin's Labor & Employment Law Blog, December 22, 2020, www.laboremploymentlawblog.com/2020/12/articles/tip-pooling/dol-tip-credit

25. Editorial Board, "Wage Theft in Restaurants," *New York Times*, March 12, 2018, www.nytimes.com/2018/03/12/opinion/tipping-restaurants-servers-cuomo-new-york.html

26. Phillip Mattera, "Darden Restaurants: Corporate Rap Sheet," Corporate Research Project, n.d, www.corp-research.org/darden

27. Corporate Research Project of Good Jobs First, "Violation Tracker Parent Company Summary," 2019, https://violationtracker.goodjobsfirst.org/parent/darden-restaurants

28. Alex N. Press, "It's Time to End the Subminimum Wage for Tipped Workers," *Jacobin*, October 2, 2020.

29. Patrick McGeehan, "After Winning a $15 Minimum Wage, Fast Food Workers Now Battle Unfair Firings," *New York Times*, February 12, 2019, www.nytimes.com/2019/02/12/nyregion/fast-food-worker-firings.html

30. "Burned: High Risks and Low Benefits for Workers in the New York City Restaurant Industry," Restaurant Opportunities Center of New York, September 11, 2009, https://rocunited.org/publications/burned-2009

31. Saru Jayaraman, "Olive Garden has Unlimited Breadsticks—Also Lots of Labor Issues, Illness Outbreaks, and an Icky Sexual Harassment Policy," *Salon*, February 1, 2016, www.salon.com/2016/02/01/olive_garden_has_unlimited_breadsticks_also_lots_of_labor_issues_illness_outbreaks_and_an_icky_sexual_harassment_policy

32. Jesse Starkey, "Restaurant Workers Speak Out about the Spread Of COVID-19 inside the Food Service Industry," ABC6/Fox28 Columbus, Ohio, July 8, 2020, https://abc6onyourside.com/news/local/restaurant-workers-speak-out-about-the-spread-of-Covid-19-inside-the-food-service-industry

33. National Employment Law Project, "Behind the Arches: How McDonald"s Fails to Protect Workers from Workplace Violence," May 22, 2019, www.

nelp.org/publication/behind-the-arches-how-mcdonalds-fails-to-protect-workers-from-workplace-violence

34. M.L. Nestel, "US Fast-Food Workers Demand Better Pay Amid Growing Violence," *The Guardian*, August 4, 2019, www.theguardian.com/food/2019/aug/04/us-fast-food-workers-demand-better-pay-amid-growing-violence

35. Zlati Meyer, "Amid McDonald's Strike, Fast-Food Workers Often Vulnerable to Sexual harassment," *USA Today*, September 18, 2018, www.usatoday.com/story/money/2018/09/18/age-few-options-make-fast-food-staff-vulnerable-sexual-harassment/1307263002

36. Sylvia A. Allegretto, Marc Doussard, David Graham, Ken Jacobs, Dan Thompson, and Jeremy Thompson, "Fast Food, Poverty Wages: The Public Cost of Low Wage Jobs in the Fast-Food Industry," University of California Berkeley, Labor Center, October 15, 2013, http://laborcenter.berkeley.edu/fast-food-poverty-wages-the-public-cost-of-low-wage-jobs-in-the-fast-food-industry

37. Manuel Madrid, "Fast-Food Blues: Workers Protest Low Wages, Sexual Harassment as McDonald's Profits Soar," *The American Prospect*, May 29, 2018, https://prospect.org/economy/fast-food-blues-workers-protest-low-wages-sexual-harassment-mcdonald-s-profits-soar

38. New York Communities for Change website, www.nycommunities.org/ABOUT

39. Sarah Jaffe, "This Group Pioneered the Fight for $15. Can They Transform the Fight for Affordable Housing Too?" *The Nation*, July 5, 2016, www.thenation.com/article/archive/this-group-pioneered-the-fight-for-15-can-they-transform-the-fight-for-affordable-housing-too

40. Ibid.

41. Josh Eidelson, "In Rare Strike, NYC Fast-Food Workers Walk Out," *Salon*, November 29, 2012, www.salon.com/2012/11/29/in_rare_strike_nyc_fast_food_workers_walk_out

42. Quoted in Kristina Bravo, "How One Protest Turned Into a Fast-Food-Worker Movement," *Takepart*, April 4, 2014, www.takepart.com/article/2014/04/04/fast-food-wages-timeline

43. Arun Gupta, "Wage Gains Won't Last, Unless Fight for 15 Builds Worker Power," *Counterpunch*, April 16, 2015, www.counterpunch.org/2015/04/16/wage-gains-wont-last-unless-fight-for-15-builds-worker-power

44. Josh Eidelson, "Fast Food Workers Plan Surprise Strike," *Salon.com*, April 4, 2013, www.salon.com/2013/04/04/fast_food_workers_plan_surprise_strike

45. Ibid.

46. Jonathan Rosenblum, "Fight for $15: Good Wins, But Where did the Focus on Organizing Go?" *Labor Studies Journal* 42, no. 4 (2017): 387–393.

47. "Hundreds of New York Fast Food Workers Protest for Better Pay," *USA News*, April 5, 2013; see also, Paul Harris, "Hundreds of Fast Food Workers Go On

Strike Over Pay," *The Guardian*, April 4, 2013, www.theguardian.com/world/2013/apr/04/new-york-fast-food-strike

48. Joel Rose, "NYC's Fast-Food Workers Strike, Demand 'Living Wages' " NPR Morning Edition, April 4, 2013, www.npr.org/post/nycs-fast-food-workers-strike-demand-living-wages#stream/0

49. Bravo, "How One Protest Turned into a Fast-Food-Worker Movement."

50. David Hudnall, "Dozens Arrested at Stand Up KC Strike at 14th and Prospect," *The Pitch*, September 4, 2014, www.thepitchkc.com/dozens-arrested-at-stand-up-kc-strike-at-14th-and-prospect; Finnegan, "Dignity."

51. Bravo, "How One Protest Turned into a Fast-Food-Worker Movement."

52. Ibid.

53. Sarah Jaffe, "In National Day of Action to Raise Minimum Wage, New Yorkers Stage Stealth Sit-In," *In These Times*, July 24, 2013, https://inthesetimes.com/working/entry/15353/in_national_day_of_action_to_raise_minimum_wage_new_yorkers_stage_sit_in

54. Ibid.

55. National Restaurant Association-SourceWatch, www.sourcewatch.org/index.php/National_Restaurant_Association

56. Lee Fang, "Where Have All the Lobbyists Gone?' *The Nation*, February 19, 2014, www.thenation.com/article/archive/shadow-lobbying-complex

57. Brendan Fischer and Mary Bottari, "The National Restaurant Association Spends Big to Keep Wages Low," *The Progressive*, May 14, 2014, https://progressive.org/dispatches/national-restaurant-association-spends-big-keep-wages-low

58. Jayaraman, *Forked*, 13.

59. Quoted in Kate Andrias, "The New Labor Law," *Yale Law Journal* 126 (2016–2017), www.yalelawjournal.org/article/the-new-labor-law; Steven Greenhouse, "Movement to Increase McDonald's Minimum Wage Broadens Its Tactics," *New York Times*, March 30, 2015, www.nytimes.com/2015/03/31/business/movement-to-increase-mcdonalds-minimum-wage-broadens-its-tactics.html

60. Noam Scheiber, "In Test for Unions and Politicians, A Nationwide Protest on Pay," *New York Times*, April 15, 2015, www.nytimes.com/2015/04/16/business/economy/in-test-for-unions-and-politicians-a-nationwide-protest-on-pay.html

61. "The Fight for $15," Gold Distinction in Government and Politics, Entered in Non-Profit, 8th Annual Shorty Awards, https://shortyawards.com/8th/the-fight-for-15

62. Andrias, "The New Labor Law."

63. Leslie Davis and Hannah Hartig, "Two-Thirds of Americans Favor Raising the Federal Minimum Wage to $15 an Hour," Pew Research Center, July 30, 2019, www.pewresearch.org/fact-tank/2019/07/30/two-thirds-of-americans-favor-raising-federal-minimum-wage-to-15-an-hour

64. Steven Greenhouse, "McDonald's Ruling Could Open Door for Unions," *New York Times*, July 29, 2014, www.nytimes.com/2014/07/30/business/nlrb-holds-mcdonalds-not-just-franchisees-liable-for-worker-treatment.html?auth=login-email&login=email

65. Whitney Filloon, "How McDonald's Labor Trial Could Affect the Entire Fast Food Industry," *Eater,* March 10, 2016, www.eater.com/2016/3/10/11192728/mcdonalds-labor-ruling

66. Eric Lipton, "Fight over Minimum Wage Illustrates Web of Industry Ties," *New York Times*, February 9, 2014, www.nytimes.com/2014/02/10/us/politics/fight-over-minimum-wage-illustrates-web-of-industry-ties.html?auth=login-email&login=email

67. Richard Berman, "The Importance of Standing Up to Activists," *Nation's Restaurant News*, August 20, 2015, www.nrn.com/opinions/importance-standing-activists

68. Chris Marr, "States with $15 Minimum Wage Laws Doubled This Year," *Bloomberg Law*, May 5, 2019, https://news.bloomberglaw.com/daily-labor-report/states-with-15-minimum-wage-laws-doubled-this-year

69. Drew Lunt, "The Mandatory Sick Leave Movement Is Gaining More Ground," *Employment Law Handbook*, February 20, 2018, www.employmentlawhandbook.com/leave-laws/mandatory-sick-leave-movement-gaining-ground

70. Yannet Lathrop, "Impact of the Fight for $15: $68 Billion, 22 Million Workers," National Employment Law Project, November 29, 2018, www.nelp.org/publication/impact-fight-for-15-2018

71. Dan LaBotz, "Immigrant Restaurant Workers Hope to Rock New York," *Dollars and Sense* (January–February 2004), www.dollarsandsense.org/archives/2004/0104labotz.html

72. Saru Jayaraman, *Behind the Kitchen Door* (Ithaca, NY & London: Cornell University Press, 2013), 4. This short book provides a good history of the early days and challenges faced by ROC.

73. Lisa Held, "Food Workers Rally for Their Rights on May Day," *Civil Eats*, May 3, 2017, https://civileats.com/2017/05/03/food-workers-rally-for-their-rights-on-may-day

74. Greg Jobin-Leeds, *When We Fight We Win: Twenty-First Century Social Movements and the Activists That Are Transforming the World* (New York: The New Press, 2016), 117–123.

75. Alana Samuels and Malcolm Burnley, "Low Wages, Sexual Harassment and Unreliable Tips. This is Life in America's Booming Service Industry," *Time*, August 22, 2019, https://time.com/magazine/us/5658416/september-2nd-2019-vol-194-no-8-u-s

76. Loryn Cesario, "States Weigh Options on Subminimum Wages for Workers with Disabilities," National Conference of State legislatures, Blog, August 28,

2019, www.ncsl.org/blog/2019/08/28/states-weigh-options-on-subminimum-wages-for-workers-with-disabilities.aspx

77. Sylvia A. Allegretto, "Should New York State Eliminate the Subminimum Wage?" Center on Wage and Employment Dynamics," Policy Brief, April 20, 2018, https://irle.berkeley.edu/files/2018/04/Should-New-York-State-Eliminate-its-Subminimum-Wage.pdf; see also, Melissa Camire and Fisher Phillips, "New York to End Subminimum Wage for Tipped Workers," *SHRM*, January 8, 2020, www.shrm.org/resourcesandtools/legal-and-compliance/state-and-local-updates/pages/new-york-to-end-subminimum-wage-for-many-tipped-workers.aspx

78. Mike Paranzino, "Federally Funded Front Group Misleads IRS, Taxpayers, Lawmakers," *The Hill*, May 23, 2013, https://thehill.com/blogs/congress-blog/labor/301503-federally-funded-front-group-misleads-irs-taxpayers-lawmakers

79. Caleb Pershan, "You've Created a Standard. But How Does That Actually Work?" *Eater*, January 24, 2020, www.eater.com/2020/1/24/21080202/colors-nyc-restaurant-roc-united-closure

80. "Gradually Raising the Minimum Wage to $15 Would be Good for Workers, Good for Business, and Good for the Economy," testimony of Ben Zipperer before the U.S. House of Representatives Committee on Education and Labor," February 7, 2019; see also, Paul J. Wolfson and Dale T. Berman, "15 Years of Research on U.S. Employment and the Minimum Wage," Tuck School of Business, Working Paper no. 2705499, December 2016.

81. David Cooper, Lawrence Mishel, and Ben Zipperer, "Bold Increases in the Minimum Wage Should be Evaluated for the Benefits of Raising Low-Wage Workers Total Earnings," Economic Policy Institute Report, April 18, 2018.

82. "Restaurants Flourish with One Fair Wage," Restaurant Opportunities Center, February 13, 2018.

83. Gupta, "Wage Gains Won't Last."

84. Zahn, "First the Fight for $15."

85. Jane McAlevey, *No Shortcuts: Organizing for Power in the New Gilded Age* (New York: Oxford University Press, 2016), 20.

86. Zahn, "First the Fight for $15."

87. Steven Greenhouse, "In Drive to Organize, Fast Food Workers Walk Off the Job," *New York Times*, November 28, 2012, www.nytimes.com/2012/11/29/nyregion/drive-to-unionize-fast-food-workers-opens-in-ny.html?auth=login-email&login=email

88. Greenhouse, "How to Get Low-Wage Workers into the Middle Class."

89. Annelise Orleck, *We Are All Fast-Food Workers Now: The Global Uprising Against Poverty Wages* (Boston: Beacon Press, 2018), 71.

90. See Steven Ashby, "Assessing the Fight for Fifteen Movement from Chicago," *Labor Studies Journal* 42, no. 4 (2017): 366–386; Rosenblum, "Fight for $15."

91. Eduardo Porter, "If Restaurants Disappear, What Happens to Cities?" *New York Times*, November 4, 2020.

92. Johnathon Maze, "The Pandemic Has Cost Restaurants 5.9 Million Jobs," *Restaurant Business*, May 8, 2020, www.restaurantbusinessonline.com/financing/pandemic-has-cost-restaurants-59-million-jobs

93. Johnathon Maze, "McDonald's Pledges to Pay Hourly Workers in Coronavirus Quarantine," *Restaurant Business*, March 10, 2020, www.restaurantbusinessonline.com/operations/mcdonalds-pledges-pay-hourly-workers-coronavirus-quarantine

94. Alex N. Press, "It's Time to End the Subminimum Wage for Tipped Workers," *Jacobin*, October 2020, https://jacobinmag.com/2020/10/tipped-restaurant-workers-waiters-coronavirus-subminimum-wage

Chapter 7

1. David Madland and Malkie Wall, "What Is Sectoral Bargaining?" Center for American Progress Action, March 2, 2020, www.americanprogressaction.org/issues/economy/news/2020/03/02/176857/what-is-sectoral-bargaining

2. Noam Scheiber, "McDonald's Notches Big Victory in Labor Board Ruling," *New York Times*, December 12, 2019, www.nytimes.com/2019/12/12/business/economy/mcdonalds-labor-board-settlement.html

3. Larry Cohen, "The Time Has Come for Sectoral Bargaining," *New Labor Forum*, June 2018, https://newlaborforum.cuny.edu/2018/06/22/the-time-has-come-for-sectoral-bargaining

4. Sarah Todd, "How Amazon Beat the Union Vote in Bessemer, Alabama," *Quartz*, April 9, 2021, https://qz.com/1994421/how-amazon-beat-the-union-vote-in-bessemer-alabama. Ironically enough, the Amazon warehouse in Bessemer, Alabama, was built on the site of a former U.S. Steel mill organized by one of the most powerful labor unions at that time in the country, the United Steel Workers of America.

5. David Rolf, *The Fight for $15: The Right Wage for a Working America* (New York & London: The Free Press, 2016), 254.

6. Dylan Matthews, "'Unions for All': The New Plan to Save the American Labor Movement," *Vox*, September 2, 2019, www.vox.com/policy-and-politics/2019/9/2/20838782/unions-for-all-seiu-sectoral-bargaining-labor-unions; David Madland, "How to Promote Sectoral Bargaining in the United States," Center for American Progress, July 10, 2019, www.americanprogressaction.org/issues/economy/reports/2019/07/10/174385/promote-sectoral-bargaining-united-states

7. Madland and Wall, "What is Sectoral Bargaining?"; see also, Kate Andrias, "Social Bargaining in Cities: Toward a More Egalitarian and Democratic Workplace Law," *Harvard Law and Policy Review on line*, Labor Law Reform Symposium (2017), https://repository.law.umich.edu/cgi/viewcontent.cgi?article=3000&context=articles

8. Cohen, "The Time Has Come."

9. Ibid.

10. New York State Department of Labor, Fast Food Wage Board, https://labor.ny.gov/workerprotection/laborstandards/wageboard2015.shtm

11. "A Growing Number of Americans Want to Join a Union," PBS News Hours, September 3, 2018, www.pbs.org/newshour/nation/a-growing-number-of-americans-want-to-join-a-union

12. U.S. Bureau of Labor Statistics, Economic News Release, "Union Members Summary," January 22, 2020, www.bls.gov/news.release/union2.nr0.htm

13. Heidi Shierholz, "Weakened Labor Movement Leads to Rising Economic Inequality," Working Economic Blog, Economic Policy Institute, January 27, 2020, www.epi.org/blog/weakened-labor-movement-leads-to-rising-economic-inequality

14. "The American Middle Class Is Losing Ground," PEW Research Center, December 9, 2015, www.pewsocialtrends.org/2015/12/09/the-american-middle-class-is-losing-ground

15. "Percent of Employment in Manufacturing in the United States," Economic Research, Federal Reserve Bank of St. Louis, June 10, 2013, https://fred.stlouisfed.org/series/USAPEFANA; Kimberly Amadeo, "US Manufacturing Statistics and Outlook," *The Balance*, October 22, 2019, www.thebalance.com/u-s-manufacturing-what-it-is-statistics-and-outlook-3305575

16. Kathleen Elkins, "Here's How Much You Have to Earn to Be in The Top 1% in Every State," CNBC Make It, July 27, 2018, www.cnbc.com/2018/07/27/how-much-you-have-to-earn-to-be-in-the-top-1percent-in-every-us-state.html; Jim Wang, "Average Income in America: What Salary in the United States Puts You in the Top 50%, Top 10%, Top 1%" (Updated for 2010), *Best Wallet Hacks*, March 10, 2020, https://wallethacks.com/average-median-income-in-america

17. Bill Fletcher Jr., and Fernando Gapasin argue that the labor movement needs to move to the left to keep pace with its membership. The actions of non-union workers is doing just that. See Bill Fletcher Jr. and Fernando Gapasin, *Solidarity Divided: The Crisis in Organized Labor and a New Path to Social Justice* (London: University of California Press, 2008).

18. Dylan Matthews, " 'Unions for All': The New Plan to save the American Labor Movement," *Vox*, September 2, 2019, www.vox.com/policy-and-politics/2019/9/2/20838782/unions-for-all-seiu-sectoral-bargaining-labor-unions; Jonathan Rosenblum, "Fight for $15: Good Wins, But Where did the Focus on Organizing Go?"; Steve Ashby, "Assessing the Fight for Fifteen Movement from Chicago"; Jane McAlevey, *No Shortcuts: Organizing for Power in the New Gilded Age.*

19. Jane McAlevey, *A Collective Bargain: Unions, Organizing and the Fight for Democracy* (New York: Harper Collins, 2020), 10–11.

20. "NYS Assembly, Senate Pass Farm Laborers Fair Labor Practices Act Despite Objections from Local Leaders," Press Releases, June 20, 2019, www.wnypapers.com/news/article/current/2019/06/20/137594/nys-assembly-senate-pass-farm-laborers-fair-labor-practices-act-despite-objections-from-local-leaders

21. Author's telephone interview with Alan Lubin, March 29, 2020.

22. Michael Williams, "Groups Seek to 'Fine-tune' Farmworker Rights Bill," *Albany Times Union*, January 7, 2020.

23. *N.Y. State Vegetable Growers Association v. Cuomo*, 19-CV-1720, https://casetext.com/case/ny-state-vegetable-growers-assn-inc-v-cuomo

24. John Meyers, "A Flood of Proposed Changes to California's AB 5 Awaits State Lawmakers," *Los Angeles Times*, February 28, 2020, www.latimes.com/california/story/2020-02-28/proposals-change-ab5-independent-contractors-labor-law-california

25. Rachel Sandler, "Judge Denies Bid from Uber, Postmate to Temporarily Halt California Gig Economy Law," *Forbes*, February 10, 2020, www.kqed.org/news/11804507/uber-and-lyft-drivers-are-organizing-but-worry-big-unions-will-sell-them-out

26. Author telephone interviews with Edward Escobar, founder and head of Alliance for Independent Workers, April 2–3, 2020.

27. Shirin Ghaffary and Alexia Fernandez Campbell, "A Landmark Law Disrupted the Gig Economy in California, But What Comes Next for Uber Drivers?" *Recode*, October 4, 2019, www.vox.com/recode/2019/10/4/20898940/uber-lyft-drivers-ab5-law-california-minimum-wage-benefits-gig-economy-disrupted

28. Jeremy B. White, "Why Uber Drivers Are Filing Claims This Month," *POLITICO*, February, 5, 2020, www.politico.com/states/california/story/2020/02/05/why-uber-drivers-are-filing-labor-claims-this-month-1259157

29. Sam Hamett, "Uber and Lyft Drivers Ramp Up Organizing Efforts, But Question Big Union's Motives," KQED, March 3, 2020, www.kqed.org/news/11804507/uber-and-lyft-drivers-are-organizing-but-worry-big-unions-will-sell-them-out

30. Author interview with Edward Escobar, April 2, 2020.

31. Elka Torpey and Andrew Hogan, "Working in a Gig Economy," U.S. Bureau of Labor Statistics, May 2016, www.bls.gov/careeroutlook/2016/article/what-is-the-gig-economy.htm

32. Jonathan Maze, "McDonald's Pledges to Pay Hourly Workers in Coronavirus Quarantine," *Restaurant Business*, March 10, 2020, www.restaurantbusinessonline.com/operations/mcdonalds-pledges-pay-hourly-workers-coronavirus-quarantine

33. Andrew Prokop, "Bernie Sanders Political Revolution, Explained," *Vox*, January 28, 2016, www.vox.com/2016/1/28/10853502/bernie-sanders-political-revolution

34. Rene Stepler, "Key Takeaways on Americans' Views of and Experiences with Family and Medical Leave," *Fact Tank*, March 23, 2017, www.pewresearch.org/fact-tank/2017/03/23/key-takeaways-on-americans-views-of-and-experiences-with-family-and-medical-leave

35. Gallup: Labor Unions, https://news.gallup.com/poll/12751/labor-unions.aspx

36. Jocelyn Kiley, "Most Continue to Say Ensuring Health Coverage Is Government's Responsibility," *FactTank*, October 3, 2018, www.pewresearch.

org/fact-tank/2018/10/03/most-continue-to-say-ensuring-health-care-coverage-is-governments-responsibility

37. Renee Stepler, "Key Takeaways on American's Views of and Experiences with family and Medical Leave."

38. Richard Fry, "Millennialls Approach Baby Boomers as Largest Generation in Electorate," *FACTANK*, Pew Research April 3, 2018, www.pewresearch.org/fact-tank/2018/04/03/millennials-approach-baby-boomers-as-largest-generation-in-u-s-electorate

39. Eric Levitz, "This One Chart Explains Why the Kids Back Bernie," *New York*, February 20, 2020, https://nymag.com/intelligencer/2020/02/this-one-chart-explains-why-young-voters-back-bernie-sanders.html

40. Kim Parker, Nikki Graf, and Ruth Igielnik, "Generation Z Looks a Lot Like Millennials on Key Social and Political Issues," Pew Research Center: Social and Demographic Trends, January 17, 2019, www.pewsocialtrends.org/2019/01/17/generation-z-looks-a-lot-like-millennials-on-key-social-and-political-issues

41. Jens Manuel Krogstadt, Mark Hugo, and Abby Budiman, "Latino Voters Favor Raising Minimum Wage, Government Involvement in Health Care, Stricter Gun Laws," *FactTank* February 20, 2020, www.pewresearch.org/fact-tank/2020/02/20/latino-voters-favor-raising-minimum-wage-government-involvement-in-health-care-stricter-gun-laws

42. "Dispatches from the New Economy: The On-Demand Economy and the Future of Work," Intuit, and Emergent Research, 2016, www.slideshare.net/IntuitInc/dispatches-from-the-new-economy-the-ondemand-workforce-57613212/13-ONDEMAND_ECONOMY_PROVIDER_DEMOGRAPHICSMenWhite_African; Aaron Smith, "Gig Work, Online Selling and Home Sharing," Pew Research Center, 2016, www.pewresearch.org/internet/2016/11/17/gig-work-online-selling-and-home-sharing; Annette Bernhardt and Sarah Thomason, "What Do We Know about Gig Work in California? An Analysis of Independent Contracting," UC Berkeley Center for Labor Research and Education, June 2017, http://laborcenter.berkeley.edu/what-do-we-know-about-gig-work-in-california

43. Alexander Burns, "Seeking: Big Democratic Ideas That Make Everything Better," *New York Times*, May 17, 2020, www.nytimes.com/2020/05/17/us/politics/joe-biden-economy-democrats.html?action=click&auth=login-email&login=email&module=Top%20Stories&pgtype=Homepage

44. Alec Tyson, "The 2018 Midterm Vote: Divisions by Race, Gender, Education," *FactTank*, November 8, 2018, www.pewresearch.org/fact-tank/2018/11/08/the-2018-midterm-vote-divisions-by-race-gender-education

45. Thomas B. Edsall, "We Aren't Seeing White Support for Trump for What It Is," *New York Times*, August 28, 2019, www.nytimes.com/2019/08/28/opinion/trump-white-voters.html

46. Quoted in Edsall, ibid.

47. Ibid.

48. Alec Tyson, "The 2018 Midterm Vote."

49. Zach Beauchamp, "The Real Reason Obama Voters Switched to Trump," *Vox*, October 16, 2018, www.vox.com/policy-and-politics/2018/10/16/17980820/trump-obama-2016-race-racism-class-economy-2018-midterm

50. Tino Sanandaji, "Are Welfare Recipients Mostly Republican?" *Wall Street Pit*, February 25, 2012, https://wallstreetpit.com/89671-are-welfare-recipients-mostly-republican

51. Erin Delmore, "This Is How Women Voters Decided the 2020 Election." NBC News, November 13, 2020, www.nbcnews.com/know-your-value/feature/how-women-voters-decided-2020-election-ncna1247746

52. Irene Tung and Paul Sonn, "The Growing Movement for $15," The National Employment Law Project. November 2015, www.nelp.org/publication/growing-movement-15

53. Josh Mound, "When Poor People Vote," *Jacobin*, April 29, 2016, www.jacobinmag.com/2016/04/bernie-sanders-poor-voters-inequality-primary

54. Frances Fox Piven and Richard A. Cloward, *Why Americans Don't Vote: Causes and Consequences* (New York: Pantheon Books, 1988); for a short summary of voter suppression of people of color, see Danyelle Solomon, Connor Maxwell, and Abril Castro, "Systematic Inequality and American Democracy," Center for American Progress, August 7, 2019, www.americanprogress.org/issues/race/reports/2019/08/07/473003/systematic-inequality-american-democracy

55. A classic work on this issue is E.E. Schattschneider, *The Semi-Sovereign People: A Realist's View of Democracy in America* (New York, Chicago, Toronto, & London: Holt, Rinehart and Winston, 1960).

56. Michelle Goldberg, "A Biden Presidency Could Be Better Than Progressives Think," *New York Times*, April 20, 2020.

57. Justine Coleman, "Major Companies Updating Sick Leave Policies in Response to Coronavirus," *The Hill*, March 11, 2020, https://thehill.com/policy/healthcare/public-global-health/486988-major-companies-updating-sick-leave-policies-in

58. Jamelle Bouie, "Trump and His Allies Are Worried about More than November," *New York Times*, April 17, 2020.

59. For a good history on voter suppression in the United States, see Alexander Keyssar, *The Right to Vote: The Contested History of Democracy in the United States* (New York: Basic Books, 2009).

60. Solomon, Maxwell, and Castro, "Systematic Inequality and American Democracy"; for a concise summary of voter suppression laws see, Theodore R. Johnson and Max Feldman, "The New Voter Suppression," Brennan Center for Justice, January 16,.2020, www.brennancenter.org/our-work/research-reports/new-voter-suppression

61. Kevin Drum, "Chart of the Day: Wisconsin Gerrymandering Was Awesome," *Mother Jones*, December 4, 2018, www.vox.com/policy-and-politics/

2018/5/8/17271766/north-carolina-gerrymandering-2018-midterms-partisan-redistricting

62. Michael Wines, "What is Gerrymandering? Why Did the Supreme Court Rule On It?" *New York Times*, June 27, 2019, www.nytimes.com/2019/06/27/us/what-is-gerrymandering.html; Elia Nilsen, "North Carolina's Extreme Gerrymandering Could Save the House Republican Majority," *Vox*, May 8, 2018, www.vox.com/policy-and-politics/2018/5/8/17271766/north-carolina-gerrymandering-2018-midterms-partisan-redistricting

63. Jessica Corbett, "Fight for $15 and Rev. Barber Announce Fast-Food Workers Strike for Racial Justice and Voting Rights," *Common Dreams*, February 1, 2018, www.commondreams.org/news/2018/02/01/fight-15-and-rev-barber-announce-fast-food-worker-strike-racial-justice-and-voting

64. Michael Sainato, "Fight for $15 Campaign is a Comeback for Labor Movement's Role in Elections," *The Guardian*, October 28, 2018, www.theguardian.com/us-news/2018/oct/28/fight-for-15-campaign-labor-movement-midterm-elections

65. "Fight for $15 Members Risk Arrest to Vote" Fight for $15 website, https://fightfor15.org/fight-for-15-members-risk-arrest-to-vote

66. "The Fight for $15," Gold Distinction in Government and Politics, Entered in Non-Profit, 8th Annual Shorty Awards, https://shortyawards.com/8th/the-fight-for-15

67. Donald J. Trump, March 30, 2020, interview with Fox and Friends News.

68. "Voting Laws Roundup: March 2021," Brennan Center for Justice, April 1, 2021. www.brennancenter.org/our-work/research-reports/voting-laws-roundup-march-2021

69. David Rolf, *The Fight for $15: The Right Wage for a Working America*; for a good review of the possibilities of wage boards, see David Madland, "Wage Boards for American Workers: Industry-level Collective Bargaining for All Workers," Center for American Progress, April 9, 2018, www.americanprogress.org/issues/economy/reports/2018/04/09/448515/wage-boards-american-workers

70. Madland, "How to Promote Sectoral Bargaining in the United States."

71. Labor Notes Staff, "Labor's Structure Stands in the Way of Organizing," *Labor Notes*, December 2, 2002, https://labornotes.org/2002/12/labor's-structure-stands-way-organizing

72. Nicholas Kristof, "McDonald's Workers in Denmark Pity Us," *New York Times*, May 8, 2020, www.nytimes.com/2020/05/08/opinion/us-denmark-economy.html

73. David Milton, *The Politics of U.S. Labor: From The Great Depression to The New Deal* (New York & London: Monthly Review Press, 1982), 167.

74. Howard Schneider and Chris Kahn, "Majority of Americans Favor Wealth Tax on Very Rich: Reuters/Ipsos Poll," Reuters, January 10, 2020, www.reuters.com/article/us-usa-election-inequality-poll/majority-of-americans-favor-wealth-tax-on-very-rich-reuters-ipsos-poll-idUSKBN1Z9141; Giovanni Russonello,

"Biden's Policies Are Popular. What Does That Mean for Republicans?" *New York Times*, February 4, 2021, updated March 3, 2021, www.nytimes.com/2021/02/04/us/politics/biden-approval-rating-republicans.html

75. Franz Neumann's brilliant essays on the tensions between the democratic and authoritarian state are even more relevant today than when they were first published more than sixty years ago. See Franz Neumann, *The Democratic and Authoritarian State* (New York: Free Press, 1957).

Index